LANDSCAPE DETAILING

Volume 2 SURFACES

LANDSCAPE DETAILING

Volume 2   SURFACES

Third Edition   Michael Littlewood

Architectural Press

OXFORD AMSTERDAM BOSTON LONDON NEW YORK PARIS
SAN DIEGO SAN FRANCISCO SINGAPORE SYDNEY TOKYO

Architectural Press
An imprint of Elsevier Science
Linacre House, Jordan Hill, Oxford OX2 8DP
225 Wildwood Avenue, Woburn, MA 01801-2041

First published 1984
Second edition 1986
Reprinted 1990
Third edition 1993
Reprinted 1994, 1995, 1997, 1998, 1999, 2001, 2002, 2003

British Library Cataloguing in Publication Data
Littlewood, Michael
  Landscape Detailing. - Vol 1 Enclosure. -
  3Rev.ed
  I. Title
  712

ISBN 0 7506 1304 1 volume 1
ISBN 0 7506 1303 3 volume 2

Library of Congress Cataloguing in Publication Data
Littlewood, Michael.
  Landscape detailing/Michael Littlewood. - 3rd ed.
  p. cm.
  Includes bibliographical references.
  Contents: v. 1. Enclosure - v. 2. Surfaces.
  ISBN 0 7506 1304 1 (v. 1) ISBN 0 7506 1303 3 (v. 2)
  1. Fences - Design and construction. 2. Garden walks - Design and
  construction. 3. Walls - Design and construction. I. Title.
  TH4965.1.58   1993   92-34847
  717-dc20   CIP

For information on all Architectural Press publications
visit our website at www.architecturalpress.com

Composition by Scribe Design, Gillingham, Kent
Printed and bound by Antony Rowe Ltd, Chippenham, Wiltshire

CONTENTS

Volume 2 SURFACES

FOREWORD

The success of both editions of *Landscape Detailing* has resulted in a review of material and data for the third edition. In view of the many more details that have been produced since the second edition it was felt that the user would prefer to have them in two volumes for ease of use. This book covers details relating to surfaces and the first volume relates to enclosures.

Many landscape architects, architects, other professionals and students responsible for the production of drawn details and specifications for landscape construction works have a need for ready reference. This book has been produced to meet that need and it can be extended by additional sheets. It has been arranged for ease of copying of sheets and it is sufficiently flexible for designers to use the details for their specific requirements.

The range of materials for external works and their possible combinations for surfaces would make it impossible to provide a definitive book of details.

It is not the intention of this book to supplant the landscape designer's own skill and experience, which is vital to the success of any project. This is still essential in evaluating the site conditions, assessing the character of the environment and creating sensitive design solutions.

It is hoped that the book, if used correctly, will allow the designer to spend more time on design details, avoiding the need to produce repetitive drawings for basic construction elements. It has been found that the details can be very useful for costing purposes and to support the preliminary design when presented to a client. To assist the designer and to save further time in writing specifications, check lists for these have been included in this edition along with technical guidance notes and tables.

Design information has been excluded; many other publications deal with this subject much more adequately than could be achieved in this book. General comments on appearance have been given only where it was felt appropriate.

ACKNOWLEDGEMENTS

I must give particular thanks to many people who have supported me in some way – no matter how small – and who have encouraged me to complete this third edition, which has been greatly enlarged.

My particular thanks must go to Caroline Mallinder and Paddy Baker of Butterworth-Heinemann – my publishers – both of whom have supported my work and put up with so many frustrating delayed publishing dates. Thank you for being so patient. Also to landscape architects Andrew Clegg, Melissa Bowers, Naila Parveen, Donna Young, Peter Dean and Craig Schofield, all of whom have succumbed to my persistence in drawing the details and reading the text.

My appreciation must also go to Colin MacGregor of NBS for his ready and willing assistance on specification matters as well as Alistair Smythe of *Specification* and Barrie Evans of the *Architect's Journal*. A very special thanks to Doris Evans for typing the text and correcting it so many times.

I am also very grateful to civil engineers John Williamson and Alan Taylor for their advice on retaining walls and to Peter Morrison of Ibstock Building Products Ltd for his kind assistance on brick walls in general.

All have contributed to this book to ensure that it eventually reaches the publishers, after such a long time.

INTRODUCTION

The landscape detail sheets have been produced in an effort to eliminate needless repetition in detailing landscape works covering hard elements. It is possible to use them without alteration, but in some cases minor modifications and additions to dimensions or specifications may be necessary. Lettering has been standardised by the use of a stencil (italic 3.5 mm). When a detail is required which is not available on a detail sheet, the new detail can be drawn by the designer using the standardised format, which will enable it to be added to the original collection of details and to be easily re-used on other projects. Readers are invited to send the publishers copies of their own details which they think would merit inclusion in future editions of this book. Appropriate acknowledgement will be made.

Each sheet portrays a detail without reference to its surroundings. This approach has been adopted because it affords to each detail the maximum number of possibilities for re-use. No attempt has been made to recommend a particular detail for a particular situation. This remains the responsibility of the landscape architect, architect or designer.

There are, of course, a great many other details which might be included on specific projects or in specific situations. In some cases, the detailing of site elements and site structures can be coordinated very carefully with the architect or building designer in order to ensure a uniformity of form and material. In yet other instances, various agencies and organisations may have standard details which must be used on their particular projects.

Notes

The notes which precede each section are intended to give only the briefest outline of main points. For more detailed guidance, the publications listed in Appendices A and B should be consulted.

Specifications

Specifications should not be written without a knowledge of the content of the relevant British Standards in Appendix C. Some British Standards contain alternative specifications which may prove more suitable in a particular case.

The task of writing specifications has now been made very much easier by the use of the word processor. Nevertheless, if a specification is to serve its purpose efficiently it must be concise and accurate, otherwise it could be misunderstood by all the people involved in the project.

To assist the designer and to ensure that he or she makes the minimum of omissions, a check list has been provided after the notes for each chapter or section. Ease of access to a particular section will encourage a contractor to read the specification and conform with its requirements. So many contractors ignore the specifications and use only the bills of quantities. Probably the best way to ensure that the completed specification is satisfactory is for the designer to read it as if he or she were the contractor and could complete the project accordingly.

Reference should be made to two main sources for specifications, namely the NBS of Newcastle-upon-Tyne and the publication *Specification*. Full details of their services are given in the Appendices.

Use of the detail sheets

The collection of detail sheets, as purchased, may if users wish be photocopied, punched and stored in a ring binder. The detail sheets have been laid out in such a way as to facilitate this operation. In the form of individual leaves the details can easily be traced or copy negatives can be made.

The sheets must be used in conjunction with a site layout drawing, preferably at 1:200. These may be more than one sheet,

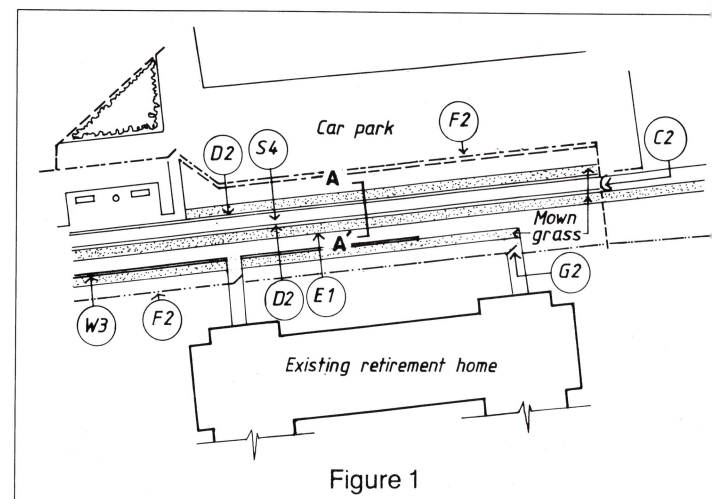

Figure 1

PLAN

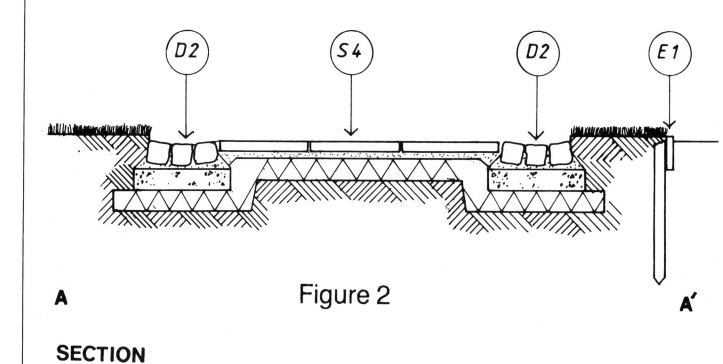

Figure 2

SECTION

depending upon the size of the project. The layout drawings will convey all information on levels, directions of falls and setting-out dimensions. They also indicate the location of the elected details and the deployment of surface finishes. (See Figure 1.) Simple conjunction of details (for example, a kerb mowing strip and channel) can be indicated by the drawing of the three relevant section lines in close proximity. (See Figure 2.)

Standards

British Standards and Codes of Practice are referred to where necessary. Users of this book living in countries where British Standards are not used should delete the reference to the British Standard and, if they feel it necessary, either insert a reference to an equivalent national standard or describe what is required in empirical terms.

Production of new detail sheets

Where the use of a detail not included in the original collection of detail sheets is required, the new detail can be produced on A4 tracing paper using a standard format. This will enable it to be added to the original collection and to be easily re-used. New details will be assigned a reference number by the design office, using their own reference system. The title of the new detail, as shown in the centre label at the foot of the drawing, can then be added to the contents list prefacing each section.

Issue of detail sheets

Detail sheets can be used in two ways. A set of photocopies can be issued to the contractor of the selected details, after completion of the title panel reference, and number-stamping each detail with the office stamp. The second method is to trace or copy a batch of details, grouped according to type and identified with key numbers, on to an A1 sheet of tracing paper and include the drawing with the contract set in the normal way.

Design detailing

The creation of good design can only come from the designer, and no amount of drawn details can be a substitute for this fact. The principles must be followed as Fraser Reekie has stated in his book *Design in the Built Environment*:

> To make an objective assessment of a design, or to set about the process of designing, consideration has to be given to the three aspects which may be summarised as:
> 1. Function: The satisfying of requirements of use or purpose;
> 2. Structure: The physical implementation of function by the best available material(s), construction, manufacture and skills as conditions permit;
> 3. Appearance: The obtaining of satisfactory visual effects (sometimes referred to as 'aesthetic values').

Other words can be used to describe these three aspects but, on analysis, whatever words are used it will be found that almost every writer on building design, which may be extended to cover the built environment, is dealing with the same three fundamentals. These three constituent parts of design are closely interrelated and each, to a greater or lesser extent, according to the nature of the subject, influences the others. An urban composition or a building or a detail that is truly well designed is one in the creation of which all three aspects have been fully considered and integrated. Integration may well be the key-word in good design. Not only does it mean the correct combining of parts into a whole but it implies, by association with integrity, soundness and honesty.

TABLES

TABLE 1. CRITERIA FOR SELECTION

Appearance will often be an important criterion in the selection of an external paving material. Some types give very pleasant mixtures of texture and colour, and different materials can often be mixed to interesting effect.

The basic functional criteria for the selection of external paving are summarised below. It should be emphasised that external paving is subject to severe weather exposure, including long periods of damp and frost. Durability is important although in some situations, such as private gardens, it will not be as crucial as in adjacent building elements. Strength is not normally critical for pedestrian use but it will be vital in areas subject to heavy vehicular loads (e.g. industrial areas). Thus different uses and situations will call for a change of emphasis between these criteria.

Durability (linked with strength and frost resistance)	The required durability will depend upon type of use, situation and budget. Premature failure of paving has been noted on housing estates where cost restrictions have necessitated the use of units of unsuitable quality. Durability is hard to assess by testing – the best evidence is satisfactory durability over a period in use of at least three years in a similar situation.
Strength	The necessary strength will depend upon the loads to be sustained. Pedestrians do not cause problems but many failures of paving are caused by casual over-riding by vehicles. Cracked pavings can form trips and early failure of paving. Most pavings have adequate strength if laid on a suitable bedding and sub-base.
Frost resistance	All external paving is subject to severe exposure, both wetting and freezing. BS 3921 notes that there is no satisfactory test for frost resistance. Some stock bricks are very absorbent but have been shown to be frost resistant in use. As with durability, reliance should be placed upon evidence of satisfactory frost resistance over a period of use of three years in a similar situation.
Freedom from efflorescence	As all external paving is subject to severe wetting/drying cycles, freedom from efflorescence is desirable for all paving and for bricks and coloured concrete pavings. Paviours, engineering pavers and concrete pavings are normally free from significant efflorescence. If facing bricks are used for paving, steps, etc., the manufacturer should be asked to give assurances that efflorescence is not worse than moderate, and preferably slight as tested to BS 3921.
Resistance to wear	The required resistance to wear will depend upon the amount of traffic (e.g. back garden compared with hypermarkets, drive-way compared to industrial access road). Softer paving materials (e.g. stock bricks) should be used in areas of light vehicular use.
Slip resistance	Good slip resistance is important in public pedestrian areas, particularly on ramps, steps, etc. Placing main running joints across the direction of traffic will help slip resistance, as will slightly recessed joints. Vehicular paving must have sufficient slip resistance and the DoT does set standards.
Colour permanence	Colour permanence is desirable but complete permanence is not possible with some paving materials.
Resistance to petrol, oil and salts	Not important for pedestrian situations. Very important for vehicular situations, particularly car parking. Clay and concrete paving have good resistance to petrol and oil in comparison with bitumen-based paving products. Paving should also be resistant to de-icing salts.
Resistance to organic growth	Importance will depend upon situation. Moss may be attractive in a garden but would be dangerous in urban pedestrian or vehicular situations. The harder and more dense the surface, the better the resistance to organic growth.

Reproduced with kind permission from AJ Information Library, 'External Paving'.

TABLE 2. PAVING CHECK LIST

Type of paving	Advantages	Disadvantages
In-situ paving – Concrete	Relatively easy to install Available with several finishes, many colours and various textures Durable surface Year-round and multiple usage Low lifetime maintenance costs Long-lasting Low heat absorbency Hard, non-resilient surface Adaptable to curvilinear forms	Joints are required Some surfaces are aesthetically unappealing Can disintegrate if not properly installed Difficult to colour evenly and permanently Light colour is reflective and can cause glare Some types can deteriorate from de-icing salts Relatively low tensile strength; can crack easily Low resiliency
– Asphalt	Low heat and light reflectivity Year-round and multiple use Durable Low maintenance costs Dust-free surface Resiliency can vary depending on mixture Water-repellent surface Adaptable to curvilinear forms Can be made porous	Will fray at edges if not supported Can soften in warm weather Soluble by gasoline, kerosene and other petroleum solvents Susceptible to freeze damage if water penetrates the base
Synthetic surfacing system (proprietary)	Can be designed for a specific purpose (e.g. court games, track) Wide colour range More resilient than concrete or asphalt Sometimes can be applied over old concrete or asphalt	Specially trained labour may be required for installation and repair More costly than asphalt or concrete
Unit paving – Brick	Non-glare surface Non-skid surface Wide colour range Good scale Easily repaired	High installation cost Difficult to clean Can disintegrate in freezing weather Susceptible to differential settlement Efflorescence
– Tiles	Polished indoor/outdoor appearance	Suitable only for milder climates High installation costs
– Adobe blocks	Fast and easy installation Can last indefinitely if base contains an adequate amount of asphaltic stabiliser Rich colour and texture	Tend to crumble at the edges Store considerable amounts of heat Fragile; require level foundations (fracture easily) Dusty Suitable only for warm and non-humid areas
– Flagstone	Very durable if properly installed Natural weathering qualities	Moderately expensive to install Might seem cold, hard, or quarry-like in appearance Colour and random pattern sometimes difficult to work with aesthetically Can become smooth and slippery when wet or worn

TABLE 2. *CONTINUED*

Type of paving	Advantages	Disadvantages
– Granite	Hard and dense Very durable under extreme weathering conditions Will support heavy traffic Can be polished to a hard gloss surface that is durable and easily cleaned	Hard and dense, difficult to work with Some types are subject to high rate of chemical weathering Relatively expensive
– Limestone	Easy to work with Rich colour and texture	Susceptible to chemical weathering (especially in humid climates and urban environments)
– Sandstone	Easy to work with Durable	Same as limestone
– Slate	Durable Slow to weather Range of colours	Relatively expensive Can be slippery when wet
Moulded units (synthetic)	Can be designed or selected for various purposes (i.e. firm, soft) Short installation time Easy installation removal, and replacement usually without specialised labour Wide colour range	Subject to vandalism Higher installation costs than asphalt or concrete
Soft paving aggregates	Economical surfacing material Range of colours	Require replenishment every few years depending on amount of use Potential for weeds Require edging
Organic materials	Relatively inexpensive Compatible with natural surroundings Quiet, comfortable working surface	Suitable only for light traffic Require periodic replenishment or replacement
Turfgrass	Colourful Non-abrasive Dust-free Good drainage characteristics Quiet, comfortable walking surface Ideal for many types of recreation Relatively low installation costs	Difficult and expensive to maintain, especially in areas of heavy use
Turf blocks	Same as turf alone but has added stability to withstand light vehicular loads	Require high levels of maintenance (frequent watering, etc.)
Artificial turf	Instant turf surface Can be used sooner after rain without wet spots Allows flat grading of playing surface No irrigation or maintenance problems as with natural turfgrass	Results in a higher number of player injuries (regarding field sports) Gives faster and higher ball roll and bounce Initial installation costs higher than natural turfgrass

Reproduced with kind permission from *Time Savers for Landscape Architectural Use*, by Morris and Dines.

TABLE 3. TYPES OF PAVING AVAILABLE

This table illustrates the common types of concrete and clay paving available, with notes on relevant British Standards, specification of materials, description of manufacture and finishes available. In terms of quantity, precast concrete flags still dominate the market; however, greater emphasis on the quality of the external environment has meant an increased use of decorative finishes to concrete slabs, and a re-awakening to the possibilities of brick paving. As stated above, flexible concrete block paving has been vigorously marketed and is now used quite widely. In addition to those materials covered in Table 2, natural stone paving (e.g. York stone and slate), is still available although it is expensive. The cost may be justified in high-quality restoration projects. Used stone paving is sometimes available and can be mixed with other materials to good effect. Granite setts are still laid as deterrent paving or in small areas for textural relief and interest.

TABLE 3. COMMON TYPES OF JOINTED EXTERNAL PAVING

Precast concrete flags (paving slabs)	Clay bricks† (including facing bricks, paviours, engineering pavers)	Flexible paving	
		Precast concrete paving blocks	Interlocking clay paviours
Relevant British Standards			
BS 368: 1973 Precast concrete flags: gives details of specification and sizes for the more basic types of paving slabs. Decorative types generally to this specification.	BS 3921: 1985 Clay bricks and blocks: defines types and qualities of bricks in general but does not specifically cover their use in paving. The British Standard for paviours is BS 6677 Pt 1 1986.	BS 6717 Pt 1 1986 provides details of specifications for these blocks for low speed road and other paved surfaces. The C&CA have produced a model specification which can be used for this work	There is no British Standard at this juncture. The paviours are produced generally to BS 3921 in terms of quality and BS 6677 Pt 1 should assist with the specifications for this type of paving.
Specification details Cement to BS 12 or BS 146. Aggregate – natural materials crushed and uncrushed to 4a and 5d of BS 882 or 4a and 5d of BS 1201 or clause 5 of BS 1047. If coloured – pigments to BS 1014. All arrises should be clean and sharp. Surface finish is to be agreed. Samples are tested for water absorption, mechanical strength of aggregate, transverse strength. Decorative patterns for purely pedestrian use may not satisfy some specification details.	Bricks used for paving should be to 'special quality'. This is defined in BS 3921 as: strength – minimum 5.2 N/mm² soluble salts – limits are given efflorescence – no sample worse than moderate

Frost resistance:
1. Proven in use, or
2. Three years exposure test, or
3. Strength not less than 48.5 N/mm² or water absorption not greater than 7%. But (3) is not very reliable so obtain assurance of satisfactory performance from manufacturer. | C&CA specification: cement to BS 12 or BS 146. Aggregate – fine and coarse to BS 882 or coarse to BS 1047: 25% of fines – natural siliceous sand. Pigments, if used, to BS 1014. Portland cement content not less than 380 kg/m³.

All arrises clean and of uniform dimensions. Slight variations in surface appearance are allowed. Wearing surface not less than 70% of plan. Minimum strength – average of 49 N/mm², 40 N/mm² for individual blocks. | Generally as bricks to 'special' quality as left. Most special bricks being produced are high strength – 70–90 N/mm². The method of manufacture ensures a surface that gives excellent skid resistance, usually wire cut.

Limits for water absorption, efflorescence, etc. ,are low. |

TABLE 3. *CONTINUED*

| Precast concrete flags (paving slabs) | Clay bricks† (including facing bricks, paviours, engineering pavers) | Flexible paving | |
		Precast concrete paving blocks	Interlocking clay paviours
Mode of manufacture Various methods are used, the most common being hydraulically pressed paving – a wet concrete mix from which surplus water is extracted by top pressure and filtered by a paper membrane. This process gives a dense and durable structure and a surface free of blow holes. The paper filter imparts the characteristic texture. Other processes have been brought in from the Continent combining pressure and vibration giving earth-dry concrete. All processes are carried out on machinery capable of large throughput with minimum labour.	Manufacture varies considerably depending on type (i.e. stocks, paviours, engineering pavers, etc.). After careful preparation of the clay, it is moulded, pressed or extruded and cut to size, then dried and fired.	Concrete paving blocks are generally produced in sophisticated vibration presses from earth-dry concrete. The temperature of the materials and moulds must be kept above freezing. After manufacture the units must be protected from frost for 24 hours and stored to prevent undue loss of moisture during curing.	There are no special procedures in the production of these bricks for 'flexible' paving. Most are extruded wire-cut bricks produced in carefully controlled conditions and fired in a normal manner.
Finishes available Colour – subdued range of greys, browns, reds, yellows and greens. Stronger colours possible with some exposed aggregates. Textures – smooth, dimpled, ribbed, machine rubbed, simulated York stone, exposed aggregate. 'Deterrent' patterns have a heavily moulded face.	Colours – a wide range is available from light brown, reds, browns, dark browns, blue, black – in multi ranges and brindled.	Colours – natural grey is cheapest, but limited range of other subdued colours, red, light brown, dark brown, buff, charcoal. Texture – slight roughness to face, most have a chamfered edge.	Colours – range of typical brick colours has recently been extended from light brown to reds to dark browns, etc. Texture – slight roughness produced during wire-cutting process.

*Natural stone paving slabs, including used stone, are still available but at considerable cost.
†Calcium silicate bricks class 4 or better with strength greater than 28 N/mm² are considered suitable for paving but are rarely used.
Reproduced with kind permission from AJ Information Library, 'External Paving'.

TABLE 4. COMPARISON OF PERFORMANCE – JOINTED PAVING

This table gives a brief comparison of the performance of different types of concrete and clay paving. The strengths and weaknesses of each type should be related to the requirements of the specific situation. Most failures of external paving relate to either the inappropriate specification of the paving material itself with regard to its strength and durability, or an inadequate sub-base upon which the paving has been laid, leading to subsidence, cracking, etc. With careful selection of the sub-base, concrete paving blocks and the special interlocking clay paviours can cope with very heavy use, although only on roads subject to a maximum speed of 50–60 km/h.

| Precast concrete flags (paving slabs) | Clay bricks (facing paviours, engineering pavers) | Flexible paving | |
		Precast concrete paving blocks	Interlocking clay paviours
Durability			
Hydraulically pressed types – 25 to 30 years; less in some urban situations. Decorative types in light-use situations – approximately 20 years.	Engineering bricks have a very long life even in paving – 40+ years. Brick paviours should last at least 25 years – one manufacturer now gives a guarantee. The durability of facing bricks and stocks will vary considerably. Get assurance from the manufacturer.	Manufacturers estimate 40 years for pedestrian areas, 25 years for heavy vehicular situations (i.e. industrial).	Manufacturers estimate a life at least equal to concrete paving blocks.
*Strength (load bearing)**			
The minimum breaking strength for flags is specified in BS 368, 63 mm thick slabs are 50% stronger than 50 mm. The general recommendations are: 38–50 mm – light pedestrian 50–63 mm – heavy pedestrian, drives, positions where overriding by vehicles 75–100 mm – medium to heavy vehicular use.	Strengths of brick used in paving vary considerably: Stocks – 20 to 40 N/mm^2 Paviours – 54 to 120 N/mm^2 Engineering: Class A > 69 N/mm^2 Class B > 48.5 N/mm^2 The general recommendations are: 35–38 – pedestrian 50–60 – light vehicular 65 – medium vehicular.	Minimum average strength 49 N/mm^2, tests show with bed equivalent to 160 mm rolled asphalt to DoT Road Note 29. The general recommendations are: 60–65 mm – pedestrian and light vehicular 80–100 mm – medium to heavy vehicular.	The strength of the small range of these special paviours varies from 52 N/mm^2 to 90 N/mm^2. Tests indicate performance similar to concrete paving blocks. They are 50 and 65 mm thick. Manufacturers believe that the 65 mm paviours will support heavy vehicular use.
Frost resistance			
Normally excellent for those produced to BS 368.	Special paviours and engineering pavers excellent. Special quality facing bricks and stocks. Good but careful selection necessary.	Careful production ensures excellent frost resistance.	Excellent frost resistance similar to engineering pavers.

7

TABLE 4. *CONTINUED*

| Precast concrete flags (paving slabs) | Clay bricks (facing paviours, engineering pavers) | Flexible paving | |
		Precast concrete paving blocks	Interlocking clay paviours
Freedom from efflorescence Normally excellent.	Depends upon brick but special quality bricks should not be subject to significant efflorescence – consult manufacturer.	Normally excellent.	Normally excellent.
Resistance to wear Normally good for those produced to BS 368. Some decorative types only fair.	Harder types – e.g. wire-cut, and engineering bricks – very good. Stocks – fair.	Very good.	Excellent.
Slip resistance Depends upon texture. Some are very good. Smooth pebble exposed aggregate can be slippery when wet.	Depends upon brick – wire-cut production gives good texture. Smooth engineering bricks may be slippery when wet.	Very good.	Excellent and hardness ensures it will be maintained.
Resistance to oil, petrol, salts‡ Good but lighter colours may suffer staining from oil.	Good in most cases, stocks may suffer stain-ing.	Good but lighter colours may suffer staining from oil.	Excellent, less easily stained than concrete and darker colours make it less obtrusive.
Freedom from organic growth* Good in most cases, heavily textured types may support organic growth in damp shaded situation.	Varies with type. Engineering pavers – excellent; Paviours – good; Facing bricks – vary from fair to good Stocks – fair and will support organic growth in damp shaded situations.	Very good.	Very good.
Colour permanence Fair – the pigments used to colour concrete are subject to fading.	Excellent	Fair – as paving flags.	Excellent.
Maintenance requirements† Replace cracked slabs or those with differential settlements as they can be dangerous. Consider relaying on more stable sub-base.	Replace bricks which suffer differential settle-ment. Consider sub-base specification	Units can be lifted if access required to services underneath, or if areas of differential settlement. Sand base is made good and units relaid. A few blocks will have to be broken to allow units to be lifted.	As concrete paving blocks.

* Strength in use will depend upon bedding and sub-base. BDA claims that the strength of the paver does *not* determine its load-bearing capacity.

† Good falls encourage quick draining so paving is wet for a shorter time, improving slip resistance and minimising organic growth.

‡ Accumulations of oil can be removed by scraping and dissolving with spirit-based thinners but this is hard work and rarely done.

Reproduced with kind permission from AJ Information Library, 'External Paving'.

TABLE 5. EXTERNAL PAVING FOR LIGHT PEDESTRIAN USE e.g. in private gardens, soft landscaping areas in parks, etc.

	Precast concrete flags 30 mm thick min[a]	Facing bricks and stocks of special quality, engineering bricks 65 mm thick	Brick paviours[b] 35 mm thick min	'Flexible' paving — Precast concrete paving blocks 60 mm thick min	'Flexible' paving — Interlocking clay paviours 50 mm thick min
1 Paving material	Precast concrete flags 30 mm thick min[a]	Facing bricks and stocks of special quality, engineering bricks 65 mm thick	Brick paviours[b] 35 mm thick min	Precast concrete paving blocks 60 mm thick min	Interlocking clay paviours 50 mm thick min
2 Site preparation/sub-grade	The preparation of the sub-grade for light pedestrian use is less crucial than in other situations as the loads to be sustained are small. In this type of paving some slight settlement over the years may be acceptable. The excavation should, however, remove any topsoil containing organic matter. The application of a weedkiller will minimise growth through the paving. The foundation should be as level as possible and ideally it should be compacted with a heavy garden roller. Falls, if required (some of these specifications are self-draining), should be formed in the foundation level.				
3 Sub-base/foundation	75 to 100 mm hardcore	75 mm coarse clinker or 150 mm hardcore	100 mm hardcore[c]	80–100 mm hardcore will be sufficient. Finished: 110 mm below finish level for 60 mm blocks / 100 mm below finish level for 50 mm bricks	
4 Edge restraint	Not essential, but if sand bed is used then must ensure it does not wash out. If edge restraint required 50 mm concrete edging to BS 340	As left, greater danger that brick edge will be displaced than with flags. If edge restraint required s/w board, concrete edging or brick on edge	Not necessary as normally laid on a firmer bedding than flags or bricks.	For small paths or patios which are not vibrated, edge restraint is not essential. Where the blocks/paviours are vibrated as described below, then an edge restraint is essential. S/w board, concrete edging, brick on edge.	
5 Bedding	25 mm sand bed is sometimes used for very light use or where plant growth is desired. 24 mm 1:4 or 5 lime/sand mortar where a firmer bedding is required. Flags are sometimes bedded on five cement/sand mortar dots,[d] (lime mortar may mark coloured flags, use 1:5 cement/sand).	50 mm sand bed is traditional and suitable for very light use or where plant growth in joints is desired. 35 mm 1:4 lime/sand mortar where a firmer bedding is required.	Paviours are normally thinner than other bricks and require a firmer bedding. A 35/40 mm 1:4 lime/sand or 1:5 cement/sand bed is recommended.	If the blocks/bricks are to be laid unvibrated then the bed of sand must be wetted and compacted before the units are laid; sand roughly 50 mm thick. The recommended method, however, is to carefully lay an uncompacted layer of sand to the required levels. The sand should be sharp, concreting quality, and is laid slightly thicker than 50 mm to allow for the compaction that occurs. The sand must be protected from footprints, etc.	
6 Jointing/pointing	Can be laid butt jointed and unfilled, or with sand filled wide joints as bricks. Normal recommendation is dry mortar mix of 1:3 cement/sand brushed into joints and carefully watered in. If wide mortar joints 6–12 mm are required. A 1:3 cement/sand mortar kept as dry as possible should be carefully used.	For a soft landscape effect wide joints can be filled with sand, pea gravel, etc. To encourage plant or moss growth joints filled with sifted or sand mixed with bone meal. Alternatively, dry 1:4 lime/sand or 1:3 cement/sand brushed into joints and watered. Engineering bricks can be butt jointed or pointed as paviours.	Normally laid with wide mortar joints 6–12 mm. These are best done as the paviour is bedded, i.e. the 'bricklayer' method. 1:3 cement/sand or 1:(1/4):3 cement/lime/sand are recommended. The addition of pigments to BS 1014 will normally improve appearance of pointing. Great care to prevent staining.	The units are carefully placed on to the sand bed butt jointed. A plate vibrator is used to vibrate the brick/blocks into the sand bed. Sand is then spread on to the units and vibrated down between the units. For unvibrated units, the sand is watered into the joints. The pattern of laying is not important for light pedestrian use.	
	Units laid on a sand bed and with sand or soil joints can be considered self-draining.			Units that are vibrated into the sand bed will quickly become impervious and should therefore be laid to falls.	

Hardcore to be clean brick, cement concrete, hard tiles, stone or ballast, broken before placing to pass 75 mm ring suitably graded, to be capable of thorough compaction and free from rubbish. Where hardcore is unobtainable 12:1 all-in ballast lean dry or lean mix can be used.

[a] The minimum suitable thickness for the situation is given in 'flexible' paving, but must be 50 mm thick min.

[b] Some brick paviours are suitable for use in 'flexible' paving. Thicker units can, of course, be used.

[c] This is the sub-base recommended by manufacturers and others. Mortar dots are not recommended by the C&CA but are sometimes used for roof terraces as this allows draining at roofing membrane level. The flexibility of the base may lead to some failures of pointing with relatively thin paviours.

[d] Mortar dots are not recommended by the C&CA but are sometimes used for roof terraces as this allows draining at roofing membrane level. Alternatively, flags on roof terraces can be laid on pads of sheathing felt. Solid mortar bedding is not recommended on roof membranes.

TABLE 6. EXTERNAL PAVING FOR HEAVY PEDESTRIAN USE e.g urban situations, housing estate footpaths, etc., also private driveways. These specifications will resist occasional overriding by heavy vehichles

	Precast concrete flags	Facing bricks / Brick paviours	'Flexible' paving
1 Paving material	Precast concrete flags 50 mm thick min[a]	Facing bricks and stocks of special quality, engineering bricks. 65 mm thick — Brick paviours 50 mm thick min	Precast concrete paving blocks 60 mm thick min — Interlocking clay paviours 50 mm thick min
2 Site preparation/sub-grade	It is important that the sub-grade is carefully prepared for situations of heavy pedestrian use. Topsoil containing organic material should be removed. Soft spots and service trenches should be backfilled and compacted in 150 mm layers. The formation should be carefully levelled to ±25 mm of true levels including falls as necessary. The formation should then be compacted using a 350 kg vibrating roller, or 2.53 tonne smooth wheeler roller or equivalent.		
3 Sub-base/foundation[b]	100 mm lean mix concrete on 100 mm hardcore. The materials used should not be susceptible to frost and should give a dense close-knit surface after compaction using the same rollers as for sub-grade.	100 mm lean mix concrete on 100 mm hardcore	To ensure that subsidence and subsequent ponding and formation of trips do not occur, a stable base is necessary. The thickness of the sub-base should be assessed in relation to the nature of the sub-grade.
4 Edge restraint	Not essential but will give greater stability to paving	Desirable to stabilise edge and helps to protect bricks from wear and displacement — Desirable as protects edge brick from displacement	Essential as flexible paving should be compacted by vibrating for heavy pedestrian use. Edge restraint must be completed prior to laying flexible paving.
5 Bedding	The recommendations for bedding of paving flags for this situation vary considerably. The concrete base will be more accurately formed than hardcore and the bedding may possibly be thinner. Recommendations for the bedding mix also vary from 1:5 lime/sand to 1:3 cement/sand. For a concrete base, the latter would seem more appropriate – say 25 mm nominal thickness of 1:3 cement/sand. The C&CA recommend a dry mix with the flags tamped to level with a paviour's maul.	Again specifications vary from sand/lime to cement/lime. The most common recommendations are: 1:4 lime/sand; 1:1:6 cement/lime/sand; 1:3 cement/sand. If the bricks are to be pointed as work proceeds a 1:(1/4):3 mix similar to the pointing will make the job more straightforward. — A thicker bed is normally provided to paviours than to flags and ordinary bricks: 35/40 mm of 1:4 sand/lime or 1:1:6 cement/sand/lime or 1:3 cement/sand. The latter would seem more appropriate on a concrete base.	The bedding sand should be sharp sand containing not more than 3% silt and clay by weight and not more than 10% retained by a 5 mm sieve. The sand is spread to give a thickness when compacted of 50 mm. This means that a surcharged thickness must be laid, usually in the order of + 15 mm. This must be determined by trials on site. To avoid the need for adjustment, keep grading and moisture content constant. The sand is carefully screeded in front of the area currently laid with blocks. The bed when screeded must not be disturbed by footprints, etc, as uneven pre-compaction would occur causing irregularities in the final paving surface.

Sub-base thickness (row 3, 'Flexible' paving):

	Heavy clay	Silt	Silty clay	Sandy clay	Well-graded sand or sandy gravel
	300	300	150	100	None required (BDA recommends 75 mm)

Edge restraint (additional, row 4): If edge restraint is required or desired, concrete edgings or kerbs, brick on edge, dwarf brick walls are suitable. Kerb-sett' or similar would also be suitable.

6 Jointing/pointing

The choice is basically between narrow butt joints and wide joints with 1:3 dry cement/sand mix brushed into joints and carefully netted. Will be longer lasting than wide mortar pointed joints and stand up to heavy use. In many cases, however, the appearance of wide joints pointed in 1:3 cement/sand mortar will be desired. Pigment to BS 1014 can be added for coloured or exposed aggregate slabs.

Traditionally dry 1:3 cement/sand or 1:4 lime/sand was brushed into joints and watered in. The appearance of this method is rarely acceptable except with smooth non-porous bricks such as engineering pavers.

A 1:3 cement/sand or 1:(1/4):3 cement/lime/sand mortar is recommended with pointing done as the work proceeds, coloured if required. For stocks the pointing should not be stronger than 1:1:6.

Paviours are best pointed in 1:3 cement/sand mortar (or 1:(1/4):3) as work proceeds and neatly flush jointed pigmented sand (or sand/lime) can be used to improve appearance of pointing.

The units are carefully placed on to the sand bed taking care that it is not disturbed and that the units are close butted. Laying the units in an interlocking pattern or the use of shaped units will aid long-term performance.

The units are vibrated into the sand bed using a plate vibrator. Care must be taken not to work too closely to the free edge.

Sand is then spread over the blocks/bricks and two or three passes of the vibrator ensures sand is forced down into the joints to achieve a good interlock. The joints will quickly seal themselves and result in an impervious paving surface. So good falls are necessary.

[a]The maximum suitable thickness for the situation is given in most cases; thicker units can, of course, be used.
[b]Specification for lean mix concrete is usually 1:10 to 1:12 cement and all-in aggregate.

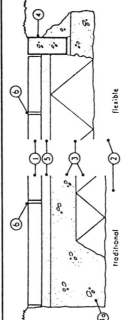

Paving laid on a rigid concrete base should have movement joints at approximately 8 m intervals in each direction.

TABLE 7. EXTERNAL PAVING FOR LIGHT VEHICULAR USE e.g. cul-de-sac, mews courts, short estate roads: maximum vehicular speed 50–60 Km/h

	Precast concrete flags 63–75 mm thick[a]	Engineering brick[b] 65 mm thick	Brick paviours[c] 50 mm thick	'Flexible' paving — Precast concrete paving blocks 60–80 mm thick[e]	'Flexible' paving — Interlocking clay paviours 50 and 65 mm thick[e]
1 Paving material					
2 Site preparation/sub-grade	It is very important that the sub-grade is carefully prepared for situations subject to vehicular traffic, even if in this case the paving is for light vehicular use, all topsoil containing organic material must be removed. These areas, soft spots and service trenches should be backfilled and carefully compacted in 150 mm layers. Trenches will require compaction with a small plate vibrator or rammer. The formation should be carefully levelled to ±25 mm of true levels including adequate falls. The formation should then be compacted using a 6–10 tonne roller or equivalent.				
3 Sub-base/foundation	For vehicular paving the sub-base must adequately support the imposed loads and the occasional lorry.			Thickness of sub-base depends upon the nature of the sub-grade.	
	100–150 mm 1:2:4 concrete on 150 mm hardcore	100 mm 1:2:4 concrete on 150 mm hardcore	100 mm 1:2:4 concrete on 150 mm hardcore		
	The materials used should not be susceptible to frost and should result in a close-knit surface after compaction using the same roller as for the sub-grade.				
4 Edge restraint	Essential to stabilise edge although these types of pavings do not rely on interlock for loadbearing capacity. Edge restraint normally achieved with concrete kerbs to BS 340 (or natural stone to BS 435) but sturdy brickwork or the new 'kerb sett' are alternatives.			Essential as flexible paving must be compacted by vibrating for light vehicular use. The edges will insure that the necessary interlock is maintained. Edge restraint must be completed prior to laying flexible paving.[d]	
5 Bedding	It is absolutely essential that the flags are solidly bedded. The C&CA method using a dry 1:3 cement/sand mix laid 25 mm nominal thickness is preferred with special care being taken in tamping them into the bed with a paviour's maul. Alternatively, a wetter 1:3 cement/sand mortar 25 mm thick can be used.	The manufacturers prefer laying by the compacted semi-dry method. A 30–50 mm 1:4 cement/coarse sand screed is laid and beaten down thoroughly. A thin 1:1 cement/sand slurry is applied and the pavers tapped into position. The bricks can be laid on a traditional wet bed with 1:3 cement/sand 25 mm thick.	A bed of 1:3 cement/sand mortar is recommended, thickness is normally 35/40 mm.	The bedding must be sharp sand containing not more than 3% silt and clay by weight and not more than 10% retained on a 5 mm sieve. The sand is spread to give a thickness when compacted of 50 mm. This means that a surcharged thickness must be laid, usually in the order of +15 mm. This must be determined by trials on site. To avoid the need for adjustment keep grading and moisture content constant. The sand is carefully screeded in front of the area currently laid with blocks. The bed when screeded must not be disturbed by footprints, etc., as uneven pre-compaction would occur causing irregularities in the final paving surface.	
6 Jointing/pointing	Wide pointed joints will not be suitable in most cases and certainly narrow butt joints filled by brushing dry 1:3 cement/sand into them will give better service. Careful wetting of the joints is necessary to avoid staining of flags, a few authorities advise leaving to hydrate naturally, but what about sudden heavy rain?	Paviours are best pointed in 1:3 cement/sand mortar (or 1:(1/4):3) as work proceeds and neatly flush jointed. Pigmented sand or sand/lime can be used to improve appearance of pointing.	If the pavers are laid butt jointed and have smooth faces they can be grouted with 1:1 cement/sand using a squeegee to force the grout into the joint. The surface is then dusted with dry 1:1 cement/sand and brushed off. With textured or studded pavers, the bricks are normally laid with a wide joint and pointed with 1:3 cement/sand (can be coloured)	The units are simply laid closely butted on to the sand taking care not to disturb the bed. For vehicular use units should be laid in an interlocking herringbone pattern or specially shaped units laid. Once laid the units can be used as a working platform. After a sufficient area is laid they are bedded down with two or three passes of a plate vibrator keeping 1 m from the free edge. Sand is then spread over the blocks/bricks and two or three more passes of the vibrator ensures sand is forced down into the joints to achieve a good interlock. Traffic can use the paving as soon as the vibration is complete. The joints will quickly seal themselves and result in an impervious paving surface, so good falls are essential.	

Sub-grade thickness (under 'Flexible' paving):

Heavy clay	Silt	Silty clay	Sandy clay	Well-graded sand or sandy gravel
400	400	190	140	80

Paving laid on a rigid concrete base should have movement joints at approximately 8 m intervals in each direction.

[a] Only flags made to the quality specification clauses of BS 368 should be used in this situation. 63 mm thick flags are suitable for very light vehicular traffic, 75 mm thick flags should be used elsewhere, smaller units are less liable to crack.
[b] Stocks and facings are not normally suitable for light vehicular use, some engineering bricks can be laid as 'flexible' paving.
[c] Some paviours can be laid as 'flexible' paving.
[d] Units must be cut (or special units used) to fit edge restraints closely. The base for the kerb must not extend under paving.
[e] 60 mm suitable for small cul-de-sacs and mews' courts, 80 mm elsewhere.

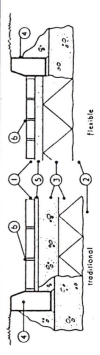

traditional

flexible

VEHICULAR PAVING

GUIDANCE NOTES

Scope

The design of roads and their associated footpaths is subject to control by the Local Authority. For this reason, any general design guidance will have to be modified in the light of local requirements and site conditions. It is assumed that most public and larger private roads will be designed by an engineer, but there are often cases of small private roads which hardly warrant such attention. They form part of the external works contract and become the responsibility of the landscape architect, land agent or builder. This information is intended for construction guidance only and is not intended to bypass the specialist. In any design problem it is preferable to decide which solution best integrates the aesthetic and practical requirements of the project. The main problems are the type of surface required and its composition; structural requirements dictated by the loading; type and strength of soil under the road; preparation of the road formation; and the costs of various materials that are available. Water must not be allowed to get in from the top or the sides of a road, otherwise frost could cause it to disintegrate. This can be overcome by having a sealed surface, appropriate falls and drainage.

Types of road construction

Road construction can be divided into two categories:

- Flexible roads (macadam, gravel).
- Rigid roads (*in-situ* concrete or precast units).

Both these types can be represented diagrammatically:

WEARING COURSE
BASE COURSE
ROAD BASE
SUB-BASE   grade
SUB-GRADE/FORMATION

Flexible roads

A flexible road is made up of layers of thoroughly compacted materials which spread the traffic load on the soil beneath. The materials used are by their nature 'flexible' and will move slightly under loading. A method of edge restraint should therefore be considered in the design to prevent the structure spreading and deforming.

Sub-Grade/Formation
This is the stable natural ground level upon which the other layers of road construction are founded. The required contour of the road surface is obtained by shaping the sub-grade.

Sub-Base
Granular material such as hoggin and shale can be used, but the material and the thickness will depend entirely on the stability of the sub-grade. It can be omitted altogether on very stable sub-grades.

Road Base
This can be lean-mix concrete, dense tar macadam, dense bitumen macadam, dry-bound macadam or wet-mix macadam, soil cement or a number of other materials. Each type of road base is specified in detail in the DOT's publication, *Specification for Road and Bridge Works*.

Base Course
A wearing course and a base course are then added to the road base. On lightly trafficked roads a single course, usually not less than 65 mm thick, is sometimes used. Greater structural strength can be obtained by using larger aggregates in a bitumen macadam. A base course may vary in thickness from 38 mm to 76 mm.

Wearing Course
Finer material is used in this layer, which will result in a more impervious surface. A wearing course may vary in thickness from

13 mm to 38 mm.

Rigid roads

General
A combination construction of continuously reinforced concrete with a bituminous surface is sometimes used for city streets, trunk roads and motorways, but is unlikely to be used on estate roads. The method by which the thickness of each structural layer is determined is set out in Road Note 29.

In-Situ Concrete
Sub-grade/formation. See notes for flexible roads.

Sub-Base
This may be of consolidated hardcore, or, if the ground is suitable, may be eliminated provided it can be compacted satisfactorily.

Road Base
This is of either reinforced or unreinforced concrete, depending upon traffic intensity.

Base Course/Wearing Course
The top surface of the concrete road base is the wearing surface of the finished road.

Precast units

Sub-Base
The requirements for category of road use and type of sub-grade may be determined by consulting Road Note 29 and the DoT's *Specification for Road and Bridge Works*. Alternatively, a thin concrete slab, of a minimum of 75 mm, laid direct on a suitable sub-grade will be satisfactory. The base can be laid without reinforcement or joints.

Laying Course
A compacted bed of sand, approximately 50 mm thick, is spread on the sub-base. The road blocks are laid on this.

Block Course
The blocks, after levelling with a vibrator, should have sand brushed over them, followed by a final vibration. All edges must be restrained to keep the blocks in compression and to prevent outward movement. The edge should be laid before the surfacing.

Design of sub-bases

The design of the sub-base is dominated by two factors:

1. The bearing capacity of the sub-grade, expressed as its California Bearing Ratio (CBR). Table 8, derived from Table 3 of Road Note 29, shows the CBR values for typical British soils. Note that the depth of water table affects the results. Sub-soil drainage should be provided if the water table is less than 600 mm below formation level.
2. The load carried in the design life of the road/paving. For design of main roads, this is usually expressed as the cumulative number of standard (8200 kg) axles expected to be imposed on it (see Road Note 29).

Table 9 shows the thicknesses of sub-bases required for typical roads and pavings, for a given CBR of sub-grade. The figures for vehicular areas are derived from Road Note 29, figures 5 and 6, and assume a design life of 40 years.

Foundations composed of sub-base and base courses give structural strength to paving surfaces. The sub-base is reasonably open and free-draining, while the base is more dense to accept laying or wearing courses. The required foundation depth depends on the load and frequency of use and on the sub-soil conditions (see Table 9).

Where a rigid base or wearing surface of reinforced concrete is laid, the minimum sub-base thickness on weak sub-soil should be 150 mm; on normal sub-soil, minimum thickness is 80 mm.

Foundations more than 200 mm deep may be made of more than one layer of sub-base or base material, while in shallow foundations (100 mm or less), only base material could be used.

Sub-soil structure and stability can now often be much improved by using filter fabrics and geogrids of artificial materials,

TABLE 8. ESTIMATED CBR VALUES FOR BRITISH SOILS

Type of soil	CBR (per cent)	
	Depth of water table below formation level	
	More than 600 mm	600 mm or less
Heavy clay	2–3	1–2
Silty clay	5	3
Sandy clay	6–7	4–5
Sand (poorly graded)	20	10
Sand (well graded)	40	15
Well-graded sandy gravel	60	20

TABLE 9. SUB-BASE THICKNESS

California Bearing Ratio (CBR) (%)	Cul-de-sacs, car parks and minor residential roads (mm)	Roads with the following numbers of public service vehicles per day in each direction			Main roads
		up to 25 mm	25–50 mm	over 50 mm	
Less than 2	550	600	630	650	700
2	400	450	480	500	550
3	300	350	360	380	430
4	230	280	290	300	330
5	190	230	240	250	280
6	140	180	180	190	220
7 or over	100	150	150	160	180

webbing mats or woven fabrics. This technique can greatly reduce development costs by reducing both the amount of excavation of unsuitable material and the importation of granular fill for the sub-base and base courses.

Choice of material for sub-base

The choice of material has no influence on the design of the sub-base: the same thickness of material is required whether it is suitably graded as-dug gravel or specially designed lean concrete (to take two contrasting examples).

It will often be advantageous to specify the same granular material for use as the sub-base to roads, etc.

SPECIFICATION CHECK LISTS

Bitumen macadam

General
There does not appear to be a single comprehensive guidance document for the designer who wishes to specify pavings without consulting a specialist in this type of work. The notes here place much reliance on BS 4987, which borders on

being a code of practice but forms the basis for a good standard of workmanship. Further information may be obtained from the British Aggregate Construction Materials Industries (BACMI) and the DTp specification together with its guidance notes which are published in a separate booklet; but the latter documents are intended for use by qualified civil engineers.

Materials

General: Specify any kerbs, drainage channels and outlets which are not more conveniently specified elsewhere (e.g. with drainage work).

Granular sub-base: Specify the type and select the thickness for one of the following:
Heavy clay
Silty clay
Sandy clay
Sandy and well-graded sandy gravel

Paving types: State types of paving to be used for coated macadam, rolled asphalt or sealed gravel, etc.

Roads and parking areas: Specify number and type of layers suitable for site roads and parking for vehicles up to about 5 tonnes. It is often convenient (especially to the contractor) to lay site roads at the beginning of the contract (e.g. multi-building development) but with the wearing course delayed until completion. In these cases a suitably strong road base and base course must be specified together with procedures for repairing any damage and preparing the used surface for the wearing course.

Workmanship

Code of practice: Comply with BS 4987: Part 2: Specification for transport, laying and compaction, subject to any qualifications given and the Department of Transport's *Specification for Highway Works*.
BS 4987: Part 2 is not catalogued as a CP by BSI but may be regarded as a CP for the purposes of the specification.
Tolerances on finishes and thicknesses are specified in the BS.

Choice of specialist firm: Ensure that macadam pavings and sub-grade are laid by specialists who are experienced in

working in accordance with BS 4987. The specification should be directed at the main contractor who must ensure that the pavings are laid by operatives experienced in road construction. Obviously this needs modification if the job specification is confined to a small area of footpath.

Compaction for pavings:Specify methods of compacting ground.

Bases:The sub-base (i.e. the layer under the bottom layer of macadam provides structural support) forms *a very important part* of the overall specification for the pavings. State method of laying and compacting.

Before laying pavings: This refers to the procedures following upon the completion of the sub-base. Specify any weedkiller required. Note if kerbs, etc., are to be executed after the pavings or if this is an option (kerbs are normally laid in separate concrete foundation but can be laid on the road base or on the finished paving). State method of protection of abutments such as manholes, drainage gullies, etc.

Laying macadam: Specify method of laying and compacting sub-base, base course and wearing course, including tolerances for levels and regularity.

Parking lines: Specify surface markings, paint and width. Many materials are suitable (e.g. thermoplastic paint, chlorinated rubber paint, reflective glass beads to BS 6088 set in epoxy resin paint). Specify details.

Protection: Specify general protection from any contamination or traffic (e.g. tracked vehicles) that could harm the paving.

Interlocking brick/block roads

General

Specification may be by reference to a standard, by proprietary name(s), or both. Delete subitems as appropriate.
For clay and calcium silicate pavers to BS 6677: Part 1, insert classification, PA or PB. Type PA pavers are suitable for areas trafficked by pedestrians, motor cars and light vans. Type PB pavers are suitable for areas trafficked by public transport and commercial road vehicles. See BS 6677: Part 1, table 1 and Part 2, clause 2.1

Setting out: State any drawing reference(s).
Bond: Describe type of bond. Herringbone bond gives the maximum amount of restraint to individual blocks/pavers and should be used in areas subject to regular vehicular traffic. Stretcher bond should be used only in pedestrian or very lightly trafficked areas. If shaped blocks/pavers are being used, stretcher bond may be acceptable for areas with light vehicular traffic. Basket weave bond is suitable for pedestrian areas only. There may be difficulties of fit with some brick pavers – check with manufacturer that the particular paver is suitable for this type of bond.
Features: Describe any features to be included. A course of headers or stretchers adjacent to raised edge restraints provides a neat finish and makes the marking of blocks/pavers for cutting much easier.

Materials
Manufacturer and reference: State precise proprietary description comprising name of manufacturer, brand or range name and colour/finish. Alternatives should be given where acceptable. The phrase 'or equivalent' may be inserted.
Size: Check with block/paver manufacturer the recommended thickness for the particular traffic situation. Brick pavers are normally:

> 210 × 105 mm
> 215 × 102.5 mm
> 200 × 100 mm

Rectangular concrete blocks are normally 200 × 100 mm on plan, shaped blocks are either 200 × 100, 225 × 112.5 or 295 × 295 mm on plan. Thicknesses of block for typical applications are:

- Industrial installations and heavily trafficked areas – 80/100 mm.
- Residential roads – 60/65/80 mm.
- Car parks and lightly trafficked areas – 60/65 mm or 80 mm if regularly trafficked by heavy commercial vehicles.

Sand for bedding: The best paving is achieved when the sand is within 1 per cent of its optimum moisture content, i.e. the moisture content at which a specified amount of compaction will produce the maximum dry density.
Sand for jointing: State details of sand for jointing. The use of mortar in joints is not recommended as the flexible nature of the paving, which is an important part of its design, will be impaired. In addition, the ease with which sections for flexible paving can be taken up and relaid for modifications to below-ground services is lost (see Interpave Information Sheet 7).
Samples: Samples may be required for block/pavers which are inherently variable in appearance, e.g. clay pavers which are selected from different parts of the kiln and mixed before delivery.
Special blocks/pavers: State requirements for special blocks such as edge restraints, starter blocks, etc.
Colour pattern: Give a basic description of appearance where specification is by reference to a standard. Chamfered edged should be used in paving subject to vehicular traffic.
Granular sub-base: State materials to be used.
Sub-base: State materials to be used. If the sub-base is used extensively by site traffic, damage is bound to occur and this should be made good prior to spreading the bedding course. The surface of the sub-base should be blinded before laying the bedding course.

Workmanship
Control samples: The specification of control samples should be related to the size and importance of the job. It may be difficult to justify control samples on small jobs. Insert type item(s) of paving reference(s), minimum size(s) and any features to be included (e.g. edgings, channels, marker blocks).
Inclement weather: State procedure for work in wet and cold weather.
Levels of paving: Paving should be set above drainage outlets to allow for future consolidation of the paving by traffic. State permissible deviation from specified levels.
Regularity: State tolerance for surface irregularity after completion.
Laying bedding: Describe laying, levelling and compacting of bedding material.

Laying blocks/pavers: Describe the method of laying blocks/pavers including checks for alignment.
Cut blocks/pavers: State how blocks are to be cut.
Compacting and jointing: Specify how blocks/pavers are to be compacted and joints filled, avoiding damaging kerbs and adjacent work during vibration.
Remedial work: Give instructions for any remedial work during the Contract of Defects Liability Period.

Precast concrete and grass paving

General
Manufacturer's recommendations vary from system to system, and should be checked before completing the specification.

Materials
Grass/concrete units: State manufacturer's name and reference. The surface area for grass not less than 85 per cent. The base area for concrete not less than 85 per cent.
Soil: Specify type of soil required.
Sand: Specify grass seed mixture
Sub-base: Specify materials to be used.

Workmanship
Sub-grade compaction: Describe method of compaction.
Sub-base: For light vehicular trafficking no sub-base is required. For more intense loadings a granular sub-base should be provided, the thickness depending upon the quality of the sub-grade and the anticipated intensity of loading. The inclusion of soil or loam in the sub-base material should provide nourishment for grass roots and encourage growth.
Sand course: A layer of sharp sand, 20 mm thick, should be placed over the sub-base (or sub-grade), screeded, then lightly rolled to form the bedding layer.
Units: Describe how units should be laid within the restrained area. The units may be laid using a staggered bond to provide increased structural integrity.
Filling: State how the cavities between the castellations should be filled and grass seed sown.

Watering: Specify number of waterings required.
Protection: Specify method of protection until grass is established.

DETAIL SHEETS

Corners (2)
Flexible
Vehicular paving (2)
Asphalt concrete
Asphalt concrete on concrete base
Bitumen macadam
Sealed gravel
Hoggin
Rigid
Concrete block (basketweave pattern)
Concrete block (herringbone pattern)
Interlocking concrete block
Interlocking concrete unit
Firepath block
Rumble block
Vehicular speed control
Cattle grid
Precast slabs
Concrete slabs and blocks
Concrete slab
In-situ
Reinforced concrete
Unreinforced concrete
Exposed aggregate

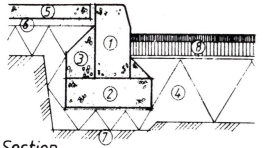

Section

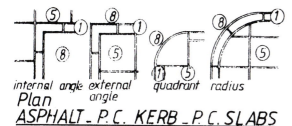

internal angle | external angle | quadrant | radius

Plan

ASPHALT_ P.C. KERB _ P.C. SLABS

1 P.C. Concrete kerb

2 Concrete foundation

3 Insitu concrete haunching

4 Consolidated hardcore

5 P.C. Paving slab

6 Sand bed

7 Sub base prepared to required level

8 Asphalt

9 Stone sett

10 Grass

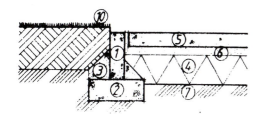

Section

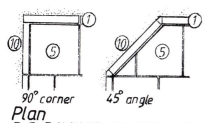

90° corner | 45° angle

Plan

P.C. PAVING SLABS _ P.C. KERB _ GRASS

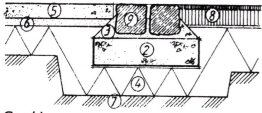

Section

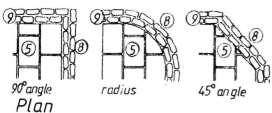

90° angle | radius | 45° angle

Plan

ASPHALT _ STONE SETTS _ P.C. SLABS

N.T.S.

CORNERS
vehicular paving

19

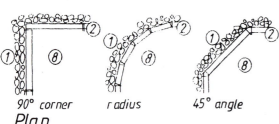

Section

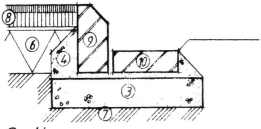

90° corner   radius   45° angle

Plan
ASPHALT _ P. C. KERB _ COBBLES

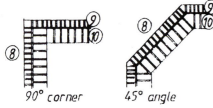

Section

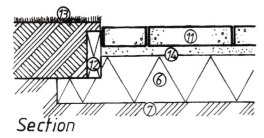

90° corner   45° angle

Plan

ASPHALT _ ENG BRICK KERB_
BRICK CHANNEL

1   Cobbles
2   P. C. Concrete kerb
3   Concrete foundation
4   Insitu concrete haunching
5   Cement & sand mortar bed
6   Consolidated hardcore
7   Sub base prepared to required level
8   Asphalt
9   Eng. brick kerb - single cant
10 Brick channel
11 Interlocking concrete block
12 Edge board
13 Grass
14 Sand bed

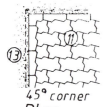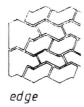

Section

45° corner   edge   end

Plan
INTERLOCKING CONCRETE BLOCKS_
P. C. EDGE _ GRASS

CORNERS
vehicular paving

N.T.S.

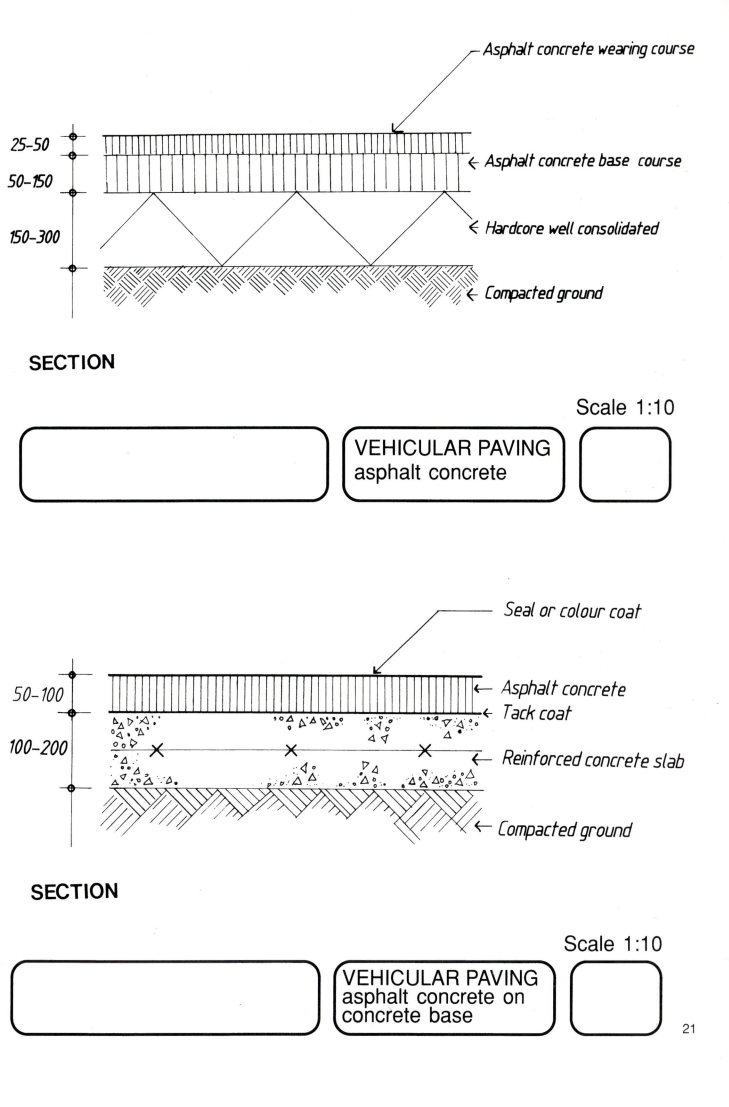

25–50 — Asphalt concrete wearing course

50–150 — Asphalt concrete base course

150–300 — Hardcore well consolidated

Compacted ground

SECTION

Scale 1:10

VEHICULAR PAVING
asphalt concrete

Seal or colour coat

50–100 — Asphalt concrete — Tack coat

100–200 — Reinforced concrete slab

Compacted ground

SECTION

Scale 1:10

VEHICULAR PAVING
asphalt concrete on
concrete base

21

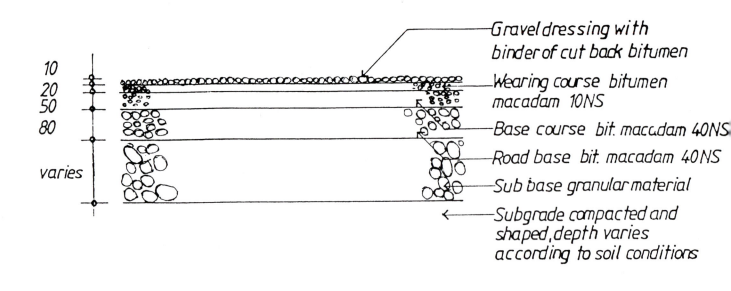

10
20
50
80

varies

Gravel dressing with
binder of cut back bitumen

Wearing course bitumen
macadam 10NS

Base course bit. macadam 40NS

Road base bit. macadam 40NS

Sub base granular material

Subgrade compacted and
shaped, depth varies
according to soil conditions

SECTION

Scale 1:10

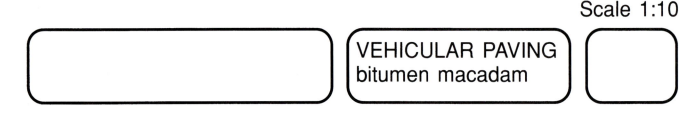

VEHICULAR PAVING
bitumen macadam

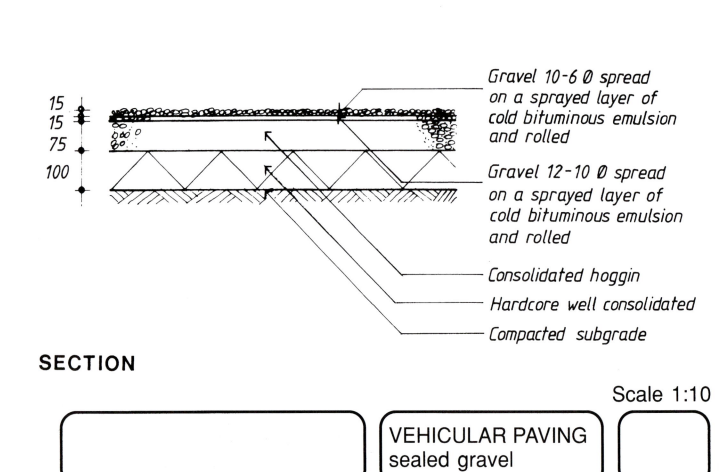

15
15
75
100

Gravel 10-6 Ø spread
on a sprayed layer of
cold bituminous emulsion
and rolled

Gravel 12-10 Ø spread
on a sprayed layer of
cold bituminous emulsion
and rolled

Consolidated hoggin

Hardcore well consolidated

Compacted subgrade

SECTION

Scale 1:10

VEHICULAR PAVING
sealed gravel

22

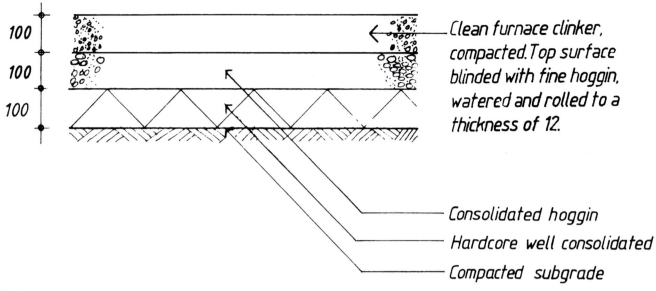

SECTION

100

100

100

Clean furnace clinker, compacted. Top surface blinded with fine hoggin, watered and rolled to a thickness of 12.

Consolidated hoggin

Hardcore well consolidated

Compacted subgrade

Scale 1:10

VEHICULAR PAVING
hoggin

23

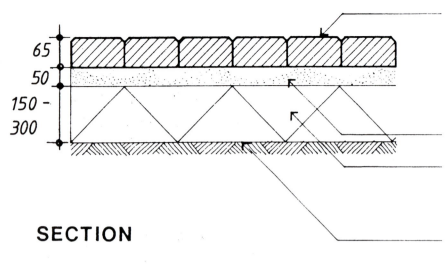

65
50
150 –
300

Precast concrete paving block *brindle* colour laid on compacted sand, joints filled with sand and blocks vibrated. Laid to falls 1:60 minimum.

Coarse sand bed compacted

Sub-base granular material depth depending on ground conditions.

Compacted sub-grade

SECTION

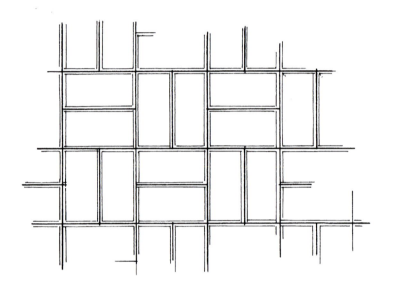

Basketweave pattern.

PLAN

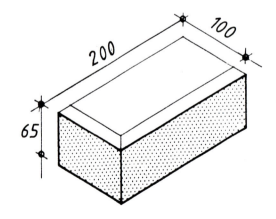

200
100
65

Scale 1:10

VEHICULAR PAVING
concrete block

24

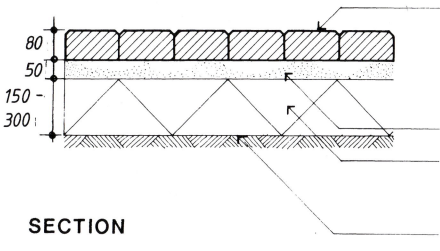

SECTION

80
50
150 -
300

Precast concrete paving block natural colour laid on compacted sand, joints filled with sand and blocks vibrated. Laid to falls 1:60

Coarse sand bed compacted

Sub-base granular material depth depending on ground conditions.

Compacted sub-grade

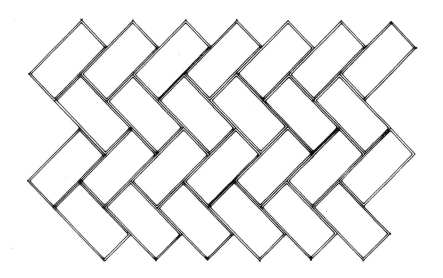

Herringbone pattern

PLAN

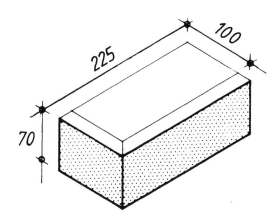

225
100
70

Scale 1:10

VEHICULAR PAVING
concrete block

25

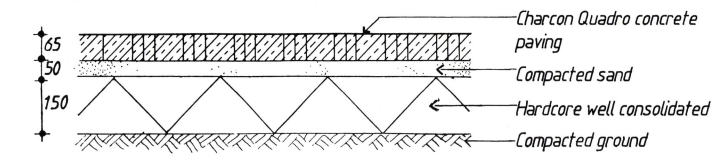

- Charcon Quadro concrete paving
- Compacted sand
- Hardcore well consolidated
- Compacted ground

65

50

150

SECTION

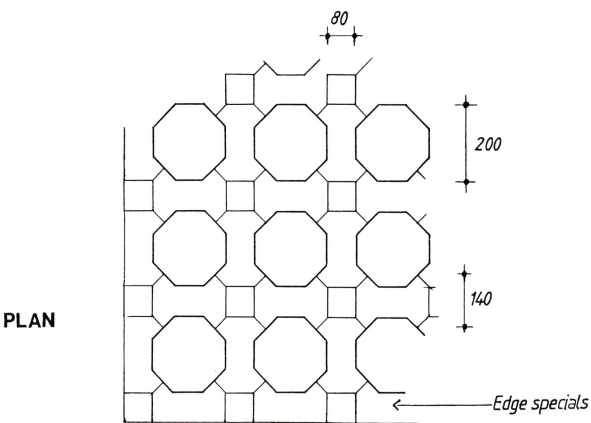

80

200

140

PLAN

- Edge specials

Scale 1:10

VEHICULAR PAVING
interlocking concrete block

26

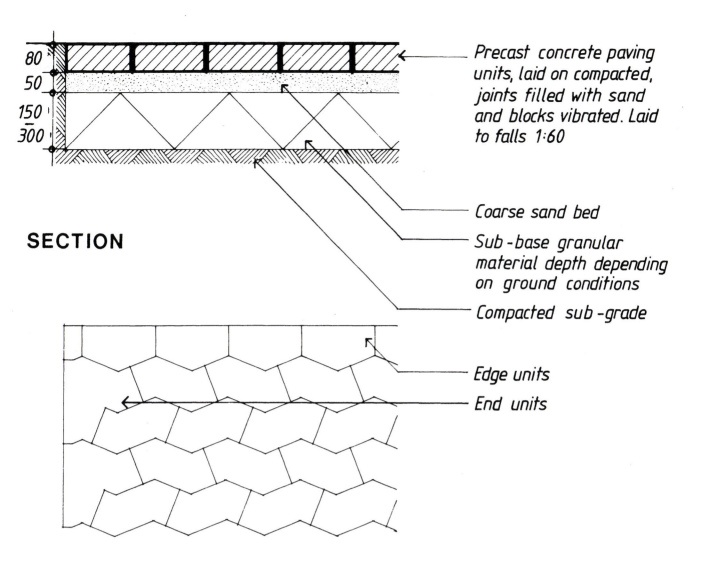

SECTION

80
50
150
300

Precast concrete paving units, laid on compacted, joints filled with sand and blocks vibrated. Laid to falls 1:60

Coarse sand bed

Sub-base granular material depth depending on ground conditions

Compacted sub-grade

Edge units

End units

PLAN

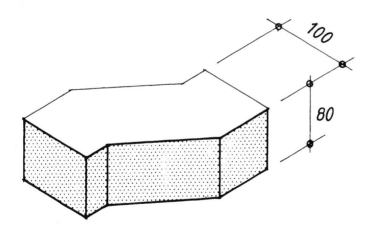

100

80

Scale 1:10

VEHICULAR PAVING
interlocking concrete
unit

27

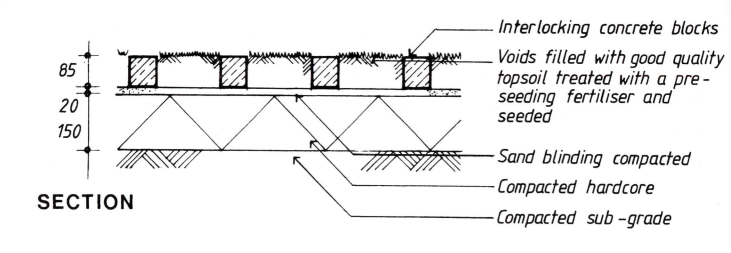

SECTION

85
20
150

Interlocking concrete blocks

Voids filled with good quality topsoil treated with a pre-seeding fertiliser and seeded

Sand blinding compacted

Compacted hardcore

Compacted sub-grade

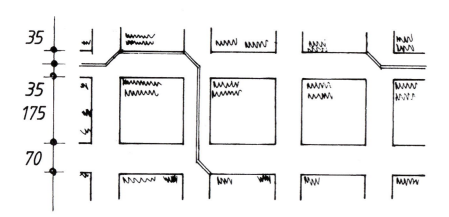

35
35
175
70

PLAN

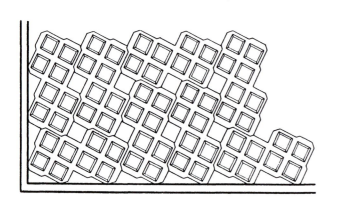

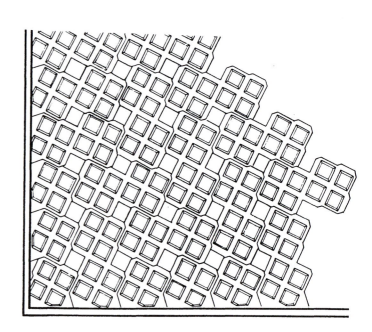

PLAN: WITHOUT EDGE BLOCKS

WITH EDGE BLOCKS   N.T.S.

Scale 1:10

VEHICULAR PAVING
firepath

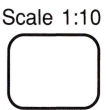

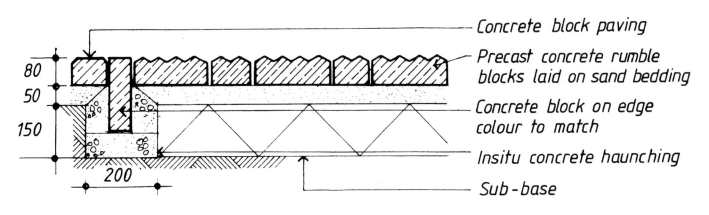

Concrete block paving

Precast concrete rumble blocks laid on sand bedding

Concrete block on edge colour to match

Insitu concrete haunching

Sub-base

80
50
150

200

SECTION

Scale 1:10

VEHICULAR PAVING
rumble block

29

SECTION

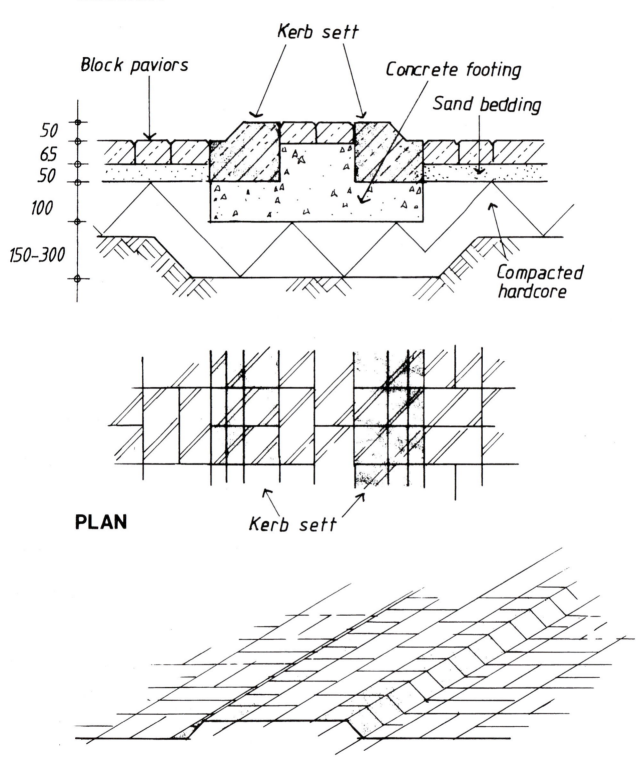

Block paviors

Kerb sett

Concrete footing

Sand bedding

50
65
50
100
150–300

Compacted hardcore

PLAN

Kerb sett

DETAIL

Scale 1:10

VEHICULAR PAVING
vehicular speed control

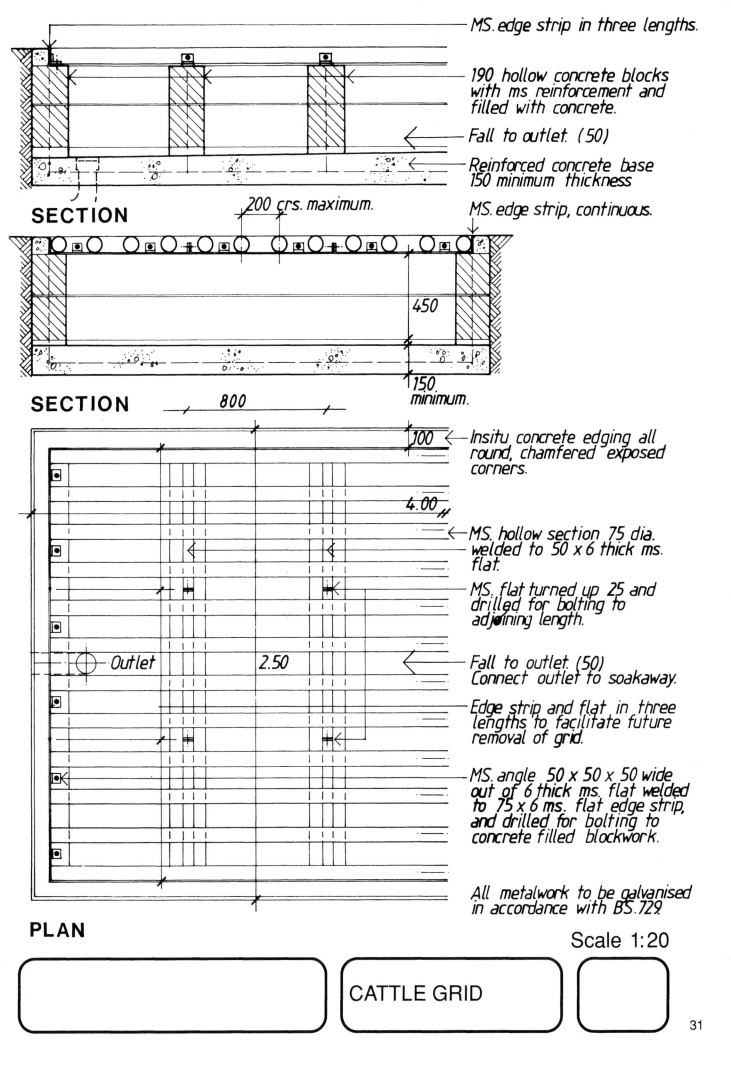

SECTION

MS. edge strip in three lengths.

190 hollow concrete blocks with ms reinforcement and filled with concrete.

Fall to outlet. (50)

Reinforced concrete base 150 minimum thickness

SECTION

200 crs. maximum.

MS. edge strip, continuous.

450

150 minimum.

800

100

PLAN

Outlet

2.50

4.00

Insitu concrete edging all round, chamfered exposed corners.

MS. hollow section 75 dia. welded to 50 x 6 thick ms. flat.

MS. flat turned up 25 and drilled for bolting to adjoining length.

Fall to outlet. (50) Connect outlet to soakaway.

Edge strip and flat in three lengths to facilitate future removal of grid.

MS. angle 50 x 50 x 50 wide out of 6 thick ms. flat welded to 75 x 6 ms. flat edge strip, and drilled for bolting to concrete filled blockwork.

All metalwork to be galvanised in accordance with BS.729

Scale 1:20

CATTLE GRID

31

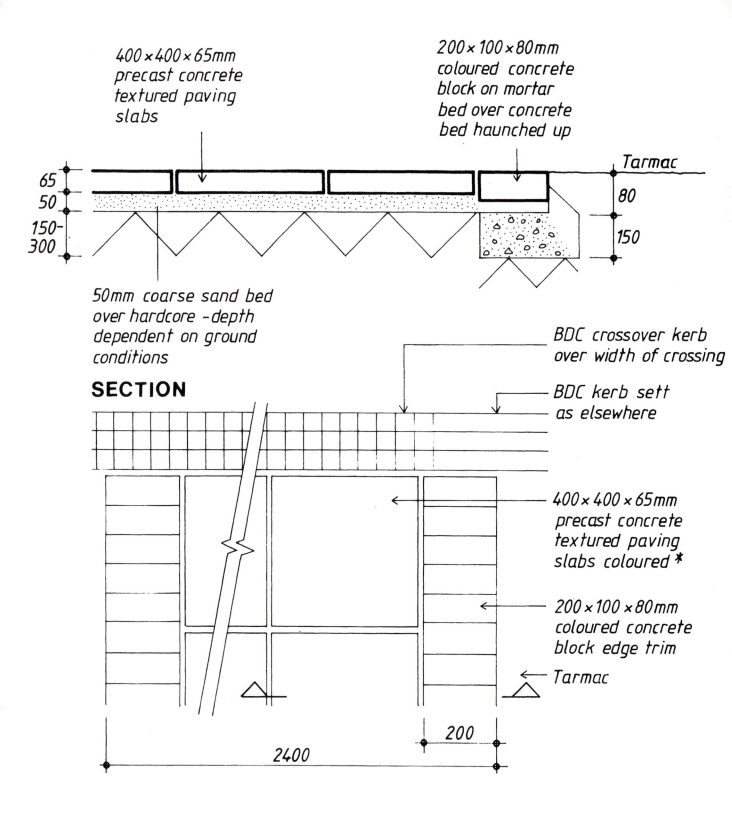

400 × 400 × 65mm
precast concrete
textured paving
slabs

200 × 100 × 80mm
coloured concrete
block on mortar
bed over concrete
bed haunched up

Tarmac

65
50
150-
300

80

150

50mm coarse sand bed
over hardcore - depth
dependent on ground
conditions

SECTION

BDC crossover kerb
over width of crossing

BDC kerb sett
as elsewhere

400 × 400 × 65mm
precast concrete
textured paving
slabs coloured *

200 × 100 × 80mm
coloured concrete
block edge trim

Tarmac

200

2400

PLAN

Paving to BS 368

* Available from:
  Charcon Ltd.
  Hulland Ward,
  Derby, DE6 3ET.

Scale 1:10

VEHICULAR PAVING
slabs

32

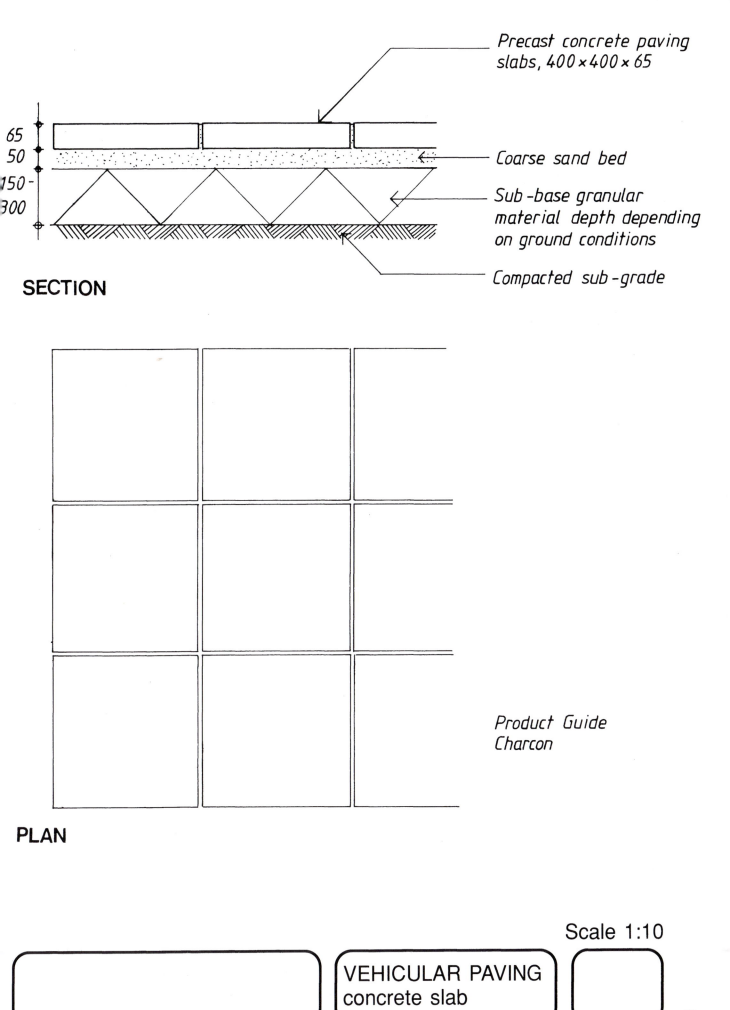

Precast concrete paving slabs, 400 × 400 × 65

65
50
150 -
300

Coarse sand bed

Sub-base granular material depth depending on ground conditions

Compacted sub-grade

SECTION

PLAN

Product Guide
Charcon

Scale 1:10

VEHICULAR PAVING
concrete slab

33

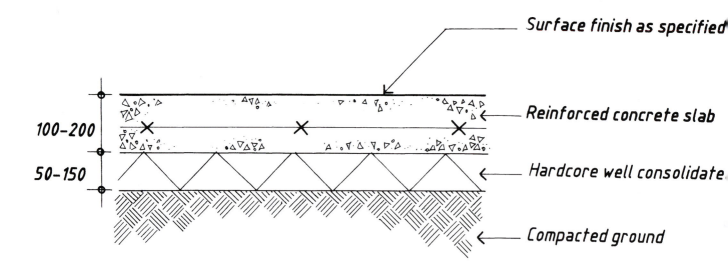

Surface finish as specified

Reinforced concrete slab

100-200

Hardcore well consolidate.

50-150

Compacted ground

SECTION

Scale 1:10

VEHICULAR PAVING
reinforced concrete

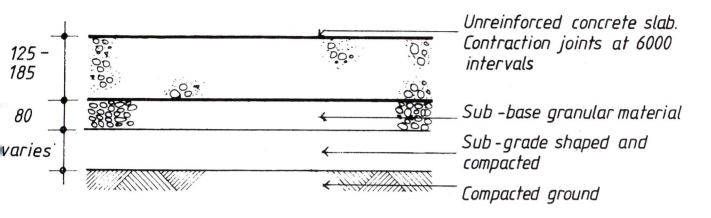

125 – 185		*Unreinforced concrete slab.* *Contraction joints at 6000* *intervals*
80		*Sub -base granular material*
varies		*Sub -grade shaped and* *compacted*
		Compacted ground

SECTION

Note

Concrete thickness can be
reduced if reinforcing mesh
is used.
Thickness depends upon
traffic intensity

Scale 1:10

VEHICULAR PAVING
concrete

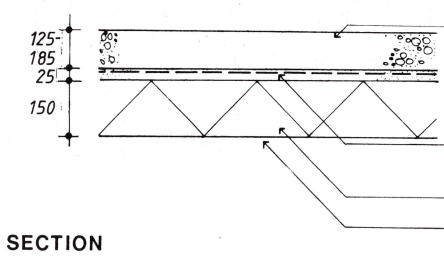

125-
185
25
150

SECTION

Concrete, with 20 maximum
aggregate. Aggregate to be
exposed by brushing and
washing. Contraction joints
at 6000 centres

Polypropylene felt lapped
10 at joints on ash blindin

Hardcore well consolidated

Compacted sub-grade

Note
Concrete thickness can be
reduced if reinforcing mesh
is used.
Thickness depends upon
traffic intensity

Scale 1:10

VEHICULAR PAVING
exposed aggregate

PEDESTRIAN PAVING

GUIDANCE NOTES

Paving patterns

Patterns for large units such as paving slabs should be kept as simple as possible, as a heavy pattern is only attractive when used to fulfil a particular function. Do not mix colours and too many different surface finishes. When introducing a texture into the paving, consider the function of the area, i.e. wheeled traffic or street furniture. When introducing an infill into a large area of smooth paving, make sure the overall design and pattern of the infill are not in conflict. In selecting colours of paving, first ensure that they blend with the building or surroundings.

Large complex patterns are difficult to design as they suffer foreshortening when seen obliquely from the ground, making them difficult for the pedestrian to comprehend. Small units such as bricks offer a variety of patterns. Setts, either granite or concrete, offer even more flexibility, such as curved and circular patterns, but their use in an area should be very carefully considered. Cobblestones, depending upon their shape, are used either as a deterrent surfacing or for walking upon. They can be used to infill corners when creating paving patterns with other materials or on their own for a path if properly laid.

Choice of materials

Hard surfaces should retain their interest throughout the year. A limited range of materials should generally be used to give coherence to a scheme, but surfaces should not become monotonous, particularly in the winter months.

The materials selected should complement each other and be suitable for the shapes they are covering. *In-situ* concrete and gravel are better for awkward or rounded shapes than square or rectangular units which require extensive cutting. The best guide to selecting appropriate paving materials is by observation; those derived from natural materials are obvious choices. New materials using, and blending with, the colours of these materials, provided they are laid correctly, generally look right.

It is preferable to reflect the local vernacular, as this creates a sense of place. The separation of pedestrian from vehicular surfacing provides an opportunity to create a far more interesting design. Where it is necessary to provide for pedestrians as well as vehicles, a mixture of materials can be used, or the same material (in a different colour) can be used for vehicles but with the appropriate increase in foundation thickness.

The main aim is to keep the areas of each material as large as possible and ensure a smooth transition from one to another. The stronger the pattern, the larger the area must be, and considerable care must be taken not to introduce too many colours. Some paving colours clash violently with the foliage of plants. Keeping the elements as natural as possible, such as granite setts, gravel and cobblestone, is one method of producing a harmonious design.

Weathering

All materials weather, but at different rates. Natural stone paving and natural materials accept moss and lichen easily. The subtle variations in light, shade and dampness are expressed by these growths, quickly giving the material a 'mature' look. Bricks, pavers, tiles and concrete lose their manufactured finishes less quickly, retaining into old age a crispness not in itself unpleasing. Weathering can be encouraged by selecting rough textured materials, or by applying organic solutions to encourage the growth of moss and lichen. The latter is not always desirable as it makes the surface damp and slippery.

Paving materials

Different paving materials should be used logically to indicate different usage of areas, changes of use, and as direction indicators.

Drainage gutters and changes in level can often be picked out in different materials to good advantage. Small-scale unit materials relating to pedestrian scale can be contrasted with more monolithic paving in areas used by vehicles. Careful choice of materials can produce an interesting and satisfying floorscape.

At a functional level, paving surfaces should not be slippery, be resistant to erosion, have a reasonable life expectancy and require limited maintenance.

Sub-grade, base and sub-base

To ensure that any surface paving material retains its final laid position, it is essential that both the surface and base materials be prepared thoroughly. Paving usually has a base and sub-grade underneath, and both of these must be thoroughly compacted.

Sub-grade
This should be well compacted either by hand or by mechanical means. The required contour of the paving is obtained by shaping the sub-grade.

Base
The base is usually of hardcore, compacted by a 3-tonne roller or a 508 kg vibrating roller.

Design of sub-base
The design of the sub-base is dominated by two factors:

1. The bearing capacity of the sub-grade, expressed as its California Bearing Ratio (CBR). Table 10 (derived from Table 3 of Road Note 29) shows the CBR values for typical British soils. Note that the depth of water table affects the results. Sub-soil drainage should be provided if the water table is less than 600 mm below formation level.
2. The load carried in the design life of the paving. For pedestrian areas design is usually on a rule of thumb basis. Table 11 shows the thicknesses of sub-bases required for typical pavings, for a given CBR of sub-grade.

Foundations on firm dry sub-soil, where light pedestrian use can be ensured, may not be required for paving units more than 500 mm square and *in-situ* concrete paving. Where small paving units are to be used, a concrete base should generally be laid, except for brick and concrete blocks, which may be laid on a flexible foundation with a sand laying course.

TABLE 10. ESTIMATED CBR VALUES FOR BRITISH SOILS

Type of soil (compacted at the natural moisture content)	CBR (per cent)	
	Depth of water table below formation level	
	More than 600 mm	600 mm or less
Heavy clay	2–3	1–2
Silty clay	5	3
Sandy clay	6–7	4–5
Sand (poorly graded)	20	10
Sand (well graded)	40	15
Well-graded sandy gravel	60	20

TABLE 11. SUB-BASE THICKNESSES

California Bearing Ratio (CBR) (%)	Footways pedestrian areas and private driveways (mm)	Footways and pedestrian areas with occasional over-riding by commercial vehicles (mm)
Less than 2	380	500
2	230	350
3	180	260
4	160	200
5	140	160
6	120	120
7 or over	100	100

Base or laying courses of mortar or sand are used to bed unit materials such as blocks, bricks and paving stones to obtain finished levels. Base courses are used for flexible surfaces like tarmacadam or cold asphalt, which may be thin or made with small particles, and have little cohesion without a base.

Choice of material for sub-base
The choice of material has no influence on the design of the sub-base; the same thickness of material is required whether it is suitably as-dug gravel or specially designed lean concrete.
If the design of the hard paved areas includes several different types of finish in close juxtaposition, consideration should be given to thicknesses of bases and sub-bases. It is obviously advantageous for the various types of finish to have a granular sub-base of a single thickness and without change of recommended bedding thickness for one or more of the finishes, cost considerations may dictate changing the levels and/or thicknesses of the sub-base.

In-situ concrete base
In considering this, a major factor may be whether or not an *in-situ* concrete base is needed for certain types of finish. Stone and concrete slab paving can normally be laid on a mortar bed on a granular sub-base. However, brick, sett and cobble

paving laid and jointed in mortar are monolithic and rigid, so that settlement may result in random stepped cracks in the surface. Such rigid finishes should therefore be laid on a concrete base with adequate movement joints. Small 'feature' panels of brick, setts and cobbles in general areas of slab paving will not, of course, be subject to such major cracking and can usually be laid direct on to the granular sub-base.

Wearing course

These can be divided into four categories:
1. Flexible (asphalt, bitumen or tarmacadam, hoggin). Flexible paving usually consists of two courses: a base course and a wearing course of a binder with variable sizes of aggregate. Wearing course aggregate size should be 6 mm; base course aggregate size 20 mm. The usual thickness for the wearing course is 6–20 mm; base course 50 mm.
2. Small concrete interlocking units are laid in contact on a dry sand bed and vibrated over a consolidated base of granular material on a compacted sub-base. Whatever unit paving is selected, the cutting of too many elements should be avoided by keeping the outlines of the paved area simple. The design should consider the size of the paving units in multiples.

3. Rigid units (bricks, stone setts, slabs, concrete units). These are usually laid on a base of consolidated hardcore granular material with a 25 mm bed of sand or 15 mm sand/lime mortar. Joints are usually sand-filled, or pointed with sand/lime mortar.
4. Rigid pavement (*in-situ* concrete). These are usually of unreinforced concrete laid directly on a consolidated sub-grade, or on a base of consolidated hardcore, depending on ground conditions. Expansion joints must be incorporated at 6 m centres. Lay concrete paths in 4 m sections.

Edges

1. Flexible pavements must be contained by a rigid edge: either a precast concrete edging with a concrete surround or a timber edging held by timber pegs.
2. Small rigid units should be contained by a row of units supported by a concrete backing.
3. Large rigid units need no edging when adjoined by turfed or flexible paved areas. Where adjoined by topsoil or planted areas, an *in-situ* concrete strip should be provided under the paving to prevent the base falling away. (See chapter on Margins, edges and trims.)
4. Rigid pavement, while not needing an edge, would benefit from one to improve the overall appearance visually.

Joints

Tight, unfilled joints are only possible with units of regular size and shape, such as precast concrete paving flags or precast concrete interlocking paving, with which tight jointing is usual. Joints between paving brick, stone setts and natural pavings are best filled with a 1:3 cement mortar or a 1:4 lime mortar. The mortar is brushed dry into the joints and then watered. This method reduces the risk of mortar staining the paving. If plant or moss growth in the joints is to be encouraged, the joints can be filled with sifted topsoil or sand mixed with bone meal.

Falls

Drainage is an integral part of paving design. Paving needs to shed water from its surface, have dry foundations to avoid frost damage, and be protected from flooding from adjacent areas. Water running down paths is usually shed by providing a cross slope with gutters making the surface domed.

The gradient of fall required to clear surface water varies according to the nature of the surface. Recommended falls are: concrete 1:60; brick paving 1:60; bituminous surfaces 1:40; paving slabs 1:70; gravel 1:30; public pavements 1:50. Over a small area the surfacing could fall to planted or grassed areas, provided the soil is well drained. For larger areas drains will be necessary, linked to a soakaway or surface water drainage system.

Surfaces around trees

Surfaces under the canopy of mature trees must be kept porous to allow air and water to reach their roots and the ground must be protected from compaction, disturbance and contamination at all times. If the ground level is to be altered specific details will be necessary.

See *Tree Detailing* for further information.

SPECIFICATION CHECK LISTS

Coated macadam/asphalt/gravel

General
It is often possible to combine layers to reduce the number of separate stages of construction. The wearing course is relatively soft when laid. Consequently it can be relatively easily marked, particularly in early life or during hot weather.

Material
Granular sub-base: Select the type and thickness for one of the following:
Heavy clay
Silty clay
Sandy clay
Sandy and well graded sandy gravel
Paving types: State type of paving to be

used – coated macadam, rolled asphalt or sealed gravel, etc.

Sub-base:

Abutments: State method of protection of abutments such as manholes, kerbs, etc.

Laying: Specify method of laying, and compacting sub-base, base course and wearing course including tolerances for levels and regularity.

Cold weather: State procedure for laying during cold weather.

Edging: Give reference to the type of edging required. See chapter on Margins, edges and trims.

Protection: Specify general protection from any contamination or traffic (e.g. tracked vehicles) that could harm the paving.

Interlocking brick/blocks

General

The ability of paving to support the loads imposed upon it will depend on the thickness of the block/paver, the design of the sub-base and the type of sub-grade.

Materials

Blocks/bricks: State type, e.g. concrete block/clay brick/calcium silicate brick, manufacturer and reference.

Size: Check with block/paver manufacturer the recommended thickness for the particular situation. Brick pavers are normally:

210 × 105 × 50/65 mm
215 × 102.5 × 50/65 mm
200 × 100 × 50/65 mm

Brick pavers less than 50 mm thick are not suitable for flexible paving. Rectangular concrete blocks are normally 200 × 100 mm on plan, shaped blocks are either 200 × 100, 225 × 112.5 or 295 × 295 mm on plan. Thicknesses of block for pedestrian areas are 50/60/65 mm.

Samples: Insert clause requesting samples to be submitted for approval.

Specials: Give details of any special blocks required such as at corners, bends or edges.

Colour/pattern: Provide information on colour of unit and any surface pattern required.

Sand for bedding: The best paving is achieved when the sand is within 1 per cent of its optimum moisture content, i.e. the moisture content at which a specified amount of compaction will produce the maximum dry density.

Sand for jointing: State details of sand for jointing. The use of mortar in joints is not recommended as the flexible nature of the paving, which is an important part of its design, will be impaired. In addition, the ease with which sections of flexible paving can be taken up and relayed for modifications to below-ground services is lost.

Setting out: Insert any drawing reference(s).

Laying patterns/bond: State type of bond to be laid (e.g. herringbone). Herringbone bond gives the maximum amount of restraint to individual blocks/pavers. Stretcher bond should be used only in pedestrian or very lightly trafficked areas. Basketweave bond is suitable for pedestrian areas only. There may be difficulties of fit with some brick pavers – check with manufacturer that the particular paver is suitable for this type of bond.

Features: Give details on any special features required such as white blocks to define edges or a course of headers or stretchers adjacent to raised edge restraints.

Workmanship

Granular sub-base: Select thickness from the following:

Heavy clay
Silky clay
Sandy clay
Sandy and well-graded sandy gravel

Specify method of laying the sub-base material. If the sub-base is used extensively by site traffic, damage is bound to occur and this should be made good prior to spreading the bedding course. The surface of the sub-base should be blinded before laying the bedding course.

Control samples: The specification of control samples should be related to the size and importance of the job. It may be difficult to justify control samples on small jobs.

Inclement weather: State procedure for work in wet and cold weather.

Level of paving: Paving should be set above drainage outlets to allow for future consolidation of the paving by traffic. State permissible deviation from specified levels.

Laying bedding: Describe method of laying, levelling and compacting bedding material.

Laying blocks/pavers: A better appearance can often be achieved by slightly altering the bond pattern at the edges of the paving by trimming some of the blocks/pavers 'in board' of the edging blocks/pavers.

State method of laying blocks/pavers. Take into account any cutting and by which process. Cutting blocks/pavers to fit around manholes, drainage outlets, etc., can be avoided by incorporating *in-situ* concrete surrounds. The appearance for this may be unacceptable. Alternatively, use very small unit pavers.

Compacting and jointing: Describe method of compacting blocks/pavers and filling joints.

Tolerances: Check if BS recommended tolerances are acceptable. State tolerance for surface irregularity after completion.

Remedial work: Advise of methods of protection and/or reinstatement during the Contract or Defects Liability Period.

Slabs, bricks, setts and cobble pavings

Materials

Base: Specify any material for bases (e.g. lean-mix concrete, local fill materials, etc.) – see chapter on Foundations.

Paving: Include reference for obtaining samples for approval, especially for clay bricks which are inherently variable in appearance (e.g. bricks which are selected from different parts of the kiln and mixed before delivery).

Concrete slabs: To BS 7263: Part 1: state colour. Sizes are 600 mm × 450, 600, 750 and 900 mm in thicknesses of 50 mm or 63 mm. smaller units are specified in BS 1197. For proprietary concrete slabs, specify details of manufacturer and reference.

Stone: Specify the type of stone and the quarry or source if known and the surface finish. Limestones should be 'joint bedded'

(i.e. natural bed vertical) and this should be specified. Ascertain sizes currently available.

Paving bricks: Ordinary walling bricks are often used for paving bedded frog down if frogged bricks are used. Note that the terms 'pavers', 'paviours' and 'paving bricks' are all common uses. Engineering bricks to BS 3921 are frequently used for pavings. Select class A or B as appropriate, class A having the higher compressive strength and lesser absorption rating. State colour, precise selection of bricks for pavings, manufacturer and reference.

Clay pavers: To comply with BS 6677: Part 1: solid bricks with durability designation FL, work size and manufacturer's reference.

Calcium silicate pavers: To BS 6677, Part 1: type PA calcium silicate pavers: solid (no voids) bricks to BS 187 with a strength class of 5 or better should be specified. State manufacturer's name and reference.

Granite setts: To BS 435: size 100 × 100 × 100 mm/100 × 100 mm in 150 to 250 mm lengths.

New setts: other sizes specified in the BS at 75 × 125 and 150 mm, 100 × 125 and 150 mm. The BS is not restricted to granite; other igneous rocks are suitable. State if stone other than granite is required along with supplier's name and reference. Second-hand setts: specify size, type of stone, etc. along with name of suppliers.

Concrete blocks (small element paving): To BS 7263: Part 1: state manufacturer's name and reference. Edges are normally chamfered and blocks are available in textured finish and coloured.

Cobbles: Hard water-smoothed stones of similar oval shape. Size with the smallest diameter in the 30 to 50 mm/50 to 75 mm/175 to 100 mm range. State size, colour range and supplier's name and reference.

Workmanship

General: BS 7263: Part 2: Code of practice for laying (PC flags, kerbs, etc.). This reflects common practice but more detailed advice could be obtained from the BCA and the NPKA for flags and the BDA for bricks.

Control samples: The specification of control samples should be related to the size and importance of the job. It may be difficult to justify control samples on small jobs. Include information on type of paving, minimum size of control sample and any features to be included in the sample area (e.g. edging, channels).

Bases under pavings: See chapter on Foundations. Specify details of thickness and method of compaction. This will depend upon the bearing capacity of the sub-grade.

If the sub-base is used extensively by site traffic, damage is bound to occur and this should be made good prior to laying paving, including any excavation through the sub-base for drainage runs.

The bedding should not be used for blinding or levelling the sub-base if it is outside the specified tolerances.

The drainage of paved areas should be designed in accordance with BS 6367: Code of Practice for drainage of roofs and paved areas: Section 3, Part 9. All gradients must be formed in the sub-base and not in the bedding course, which must be of constant thickness.

Levels of paving: Paving should be set above drainage outlets to allow for future settlement under trafficking.

Laying concrete slabs: On sand: An econo-mical method of providing paving for light foot traffic. Normally laid on a fill material such as hoggin or hardcore. Sand joints tend to get washed out or grow weeds; weak mortar joints prevent this but still enable the slabs to be easily lifted for access or re-use. On mortar dabs: This is a commonly used method that facilitates laying and levelling. Joints are dry butted.

Bedded solid: This method is normally used to support vehicular traffic and, given a well-compacted adequate base, should not crack or move, particularly if the thicker (63 mm) flags to BS 7263: Part 1 are used.

Laying stone flags: Solid rather than spot bedding should be specified. Specify joint widths suited to the type of stone. Riven sandstone laid random pattern may need joints up to 20 mm wide while accurately sized stone may lend itself to narrow joints and poured grout.

Laying bricks: On sand: This is for walling-type bricks (not paviours as described) laid on sand and must not be confused with the block pavings. Bricks laid on sand, either with distinct sand joints or laid close butted with sand brushed into the unavoidable spaces, make a simple but effective constructed paving for pedestrian traffic.

On mortar: This paving uses bricks as stated above. The bricks can be jointed as the work proceeds but the method of brushing completely dry or very dry mortar into open joints as a separate operation overcomes the risks of unsightly mortar stains on the pavings.

Laying block/brick pavers: Small element units are usually laid as for interlocking block/brick pavers. If pavers are required to be jointed with acid-resisting mortar or grout, this is specialist work and needs careful specification.

Laying granite setts: On sand: Specify details as for bricks. If it is required to lay these to an interlocking pattern to receive vehicular traffic, specify them as for interlocking block pavings.

Cobble paving: Specify height above ground level, type of bedding, size and type of joints. If being specified in renovation, the pavings are best specified as 'to match existing'.

Mortar bedding: For very firm bonding to the base, it might be advisable to specify dusting the compacted and levelled bedding with finely sieved cement and coating the backs of slabs with a cement slurry at time of laying. A form of bedding, strongly recommended for block, tile and slab flooring, is the semi-dry or 'thick bed' method.

Jointing and grouting: The jointing methods should be written into the descriptions of the methods of laying the paving followed by details of protection of the work. State either dry mortar or mortar pointed or sand-filled joints along with size of joints.

Dry mortar joints: This method of jointing is recommended for any type of absorbent paving (e.g. brick or concrete) from which it is very difficult to remove the marks of mortar or grout. It can be applied quite dry or mixed almost dry, which facilitates compaction to form a very dense joint.

Mortar-pointed joints: Due to relative movement and frost, mortar-pointed joints tend to deteriorate in time, and repointing may be necessary every few years. The use of a fairly coarse sand (rather than an ordinary building sand) will improve durability of the joints.

Sand-filled joints: Sand-filled joints will allow the development of moss and other plant growth, which may be considered desirable. For narrow (3 mm) joints a grade F sand will be appropriate, but for wider joints grade C (coarse) may be preferred.

Movement joints: Specify any movement joints required.

Protection: Specify methods of protection of work from both inclement weather and any traffic.

In-situ concrete

General

Concrete in situ is one of the cheapest forms of paving although its popularity with landscape architects has not been high due to its appearance. There has been an unimaginative use of the various surface finishes that are available and poor edge detailing along with a shortage of skilled and interested contractors. The use of 'stamped coloured' concrete popular mainly in the USA has not received the same support in the UK due, no doubt, to its costs.

Sub-base

In-situ concrete may not generally need a sub-base and in some cases a base may not be required, either of which results in savings of both materials and labour. However, in formulating the design, the paving, the sub-grade and the sub-base are each considered, depending upon the final use.

Materials

Steel reinforcement: This is not necessary in pedestrian pavings although some lightweight material in the slab could help to distribute evenly the forces resulting from both contraction and use, especially in a long length of paving. Specify type of steel reinforcement and method of fixing.

Cement(s): In most cases it will be appropriate to insert as BS 5328. Particular type(s) of cement can be specified if required (the readily available types).

Aggregate(s): In most cases it will be appropriate to insert as BS 5328. Particular type(s) can be specified by inserting BS numbers from the following:

Coarse	Fine	
BS 882	BS 882	Coarse and fine aggregates from natural sources
BS 877	BS 877	Foamed or expanded blastfurnace slag lightweight aggregates
BS 1047	–	Air-cooled blastfurnace slag coarse aggregate
BS 1165	BS 1165	Clinker aggregate

Aggregates for watertight concrete should be to BS 882 and/or BS 1047.

BS 5328 also permits lightweight aggregates to BS 3797, including pumice, expanded clay, expanded shale and sintered PFA. These have quite different properties and if a lightweight aggregate is required, the type should be stated. Alternatively, a proprietary lightweight aggregate can be specified.

Normal maximum size of aggregate: Standard sizes are 40, 20, 14 and 10 mm: 20 mm is normal; 40 mm is often more economic but is too large for most reinforced work; 14 mm is not normally available. State single size if required.

Workmanship

Concrete mix: Mix on-site: Concrete is made from a mixture of cement, sand, aggregate and water. All should have their information specified and the proportions of mix; for example:

1 part of cement
2 parts of sand ⎫ by volume
4 parts of aggregate ⎭

This can be mixed on-site.

Concrete mix: ready-mix: Alternatively, ready-mixed concrete can be specified. Table 1 of BS 5328 (Methods for specifying concrete, including ready-mixed concrete) defines the proportions of cement and aggregates in a range of 'Ordinary prescribed mixes' which can be expected to have at least the strength indicated by the grade number. A typical designation is C20P, in which 'C' means compressive strength, the number indicates the 28-day characteristic strength in N/mm^2, and 'P' means ordinary prescribed mix. Strength testing is not used to judge compliance, the producer's responsibility being only to produce concrete of the specified proportions. Ordinary prescribed mixes are therefore suitable for use on small projects. Contrary to popular belief, structural strength is not usually the main consideration when specifying concrete mixes, particularly for small projects. Durability of the concrete will invariably require the choice of a higher grade of concrete, to resist:

- Exposure of the elements, particularly in industrial or marine environments. Protection of the reinforcement will usually be even more critical than the durability of the concrete itself.
- Wearing of self-finished slabs and pavements.
- Attack by sulphates in the ground, ground water or fill materials.

Concrete mixes
Ready-mix concrete may be used provided that it is obtained from a plant which holds a current Certificate of Conformity under the Quality Scheme for Ready-mixed Concrete. Each mix must be obtained from only one source unless otherwise approved. Confirm name and address of depot(s) to Local Authority before any concrete is delivered. Retain all delivery notes for inspection.

CONCRETE GRADES FOR USE IN MINOR WORKS

Blinding, backfilling of trenches	C10P using OPC

Plain concrete foundations, oversite concrete, manholes	
– Sulphate class 1	C20P using OPC
– Sulphate class 2, 3 or 4	C30P using SRPC

Reinforced non-structural concrete ground floor slabs:	
– Sulphate class 1, or higher class where effectively protected, e.g. by an underslab damp proof membrane	C25P using OPC
– Sulphate class 2, 3 or 4	C30P using SRPC

Reinforced structural concrete not exposed to severe weathering, and with 35 mm cover to reinforcement on external faces:	

Plain concrete external *in-situ* paving	C30P using OPC

Additives: Specify if any additives are required in the concrete mix. Note that they are likely to change the surface colour of the slab and must be used consistently.
Formwork: Specify materials (either steel or timber for formwork), method of construction (ensuring no loss through joints) and treatment before concrete is placed. Also if materials are to be re-used.
Placing and compaction: It is vital to control the workability (slump) of the concrete. If the workability is too high, the free water/cement ratio will also be too high, the permeability of the concrete will be increased and durability will be inadequate. See British Cement Association publication 45.112, *Man on the job: Testing for workability*.
State that the surfaces to receive concrete are to be clean, that the temperature is not less than 5°C and that compaction is to be to the full depth – until air bubbles cease to appear on the top surface.
Full compaction is generally taken to mean the virtual exclusion of air voids from the concrete. The ability of concrete to protect reinforcement and to resist frost and sulphate attack will be severely reduced if not fully compacted. It is not normally necessary to vibrate elements in which strength and durability are not critical. Insert appropriate details.
Curing and protecting: There is a temptation to think that early curing is not necessary, and that it can be deferred until,

say, after the initial set. However, during this period, particularly if there is a breeze or it is hot, surface evaporation from the concrete can be at a very high level. The top layer can dry and shrink, leading to plastic shrinkage cracking, particularly in slabs.

Joints: State type of expansion/contraction joints and their location. There are three methods:

Alternate bay construction
Dummy construction joints
Saw joints

Finishes: Describe the methods of finish to the concrete surface. These can be by the application of a patterned steel grid with weight or by exposing the aggregates either by hand or mechanical means, or by giving the surface a texture by using a brush, broom or other device. The surface can also be coloured by the use of a pigment. See *Textures for in-situ concrete road and footway pavings* by Brian J.C. Walker, Techniques No. 2, published by The Landscape Institute.

DETAIL SHEETS

Corners (2)
Paving patterns bricks/blocks (2)
Paving patterns granite sett (square)
Paving patterns textured concrete
Paving patterns tiles
Paving patterns stone pavers
Flexible
Asphalt
Loose gravel
Sealed gravel
Sealed gravel on concrete
Sealed gravel on hoggin
Compacted hoggin
Pine bark
Rigid
Brick (basketweave)
Brick (herringbone)
Brick (stretcherbond)
Engineering brick
Cobbles laid flat
Cobbles loose laid
Concrete
Concrete and brick
Concrete block (3)
Concrete broom finish
Concrete flag
Concrete rounds
Concrete slab (2)
Concrete sett
Concrete slab/brick
Concrete slabs/blocks
Concrete slab and gravel (2)
Exposed aggregate (2)
Granite sett (2)
Granite sett and gravel
Natural York stone
Reconstituted stone
Stepping stones
Timber boardwalk
Timber block

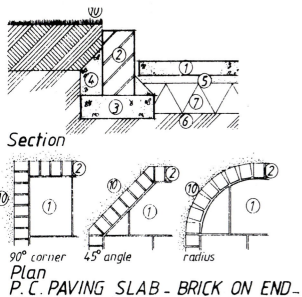

Section

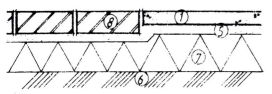

90° corner 45° angle radius

Plan
P.C. PAVING SLAB - BRICK ON END -
GRASS

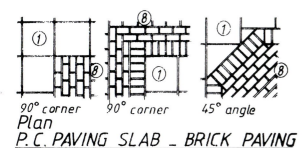

Section

90° corner 90° corner 45° angle

Plan
P.C. PAVING SLAB - BRICK PAVING

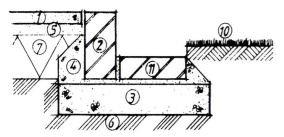

Section

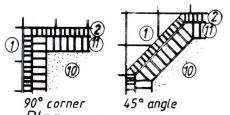

90° corner 45° angle

Plan
P.C. PAVING SLAB - BRICK ON END -
BRICK CHANNEL

1 P.C. Paving slab
2 Brick on end
3 Concrete foundation
4 Insitu concrete haunching
5 Cement & sand mortar bed
6 Sub base prepared to required level
7 Consolidated hardcore
8 Brick paving
9 Asphalt
10 Grass
11 Brick channel

N.T.S.

CORNERS
pedestrian paving

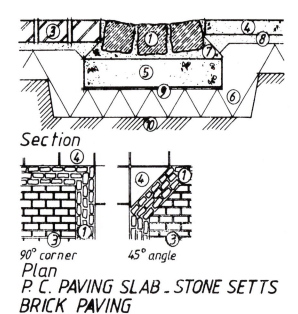

Section

90° corner   45° angle
Plan
P. C. PAVING SLAB _ STONE SETTS
BRICK PAVING

1   Stone sett
2   Cobbles
3   Brick paving
4   P.C. Paving slab
5   Concrete foundation
6   Consolidated hardcore
7   Insitu concrete haunching
8   Cement & sand mortar bed
9   Blinding
10 Sub base prepared to required level
11 Concrete footing
12 Brick on edge

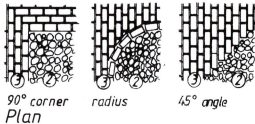

Section

90° corner   radius   45° angle
Plan
BRICK PAVING _ COBBLES

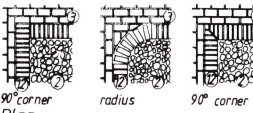

Section

90° corner   radius   90° corner
Plan
BRICK PAVING _ BRICK ON EDGE _ COBBLES

Scale 1:10

CORNERS
pedestrian paving

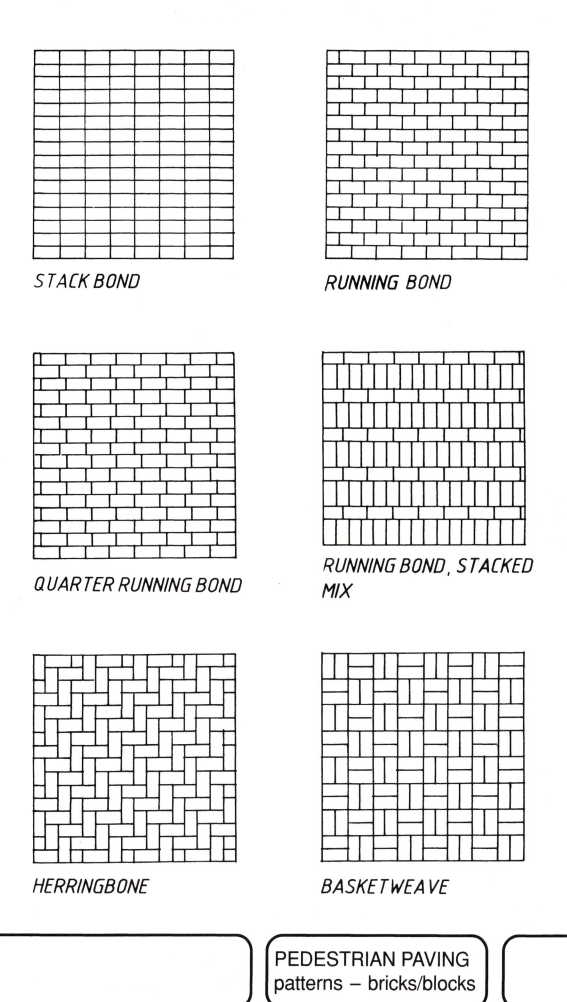

STACK BOND

RUNNING BOND

QUARTER RUNNING BOND

RUNNING BOND, STACKED MIX

HERRINGBONE

BASKETWEAVE

PEDESTRIAN PAVING
patterns – bricks/blocks

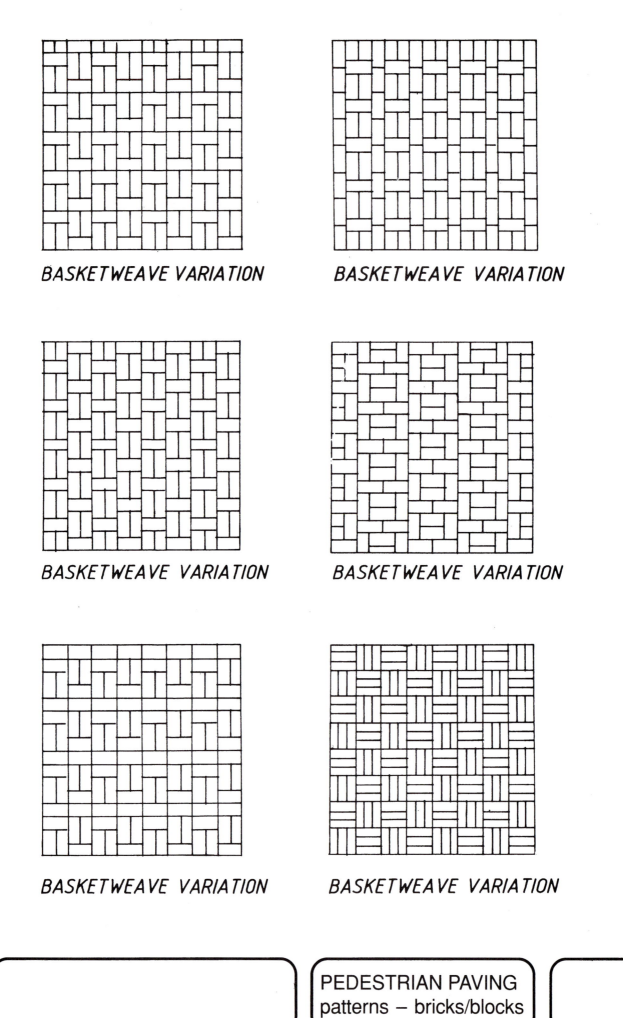

BASKETWEAVE VARIATION

BASKETWEAVE VARIATION

BASKETWEAVE VARIATION

BASKETWEAVE VARIATION

BASKETWEAVE VARIATION

BASKETWEAVE VARIATION

PEDESTRIAN PAVING
patterns – bricks/blocks

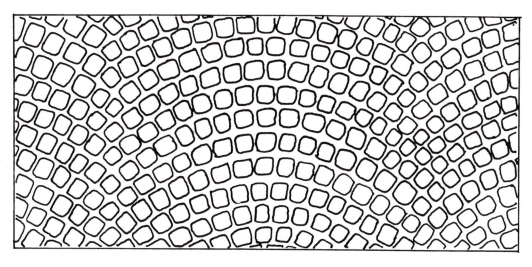

Plan *CURVED*

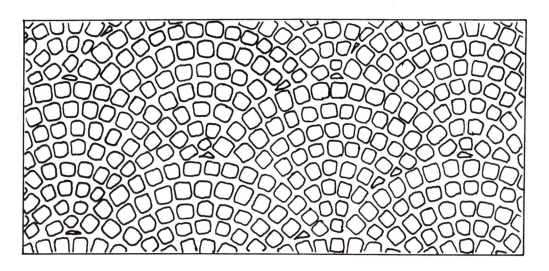

Plan *FANTAIL*

Scale 1:20

PEDESTRIAN PAVING
patterns – granit set
(square)

51

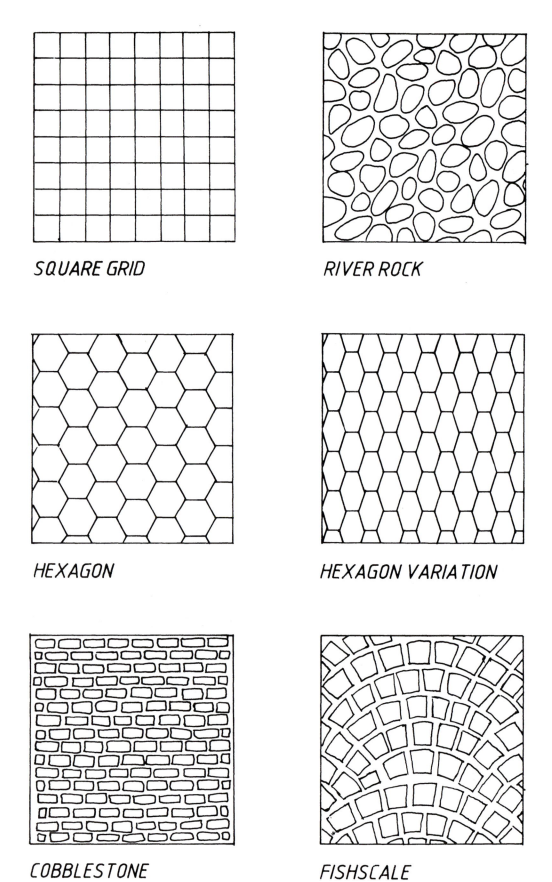

SQUARE GRID

RIVER ROCK

HEXAGON

HEXAGON VARIATION

COBBLESTONE

FISHSCALE

PEDESTRIAN PAVING
patterns – textured
concrete

VARIOUS SIZE PATTERN

SQUARE GRID

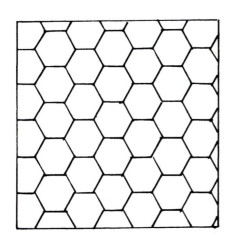

HEXAGONAL

CONCENTRIC CIRCLES

PEDESTRIAN PAVING
patterns – tiles

RECTANGULAR (LIMITED SIZE)

RANDOM RECTANGULAR

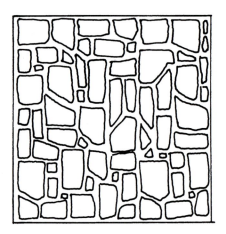

SEMI-IRREGULAR

IRREGULAR (FITTED)

PEDESTRIAN PAVING
patterns – stone pavers

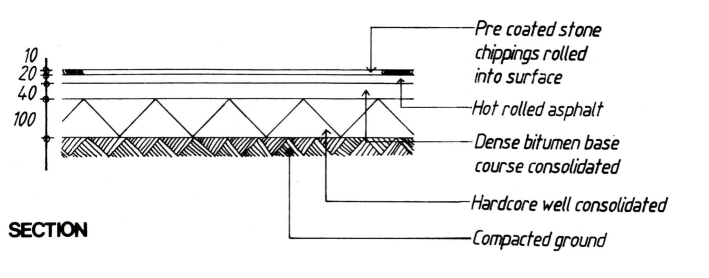

10
20
40
100

Pre coated stone chippings rolled into surface

Hot rolled asphalt

Dense bitumen base course consolidated

Hardcore well consolidated

Compacted ground

SECTION

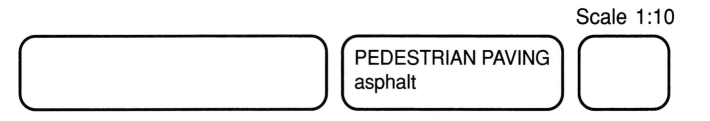

Scale 1:10

PEDESTRIAN PAVING
asphalt

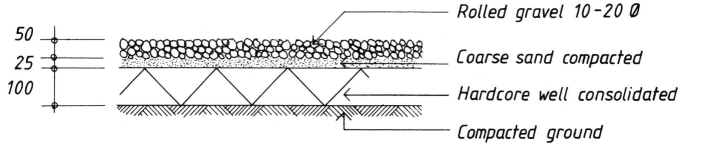

50
25
100

Rolled gravel 10-20 Ø

Coarse sand compacted

Hardcore well consolidated

Compacted ground

SECTION

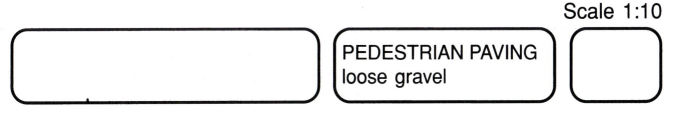

Scale 1:10

PEDESTRIAN PAVING
loose gravel

55

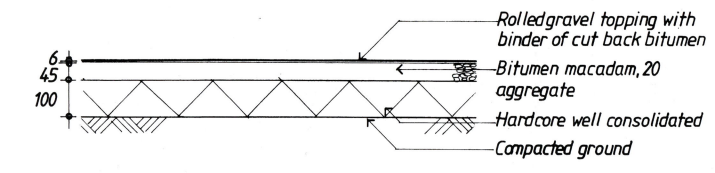

6 ───Rolled gravel topping with binder of cut back bitumen
45 ───Bitumen macadam, 20 aggregate
100 ───Hardcore well consolidated
───Compacted ground

SECTION

Scale 1:10

| | PEDESTRIAN PAVING sealed gravel | |

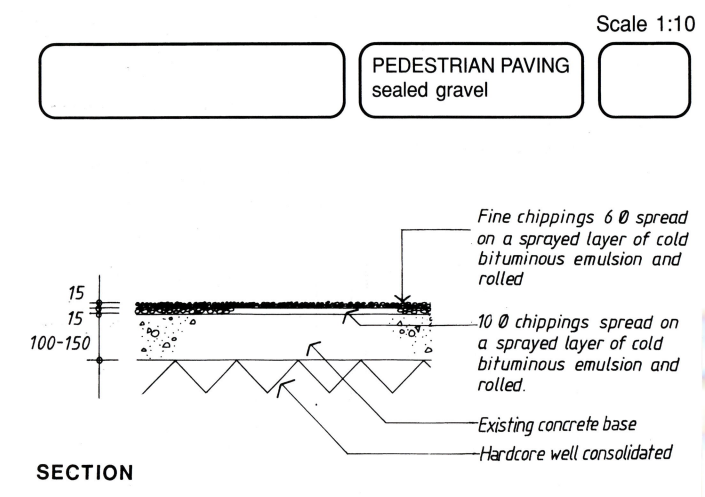

15 ───Fine chippings 6 Ø spread on a sprayed layer of cold bituminous emulsion and rolled
15 ───10 Ø chippings spread on a sprayed layer of cold bituminous emulsion and rolled.
100-150 ───Existing concrete base
───Hardcore well consolidated

SECTION

Scale 1:10

| | PEDESTRIAN PAVING sealed gravel on concrete | |

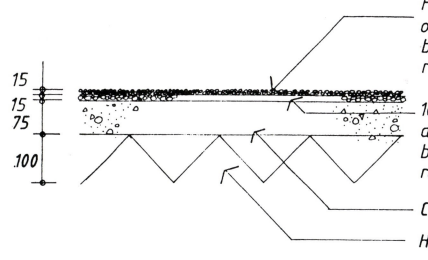

15
15
75

.100

Fine chippings 6 Ø spread on a sprayed layer of cold bituminous emulsion and rolled

10 Ø chippings spread on a sprayed layer of cold bituminous emulsion and rolled.

Consolidated hoggin

Hardcore well consolidated

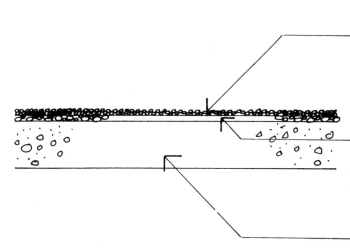

Fine chipping 6Ø spread on a sprayed layer of cold bituminous emulsion and rolled

10 Ø chippings spread on a sprayed layer of cold bituminous emulsion and rolled

Existing 'hard surfacing'

Scale 1:10

PEDESTRIAN PAVING
sealed gravel on hoggin

57

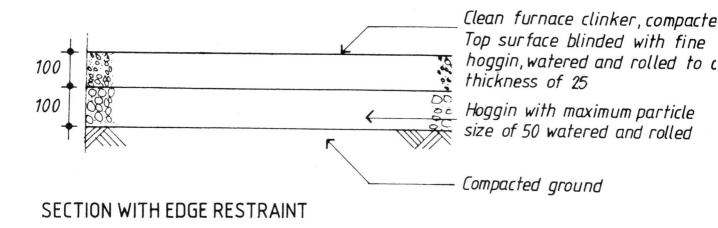

100

100

Clean furnace clinker, compacte
Top surface blinded with fine
hoggin, watered and rolled to c
thickness of 25

Hoggin with maximum particle
size of 50 watered and rolled

Compacted ground

SECTION WITH EDGE RESTRAINT

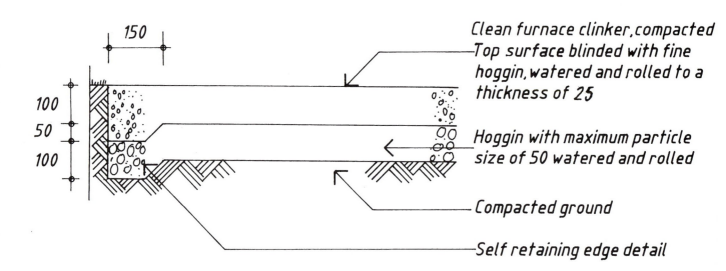

150

100

50

100

Clean furnace clinker, compacted
Top surface blinded with fine
hoggin, watered and rolled to a
thickness of 25

Hoggin with maximum particle
size of 50 watered and rolled

Compacted ground

Self retaining edge detail

SECTION WITH SELF EDGE RESTRAINT

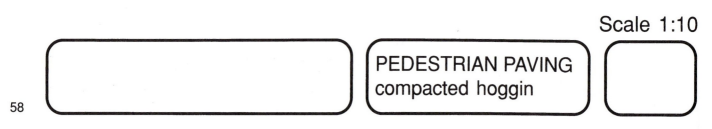

Scale 1:10

PEDESTRIAN PAVING
compacted hoggin

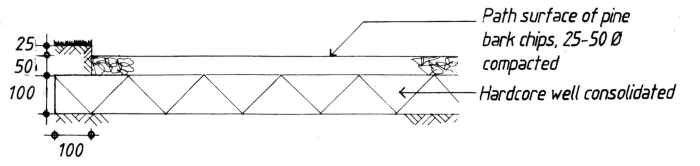

25
50
100

100

SECTION

Path surface of pine
bark chips, 25-50 Ø
compacted

Hardcore well consolidated

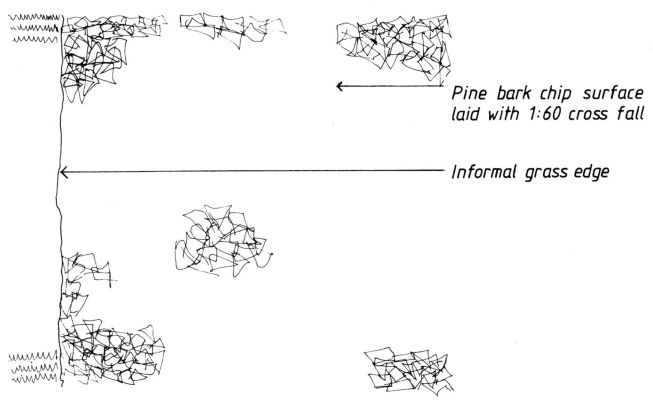

Pine bark chip surface
laid with 1:60 cross fall

Informal grass edge

PLAN

Note
For edge details see
separate drawing(s)

Scale 1:10

PEDESTRIAN PAVING
pine bark

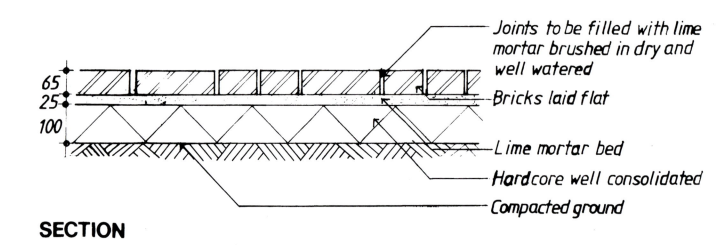

Joints to be filled with lime mortar brushed in dry and well watered

Bricks laid flat

Lime mortar bed

Hardcore well consolidated

Compacted ground

65
25
100

SECTION

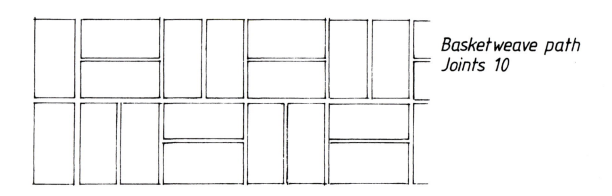

Basketweave path
Joints 10

PLAN

Scale 1:10

PEDESTRIAN PAVING
brick (basket weave)

60

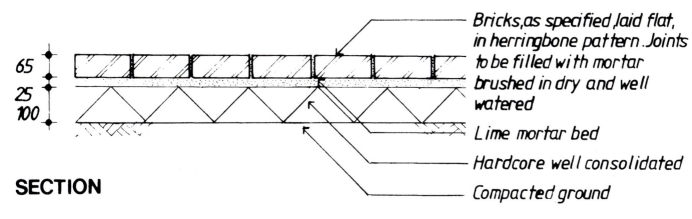

65
25
100

Bricks, as specified, laid flat, in herringbone pattern. Joints to be filled with mortar brushed in dry and well watered

Lime mortar bed

Hardcore well consolidated

Compacted ground

SECTION

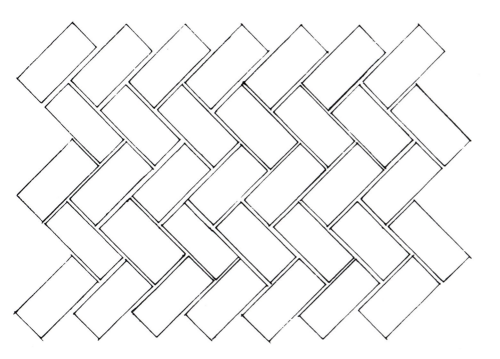

PLAN

Scale 1:10

PEDESTRIAN PAVING
brick (herringbone)

61

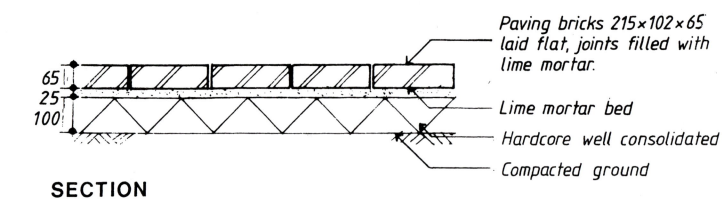

65
25
100

SECTION

Paving bricks 215×102×65 laid flat, joints filled with lime mortar.

Lime mortar bed

Hardcore well consolidated

Compacted ground

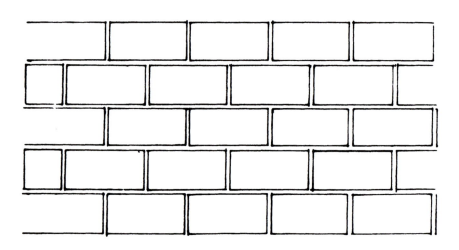

PLAN

Scale 1:10

PEDESTRIAN PAVING
brick (stretcherbond)

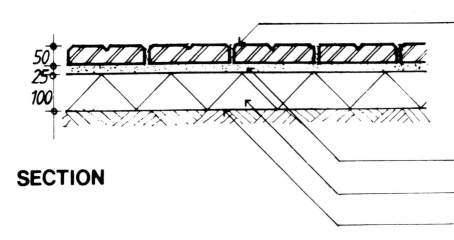

SECTION

50
25
100

Staffordshire blue engineering paving bricks with two raised panels laid stretcher bond. Joints to be filled with lime mortar brushed in dry and well watered

Lime mortar bed

Hardcore well consolidated

Compacted ground

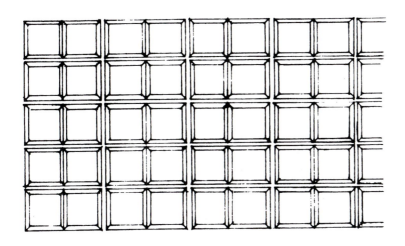

PLAN

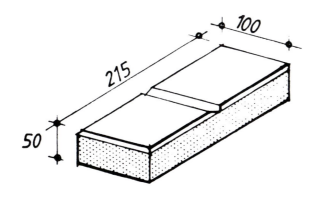

100

215

50

UNIT

Scale 1:10

PEDESTRIAN PAVING
brick (engineering)

63

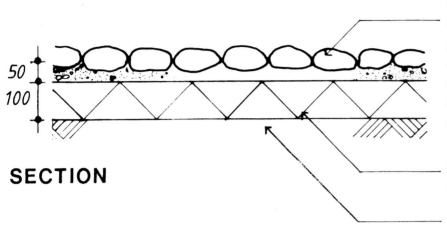

SECTION

50
100

Kidney flint cobbles laid flat with their long axes parallel in small aggregate concrete. Cobbles to be embedded by hand, tight butted, to a depth of half their thickness

Hardcore base well consolidated

Compacted ground

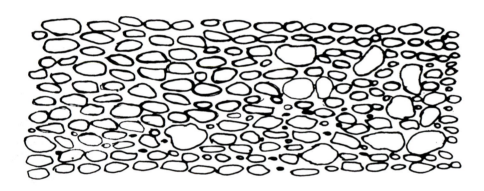

PLAN

Scale 1:10

PEDESTRIAN PAVING
cobbles laid flat

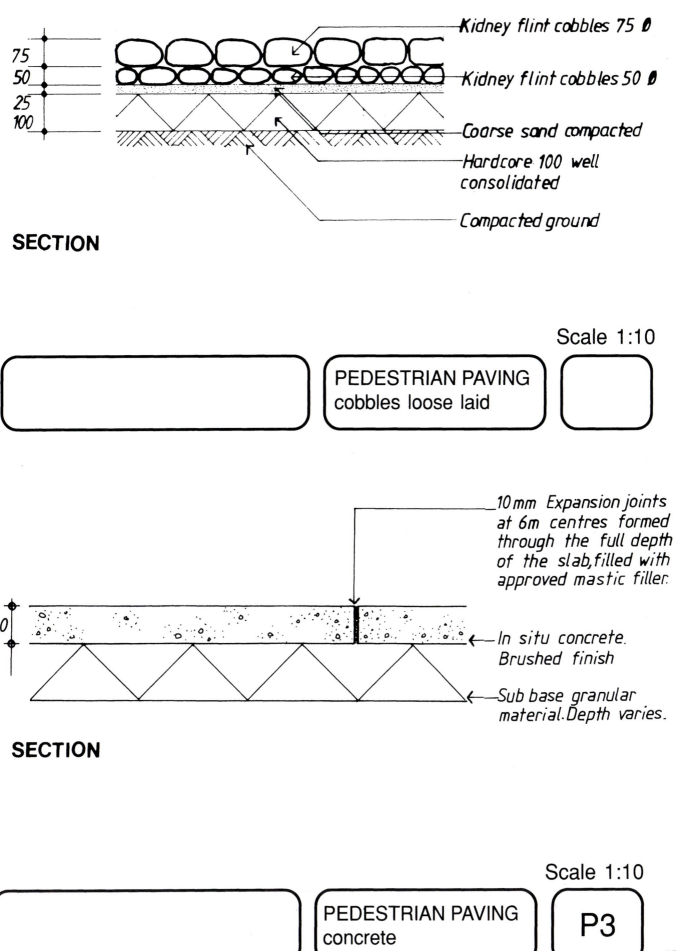

75
50
25
100

Kidney flint cobbles 75 Ø

Kidney flint cobbles 50 Ø

Coarse sand compacted

Hardcore 100 well consolidated

Compacted ground

SECTION

Scale 1:10

PEDESTRIAN PAVING
cobbles loose laid

100

10 mm Expansion joints at 6m centres formed through the full depth of the slab, filled with approved mastic filler.

In situ concrete. Brushed finish

Sub base granular material. Depth varies.

SECTION

Scale 1:10

PEDESTRIAN PAVING
concrete

P3

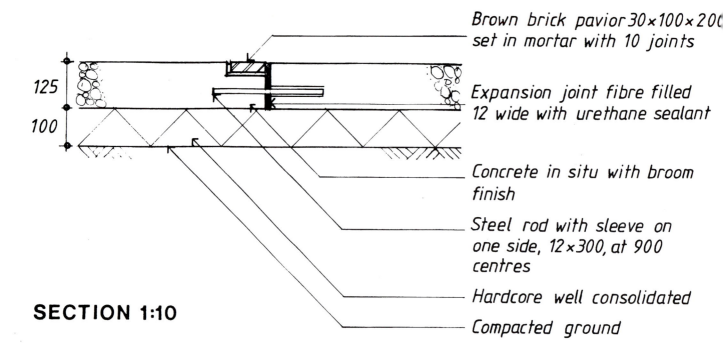

SECTION 1:10

125
100

Brown brick pavior 30×100×200
set in mortar with 10 joints

Expansion joint fibre filled
12 wide with urethane sealant

Concrete in situ with broom
finish

Steel rod with sleeve on
one side, 12×300, at 900
centres

Hardcore well consolidated

Compacted ground

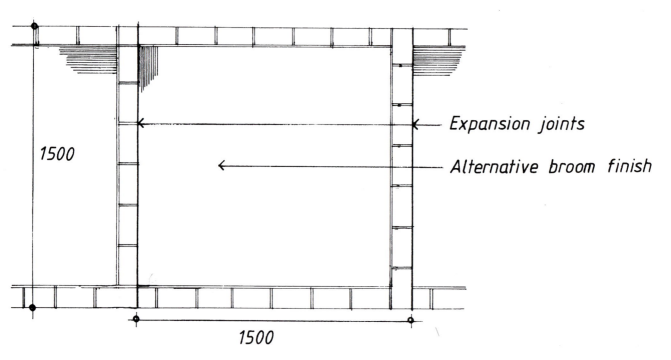

1500

1500

Expansion joints

Alternative broom finish

PLAN 1:20

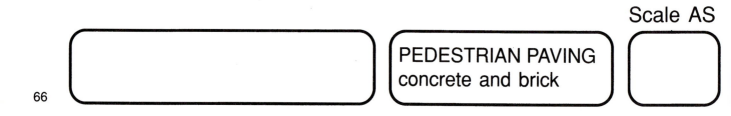

Scale AS

PEDESTRIAN PAVING
concrete and brick

66

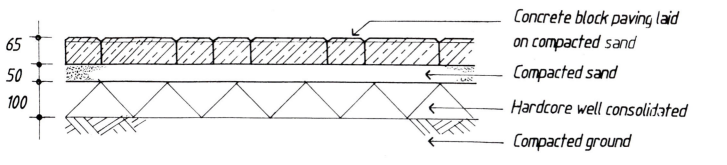

65
50
100

Concrete block paving laid on compacted sand

Compacted sand

Hardcore well consolidated

Compacted ground

SECTION

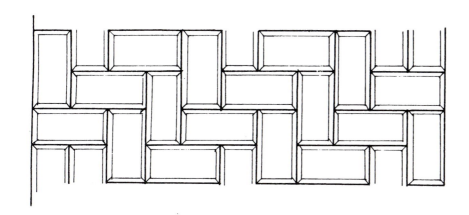

PLAN

Scale 1:10

PEDESTRIAN PAVING
concrete block

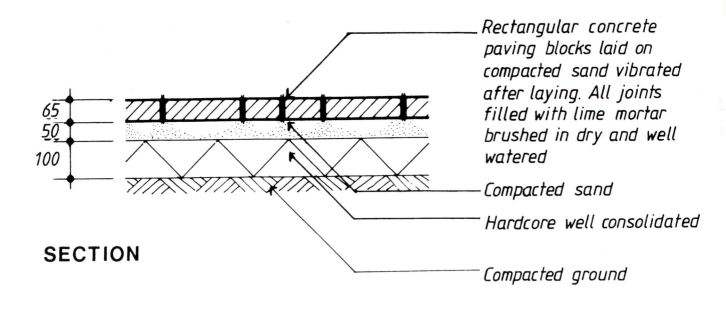

65
50
100

SECTION

Rectangular concrete paving blocks laid on compacted sand vibrated after laying. All joints filled with lime mortar brushed in dry and well watered

Compacted sand

Hardcore well consolidated

Compacted ground

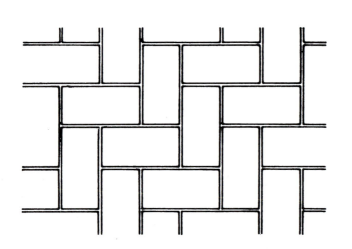

PLAN

Rectangular concrete paving laid in herringbone pattern with 1:40 cross fall

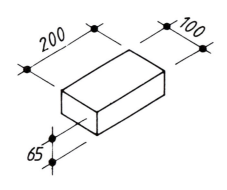

200
100
65

UNIT

Rectangular concrete paving block

Scale 1:10

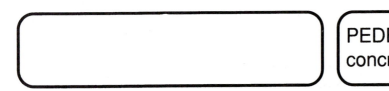

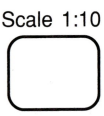

PEDESTRIAN PAVING
concrete block

68

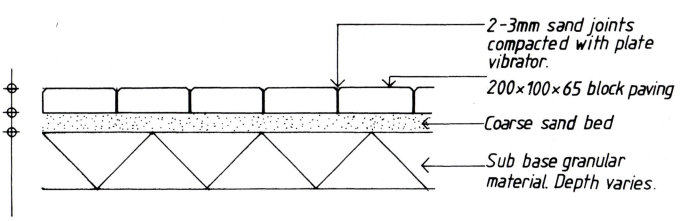

2-3mm sand joints compacted with plate vibrator.

200×100×65 block paving

Coarse sand bed

Sub base granular material. Depth varies.

SECTION

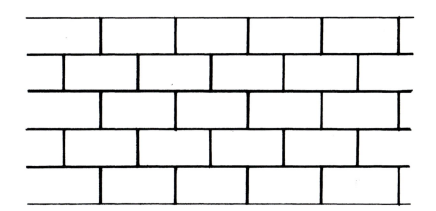

Brindled coloured Charcon Europa block paving

Paving to be laid in accordance with manufacturers instructions.

PLAN

Scale 1:10

PEDESTRIAN PAVING
concrete block

69

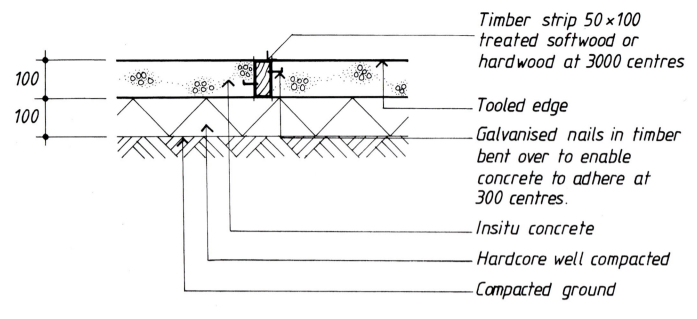

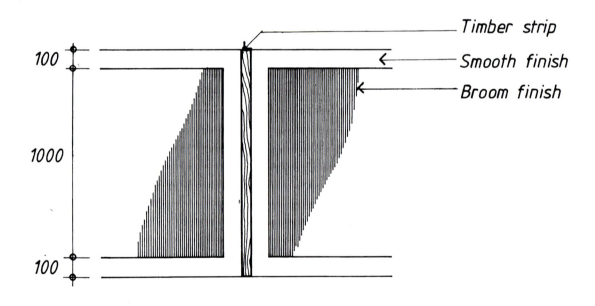

100
100

SECTION 1:10

Timber strip 50 × 100
treated softwood or
hardwood at 3000 centres

Tooled edge

Galvanised nails in timber
bent over to enable
concrete to adhere at
300 centres.

Insitu concrete

Hardcore well compacted

Compacted ground

100
1000
100

Timber strip

Smooth finish

Broom finish

PLAN 1:20

Scale AS

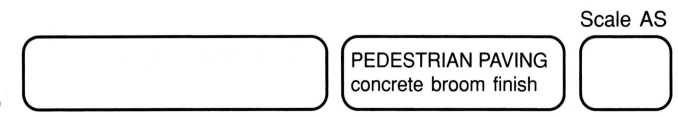

PEDESTRIAN PAVING
concrete broom finish

70

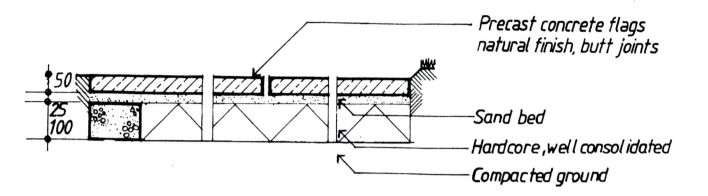

Precast concrete flags natural finish, butt joints

50
25
100

Sand bed

Hardcore, well consolidated

Compacted ground

SECTION 1:10

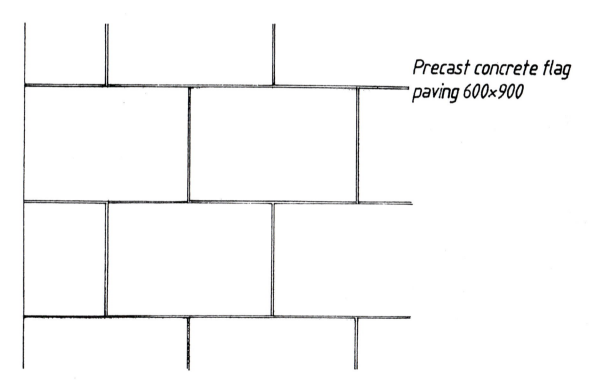

Precast concrete flag paving 600×900

PLAN 1:20

Scale AS

PEDESTRIAN PAVING
concrete flag

71

SECTION 1:10

50
50
100

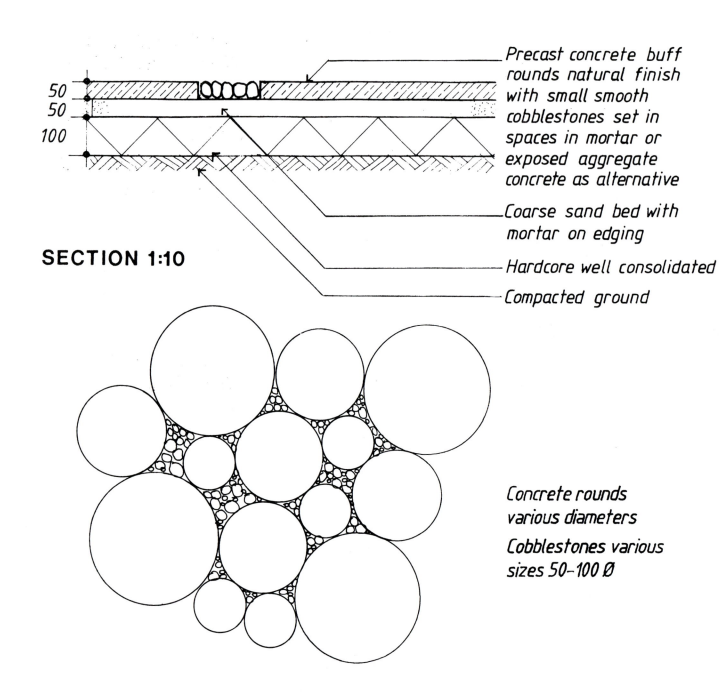

Precast concrete buff
rounds natural finish
with small smooth
cobblestones set in
spaces in mortar or
exposed aggregate
concrete as alternative

Coarse sand bed with
mortar on edging

Hardcore well consolidated

Compacted ground

Concrete rounds
various diameters

Cobblestones various
sizes 50-100 Ø

PLAN 1:20

Scale AS

PEDESTRIAN PAVING
concrete rounds

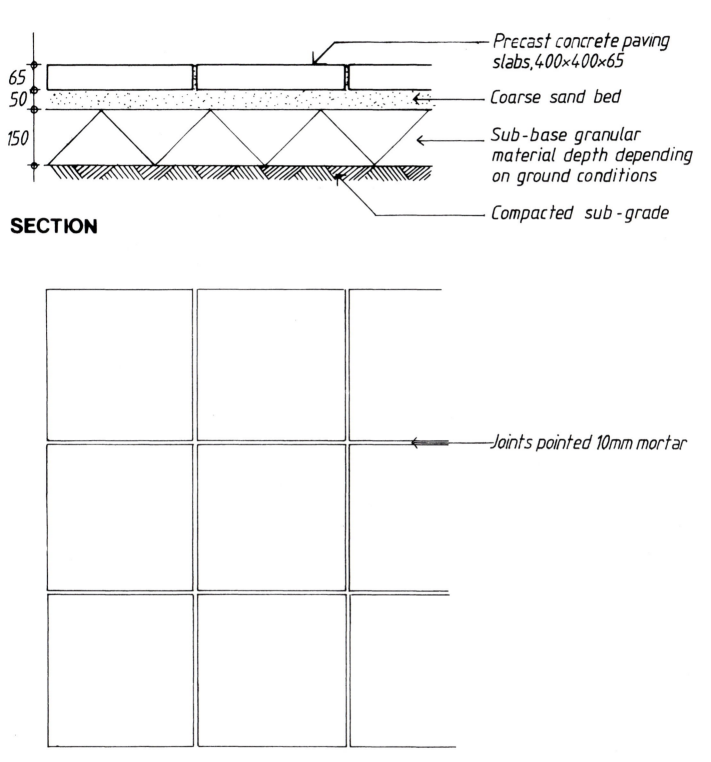

SECTION

65
50
150

Precast concrete paving
slabs, 400×400×65

Coarse sand bed

Sub-base granular
material depth depending
on ground conditions

Compacted sub-grade

Joints pointed 10mm mortar

PLAN

Scale 1:10

PEDESTRIAN PAVING
concrete slab

73

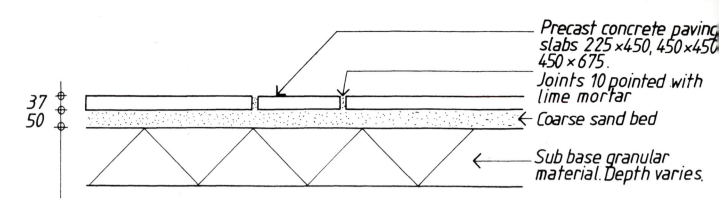

Precast concrete paving slabs 225×450, 450×450, 450×675.

Joints 10 pointed with lime mortar

← Coarse sand bed

← Sub base granular material. Depth varies.

37
50

SECTION 1:10

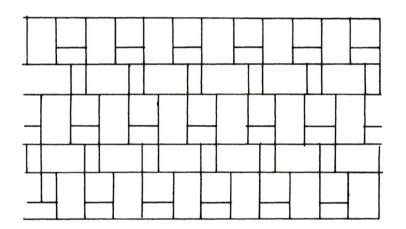

Buff coloured smooth paving slab by Charcon "Derbyshire"

PLAN 1:50

Scale AS

PEDESTRIAN PAVING
concrete slab

74

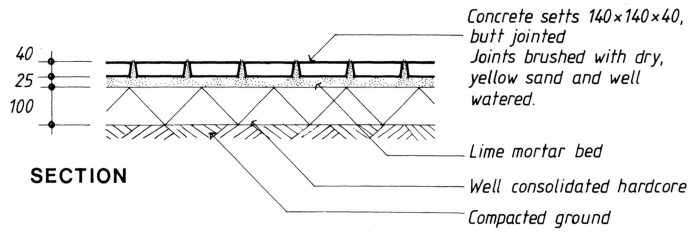

40
25
100

SECTION

Concrete setts 140×140×40,
butt jointed
Joints brushed with dry,
yellow sand and well
watered.

Lime mortar bed

Well consolidated hardcore

Compacted ground

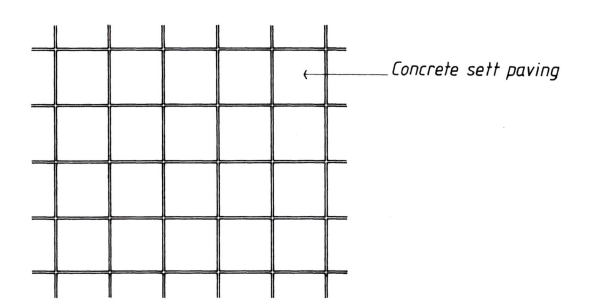

Concrete sett paving

PLAN

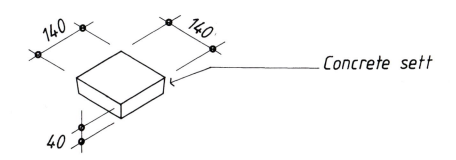

140   140

Concrete sett

40

Scale 1:10

PEDESTRIAN PAVING
concrete sett

75

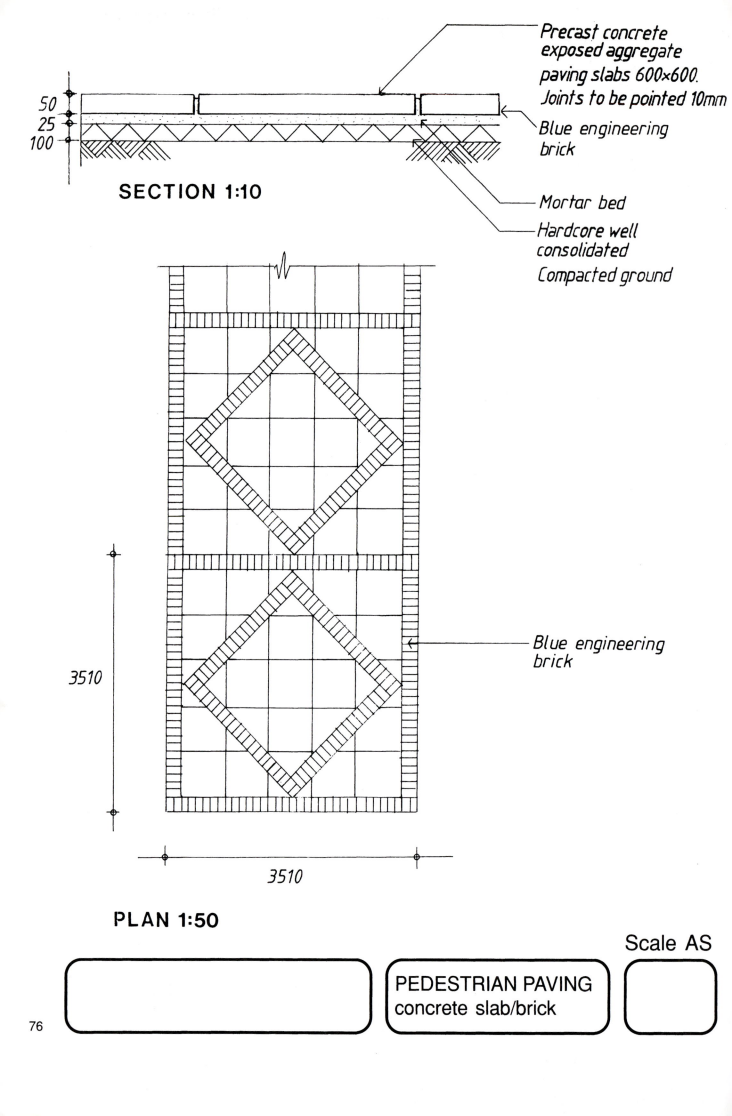

Precast concrete
exposed aggregate
paving slabs 600×600.
Joints to be pointed 10mm

Blue engineering
brick

50
25
100

SECTION 1:10

Mortar bed

Hardcore well
consolidated

Compacted ground

Blue engineering
brick

3510

3510

PLAN 1:50

Scale AS

PEDESTRIAN PAVING
concrete slab/brick

76

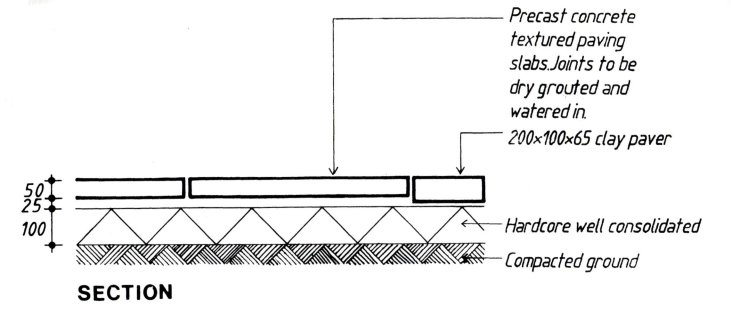

Precast concrete textured paving slabs. Joints to be dry grouted and watered in.

200×100×65 clay paver

50
25
100

Hardcore well consolidated

Compacted ground

SECTION

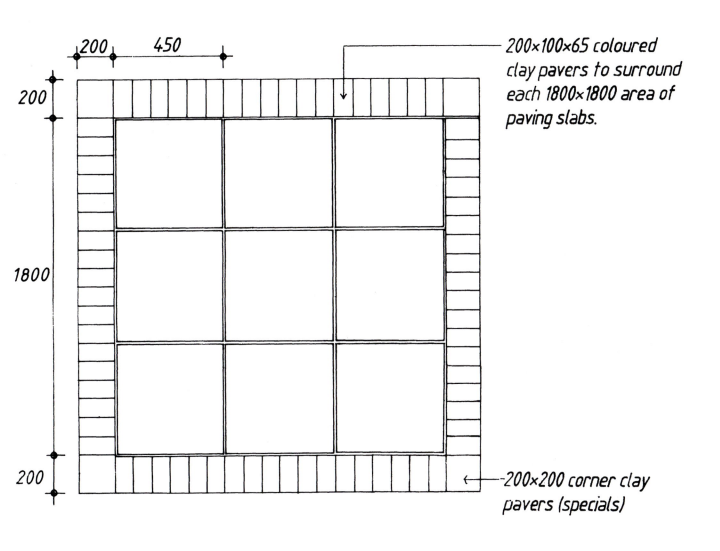

200
450

200

1800

200

200×100×65 coloured clay pavers to surround each 1800×1800 area of paving slabs.

200×200 corner clay pavers (specials)

PLAN 1:20

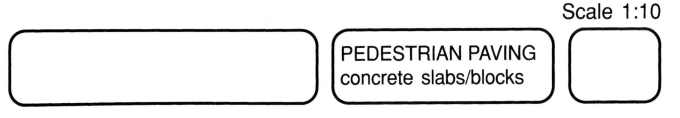

Scale 1:10

PEDESTRIAN PAVING
concrete slabs/blocks

77

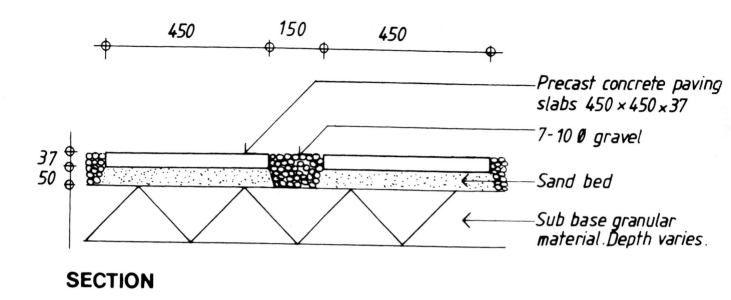

450   150   450

— Precast concrete paving
slabs 450 × 450 × 37

— 7-10 Ø gravel

37
50

— Sand bed

— Sub base granular
material. Depth varies.

SECTION

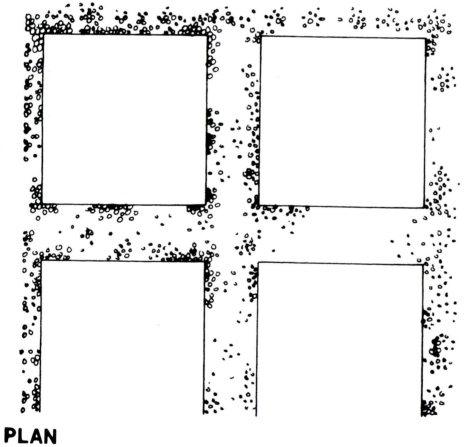

Paving slabs natural
coloured textured by
Charcon "Derbyshire"

Rustic coloured gravel
by Border Hardcore &
Rockery.

PLAN

Scale 1:10

PEDESTRIAN PAVING
concrete slab & gravel

78

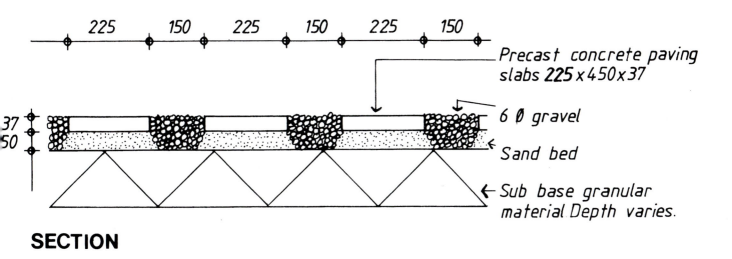

225   150   225   150   225   150

Precast concrete paving
slabs *225 x 450 x 37*

37

50

6 Ø gravel

Sand bed

Sub base granular
material Depth varies.

SECTION

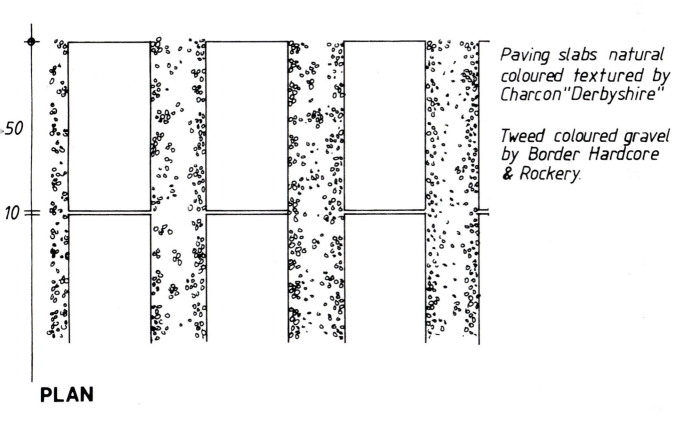

50

10

Paving slabs natural
coloured textured by
Charcon "Derbyshire"

Tweed coloured gravel
by Border Hardcore
& Rockery.

PLAN

Scale 1:10

PEDESTRIAN PAVING
concrete slab & gravel

79

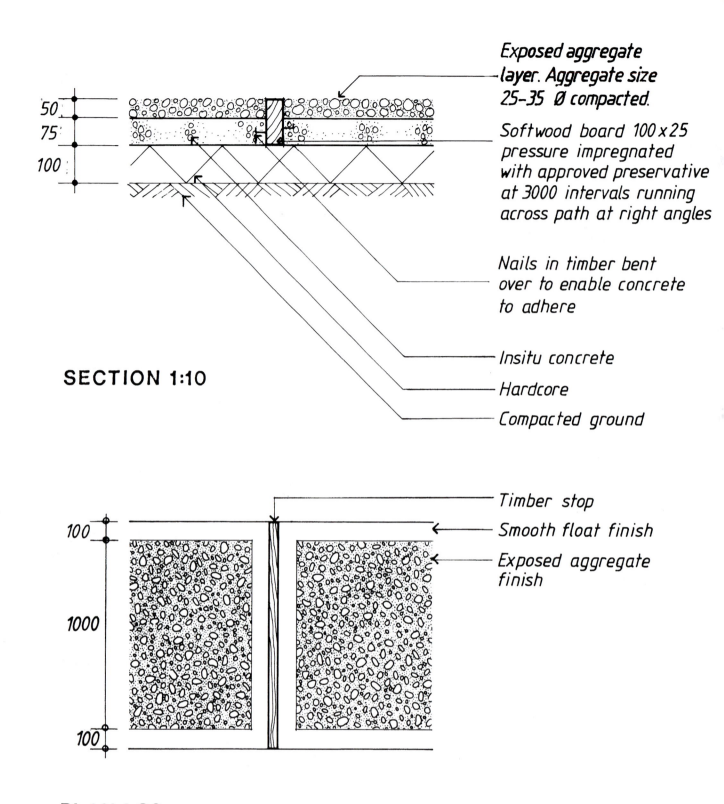

SECTION 1:10

50
75
100

Exposed aggregate
layer. Aggregate size
25-35 Ø compacted.

Softwood board 100 x 25
pressure impregnated
with approved preservative
at 3000 intervals running
across path at right angles

Nails in timber bent
over to enable concrete
to adhere

Insitu concrete

Hardcore

Compacted ground

PLAN 1:20

100
1000
100

Timber stop

Smooth float finish

Exposed aggregate
finish

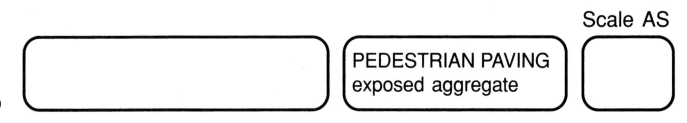

Scale AS

PEDESTRIAN PAVING
exposed aggregate

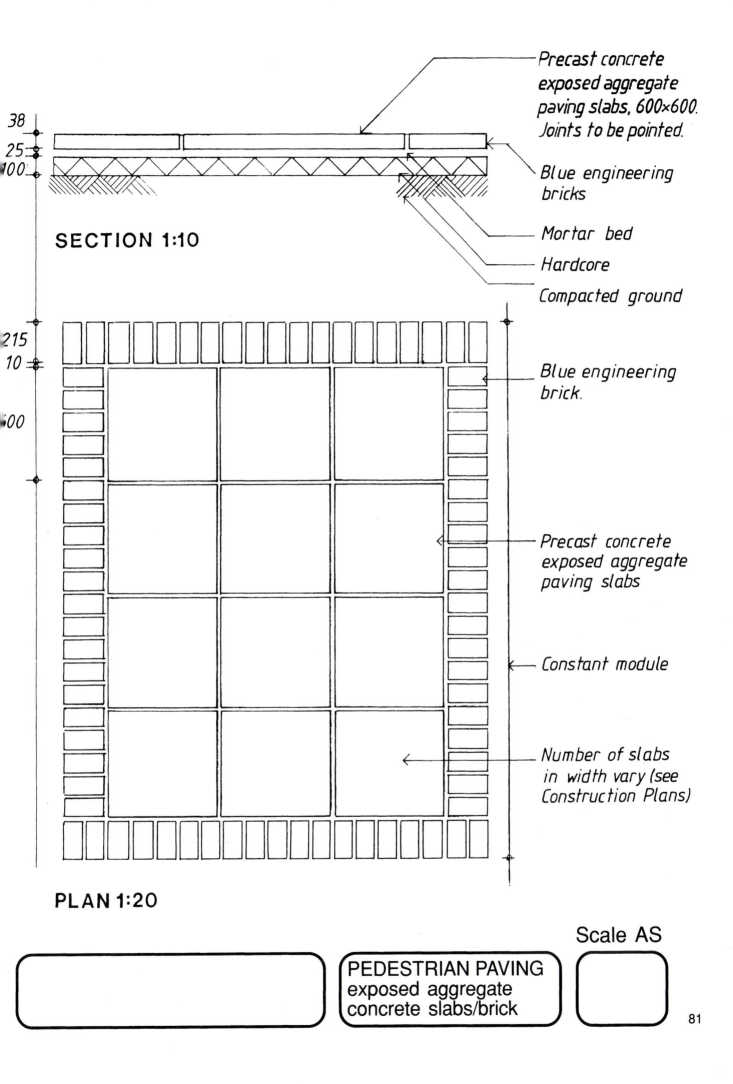

38
25
100

SECTION 1:10

Precast concrete
exposed aggregate
paving slabs, 600×600.
Joints to be pointed.

Blue engineering
bricks

Mortar bed

Hardcore

Compacted ground

215
10

600

Blue engineering
brick.

Precast concrete
exposed aggregate
paving slabs

Constant module

Number of slabs
in width vary (see
Construction Plans)

PLAN 1:20

Scale AS

PEDESTRIAN PAVING
exposed aggregate
concrete slabs/brick

81

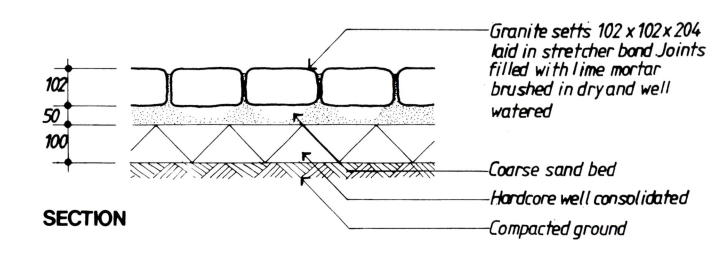

102

50

100

Granite setts 102 x 102 x 204
laid in stretcher bond Joints
filled with lime mortar
brushed in dry and well
watered

Coarse sand bed

Hardcore well consolidated

Compacted ground

SECTION

PLAN

Scale 1:10

PEDESTRIAN PAVING
granite sett

82

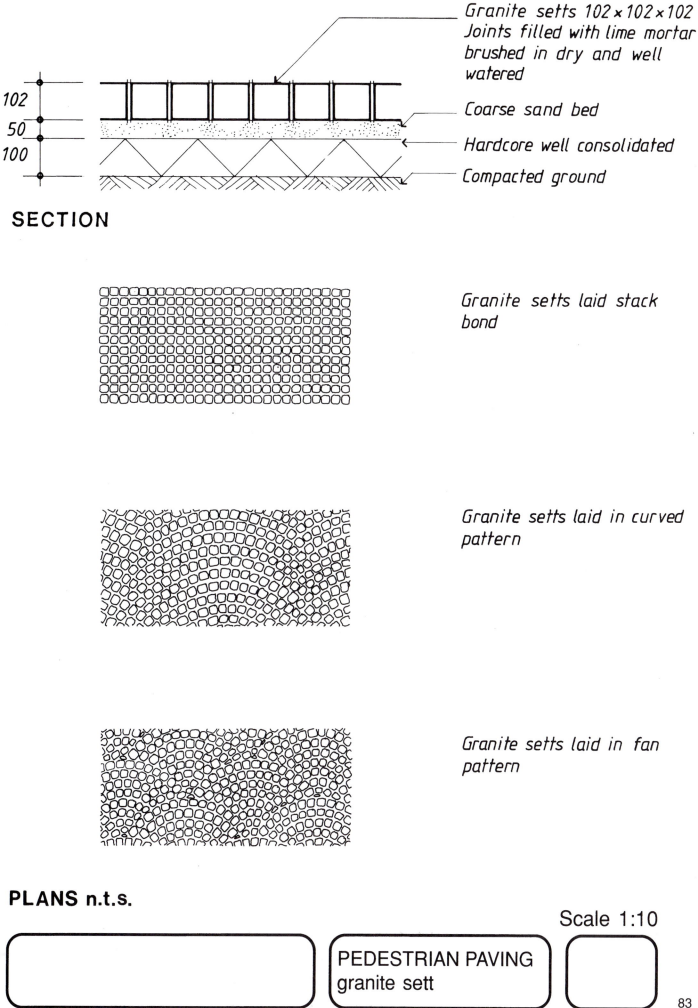

Granite setts 102 × 102 × 102
Joints filled with lime mortar
brushed in dry and well
watered

Coarse sand bed

Hardcore well consolidated

Compacted ground

102
50
100

SECTION

Granite setts laid stack
bond

Granite setts laid in curved
pattern

Granite setts laid in fan
pattern

PLANS n.t.s.

Scale 1:10

PEDESTRIAN PAVING
granite sett

83

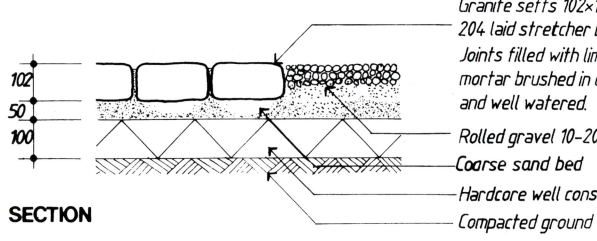

Granite setts 102×102× 204 laid stretcher bond Joints filled with lime mortar brushed in dry and well watered.

Rolled gravel 10-20 Ø

Coarse sand bed

Hardcore well consolidated

Compacted ground

102

50

100

SECTION

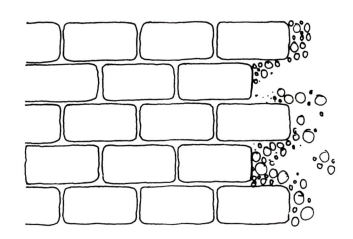

PLAN

Scale 1:10

PEDESTRIAN PAVING
granite sett & gravel

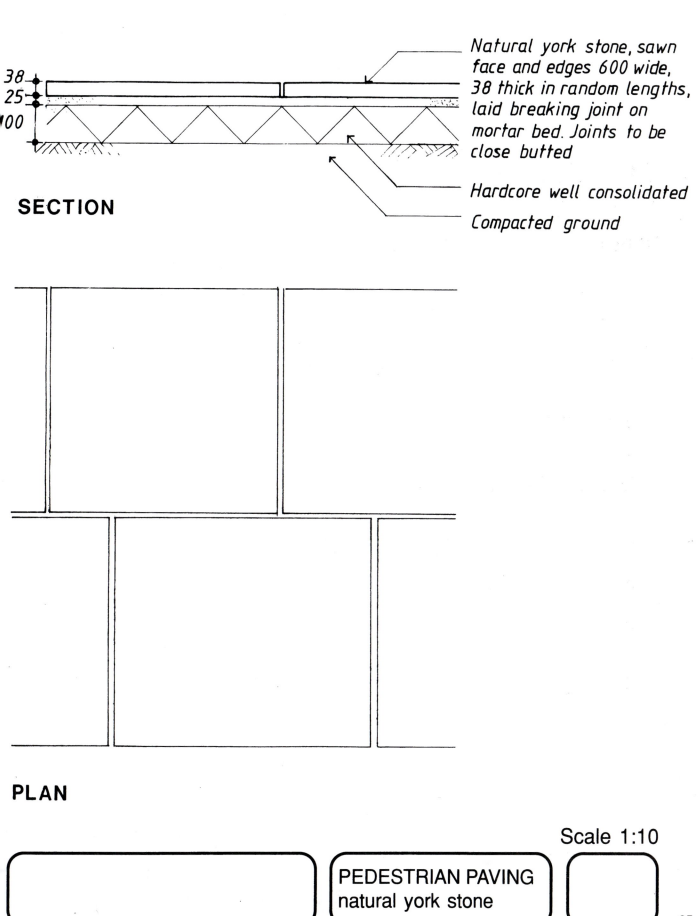

SECTION

38
25
100

Natural york stone, sawn
face and edges 600 wide,
38 thick in random lengths,
laid breaking joint on
mortar bed. Joints to be
close butted

Hardcore well consolidated

Compacted ground

PLAN

Scale 1:10

PEDESTRIAN PAVING
natural york stone

85

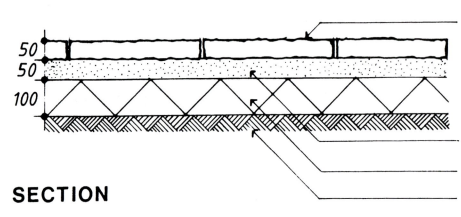

SECTION

50
50
100

Reconstituted stone sett 180 × 360 × 50 laid stack bond. Joints filled with mortar brushed in dry and well watered

Coarse sand bed

Hardcore well consolidated

Compacted ground

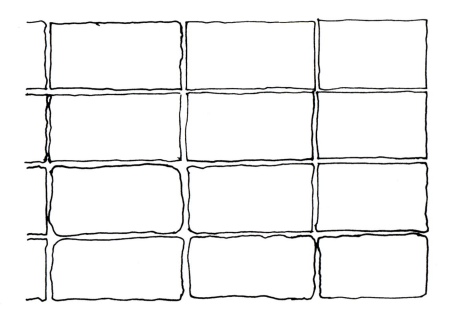

PLAN

Scale 1:10

PEDESTRIAN PAVING
reconstituted stone

86

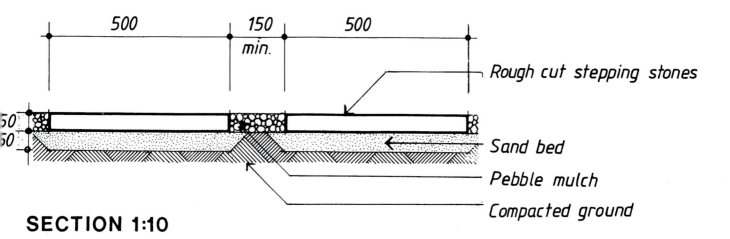

| 500 | 150
min. | 500 |

Rough cut stepping stones

Sand bed

Pebble mulch

Compacted ground

SECTION 1:10

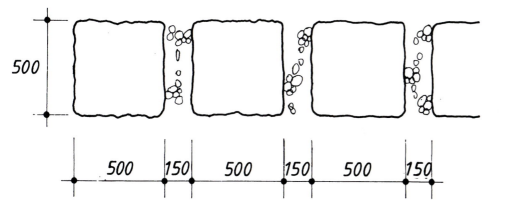

500

| 500 | 150 | 500 | 150 | 500 | 150 |

PLAN 1:20

PEDESTRIAN PAVING
stepping stones

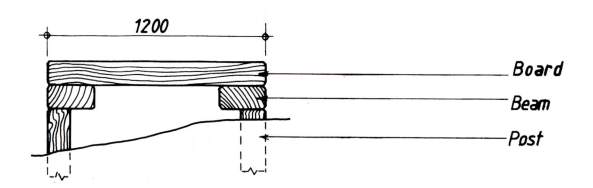

SECTION

Board

Beam

Post

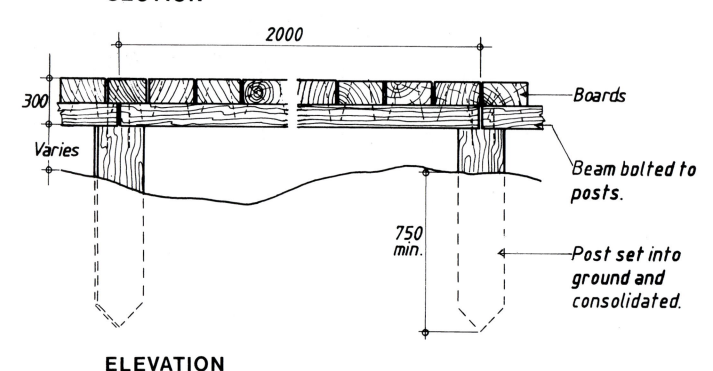

1200

2000

300

Varies

750 min.

Boards

Beam bolted to posts.

Post set into ground and consolidated.

ELEVATION

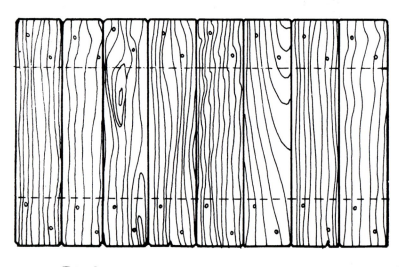

PLAN

Note
All timbers 200×150 ex railway sleepers.
The top surface may be made slip resistant by spraying with hot tar into which coarse sand is sprinkled.

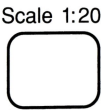

Scale 1:20

BOARDWALK
timber

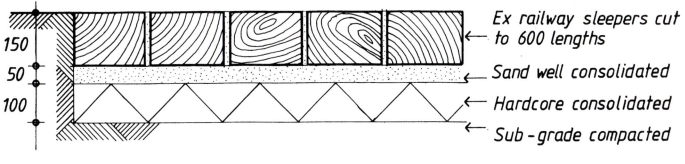

150 — Ex railway sleepers cut to 600 lengths

50 — Sand well consolidated

100 — Hardcore consolidated

Sub-grade compacted

SECTION

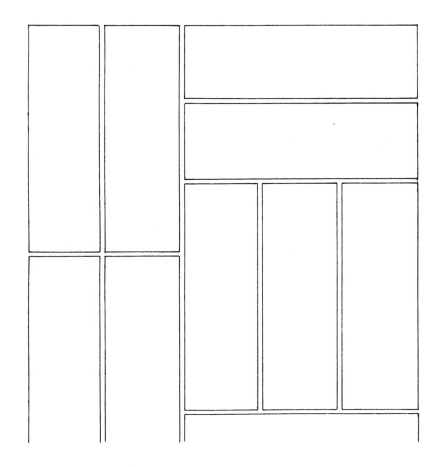

PLAN

Scale 1:10

PEDESTRIAN PAVING
timber block

89

STEPS AND RAMPS

GUIDANCE NOTES

Appearance

Steps should be gentle, low and wide, as too steep a flight will quicken the pace unnecessarily; constructing them wide will have the effect of making them look inviting. The materials used for the construction of steps will dictate their form. The materials used at the top and bottom of the steps or for any nearby retaining walls will also play an important part in the overall design. Let the steps reinforce the character of the site. A change in direction and a landing can greatly assist in making the design more interesting than steps going straight up and down a slope. It is quite common for the materials chosen for the facing to dictate the precise size of the riser to be used as well as the nosing.

Risers and treads do not always have to be of the same materials but should be chosen with care, as steps receive considerable wear. It is very important in the design of steps next to grassed or planted banks to consider the edge detail to ensure ease of maintenance.

Steps

The two main components of steps are risers and treads, and their size plays a significant part in their overall appearance. External steps can be far more generous in their size than internal ones, but they should have a rise of between 80 mm and 170 mm. The outdoor scale makes the use of any formula for calculating the size of risers and treads extremely difficult. Single steps used in isolation are dangerous as they are easily overlooked.

Treads

These should not be less than 350 mm, their width not being less than the going. Each tread should have a fall of 5 mm to ensure that no water is retained which might make the steps dangerous, especially in very cold weather. Non-slip materials are preferable. Where slab treads are used they should overhang the risers by 15 mm. Falls will affect the total rise of long flights.

Risers

These should be well marked, especially where the material used is different from the treads.

Landings

Long flights of steps should be broken up by generous landings of between one and two metres wide, with the maximum number of steps between landings limited to twelve. Flights should not exceed nineteen steps.

Handrails

If extensive use by old people is anticipated, or if the vertical drop at the side of the steps exceeds 600 mm, a handrail should be included. Reference should also be made to the building regulations.

Construction

Most flights of steps will usually involve the use of a concrete structure, possibly mesh reinforcement. In most cases it will be possible to cast the concrete *in situ* as a continuous mass element. The use of reinforcement is recommended in all but the most stable of ground, to guard against any differential movement. When flights of steps are flanked by retaining walls, the overall appearance, as well as the structural stability, would be better if the steps were built into the walls. This is especially important if the ground has been backfilled and there is some danger of movement.

Stepped ramps

Stepped ramps are generally used on ground slopes of between 1 in 12 (8.3 per cent) and 1 in 4 (25 per cent). The ramp going should have a constant slope of 1 in 12 (8.3 per cent) and the step riser height should be varied to suit the slope of the land.

Stepped ramps can be used to reduce the apparent steepness of a long ramp. To allow easy negotiation by prams and wheelchairs, riser dimension should not exceed 100 mm and tread dimension should be not less than 900 mm and preferably 1,500 mm. Allow for three paces to each tread. Nosings of treads should be clearly defined by a change of colour or texture.

Ramps

Ramps should have a maximum gradient of 1:10. For wheelchairs the maximum should be 1:12. The surface should be non-slip and surface water should be shed across the ramp, preferably into a drainage channel. Ramp lengths should not exceed 10 m. Level landings should be provided at intervals. Ramps that are parallel to a street are safer than those at right angles to it.

SPECIFICATION CHECK LIST

General

Specifiers are advised to complete the detailing of paving junctions and edges before completing this section of the specification. Such assembly drawings can be cross-referenced to the clauses in this section. Exact location and extent of each type should be shown on drawings. A separate clause for each main type of unit will permit their separate referencing on the drawn detail.

Materials

Base
Specify any material for bases (e.g. lean-mix concrete, local fill materials, etc.) – see chapter on Foundations.

Paving
Samples: Include reference for obtaining samples for approval, especially for clay bricks which are inherently variable in appearance (e.g. bricks which are selected from different parts of the kiln and mixed before delivery).

Concrete slabs
To BS 368 hydraulically pressed. State colour. Sizes are 600 mm × 450, 600, 750 and 900 mm in thicknesses of 50 mm or 63 mm. Smaller units are specified in BS 1197. For proprietary concrete slabs, specify details of manufacturer and reference.

Stone
Specify the type of stone and the quarry or source if known and the surface finish. Limestones should be 'joint bedded' (i.e. natural bed vertical) and this should be specified. Ascertain sizes currently available.

Paving bricks
This clause is for ordinary walling bricks which are often used for paving bedded frog down if frogged bricks are used. Note that the terms 'pavers', 'paviours' and 'paving bricks' are all common uses. Engineering bricks to BS 3921 are frequently used for pavings.
Select class A or B as appropriate, class A having the higher compressive strength and lesser absorption rating. State colour, precise selection of bricks for pavings, manufacturer and reference.

Clay pavers
To comply with BS 6677: Part 1: solid bricks with durability designation FL, work size and state manufacturer's name and reference.

Calcium silicate pavers
To BS 6677: Part 1: type PA: calcium silicate pavers. Solid (no voids) bricks BS 187 with a strength class of 5 or better should be specified. State manufacturer's name and reference.

Granite setts
To BS 435: size 100 × 100 × 100 mm/100 × 100 mm in 150 to 250 mm lengths.

New setts: other sizes specified in the BS are 75 × 125 and 150 mm, 100 × 125 and 150 mm. The BS is not restricted to granite; other igneous rocks are suitable. State if stone other than granite is required along with supplier's name and reference. Second-hand setts: specify size, type of stone, etc., along with name of supplier.

Concrete blocks (small element paving)
To BS 6273: Part 1: state manufacturer's name and reference.
Edges are normally chamfered and blocks are available in textured finish and coloured.

Cobbles
Hard water-smoothed stones of similar oval shape. Size with the smallest diameter in the 30 to 50 mm/50 to 75 mm/175 to 100 mm range.
State size, colour range and supplier's name and reference.

Workmanship

General
BS 7263: Part 2: Code of practice for laying (PC flags, kerbs, etc.). This reflects common practice but more detailed advice could be obtained from the BCA and the NPKA for flags and the BDA for bricks.

Control samples
The specification of control samples should be related to the size and importance of the job. It may be difficult to justify control samples on small jobs. Include information on type of paving, minimum size of control sample and any features to be included in the sample area (e.g. edging, channels).

Bases
If the steps are to be in precast units then the foundations are extremely important and require to be specified. In certain circumstances where the ground cannot be thoroughly compacted *in-situ* concrete should be specified.
Specify details of thickness and method of compaction. This will depend upon the bearing capacity of the sub-grade.
If the sub-base is used extensively by site

traffic, damage is bound to occur and this should be made good prior to laying paving, including any excavation through the sub-base for drainage runs.
The bedding should not be used for blinding or levelling the sub-base if it is outside the specified tolerances.
The drainage of paved areas should be designed in accordance with BS 6367: Code of practice for drainage of roofs and paved areas: Section 3, Part 9. All gradients must be formed in the sub-base and not in the bedding course which must be of constant thickness.
Laying: All precast units will require to be laid on a solid bed of mortar or a sand/cement dry mix both on hardcore.
Jointing and grouting: The jointing methods should be written into the descriptions of the methods of laying the paving followed by details of protection of the work. State either dry mortar or mortar-pointed or sand-filled joints along with size of joints.
Dry mortar joints: This method of jointing is recommended for any type of absorbent paving (e.g. brick or concrete) from which it is very difficult to remove the marks of mortar or grout. It can be applied quite dry or mixed almost dry which facilitates compaction to form a very dense joint.
Mortar-pointed joints: Due to relative movement and frost, mortar-pointed joints tend to deteriorate in time, and repointing may be necessary every few years.
The use of a fairly coarse sand (rather than an ordinary building sand) will improve durability of the joints.
Protection: Specify methods of protection of work from both inclement weather and any traffic.

DETAIL SHEETS

Steps
Brick (3)
Brick and concrete flag
Brick and granite sett
Brick and paving slab (4)
Brick and stone
Brick/block
Concrete block paviors
Concrete *in-situ* (2)
Concrete slab (3)
Concrete units
Granite sett
Natural stone
Natural York stone
Reconstituted stone (2)
Railway sleepers
Railway sleepers and hoggin
Timber (5)
Timber and aggregate (2)
Timber and hoggin
Split timber and chippings
Stepped ramps
Concrete and brick
Cobbled stepped ramp
Railway sleeper ramp
Timber log ramp
Brick pavior
'Embankments'
Brick (2)
Slate

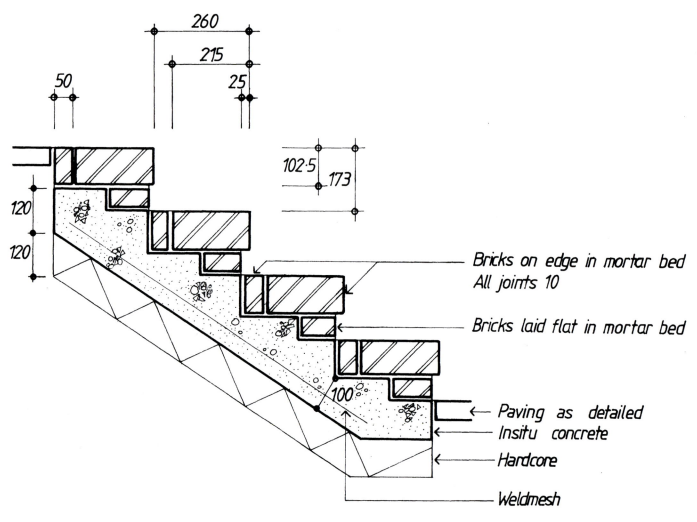

260

215

25

50

120

120

102·5

173

100

Bricks on edge in mortar bed
All joints 10

Bricks laid flat in mortar bed

Paving as detailed
Insitu concrete

Hardcore

Weldmesh

SECTION

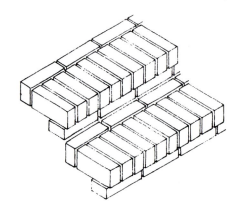

Scale 1:10

STEPS
brick

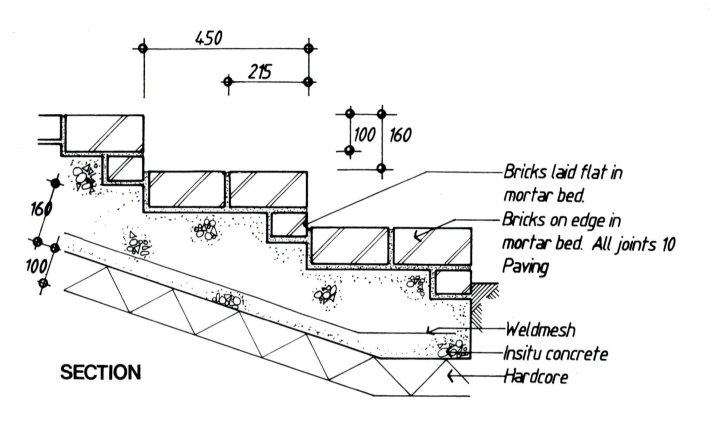

450

215

100 | 160

Bricks laid flat in mortar bed.

Bricks on edge in mortar bed. All joints 10 Paving

160

100

SECTION

Weldmesh

Insitu concrete

Hardcore

Scale 1:10

STEPS
brick

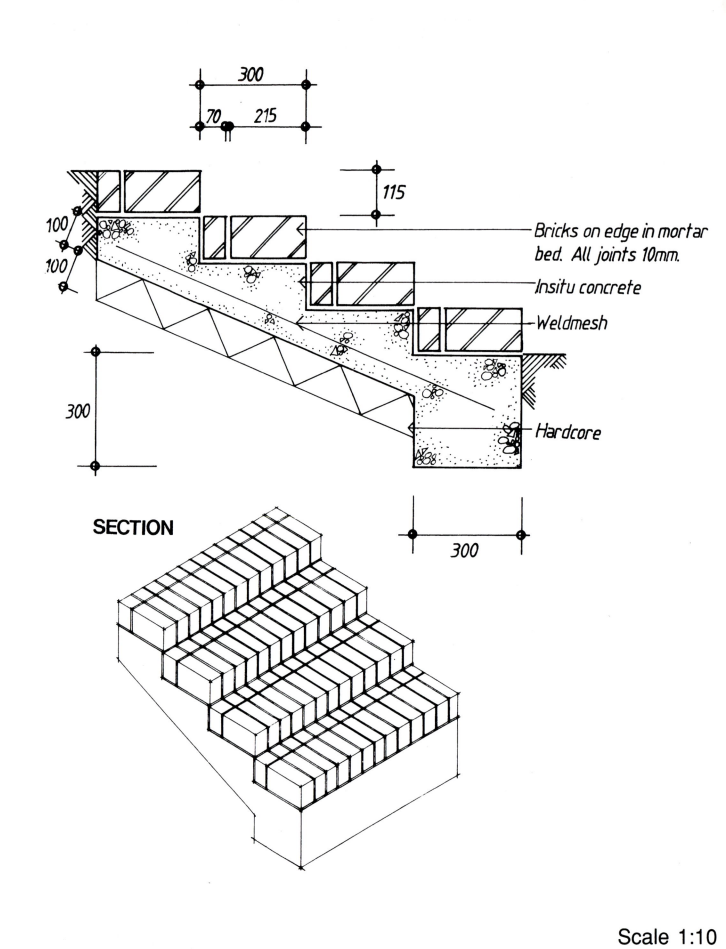

300

70 215

115

100

100

300

Bricks on edge in mortar bed. All joints 10mm.

Insitu concrete

Weldmesh

Hardcore

300

SECTION

Scale 1:10

STEPS
brick paving

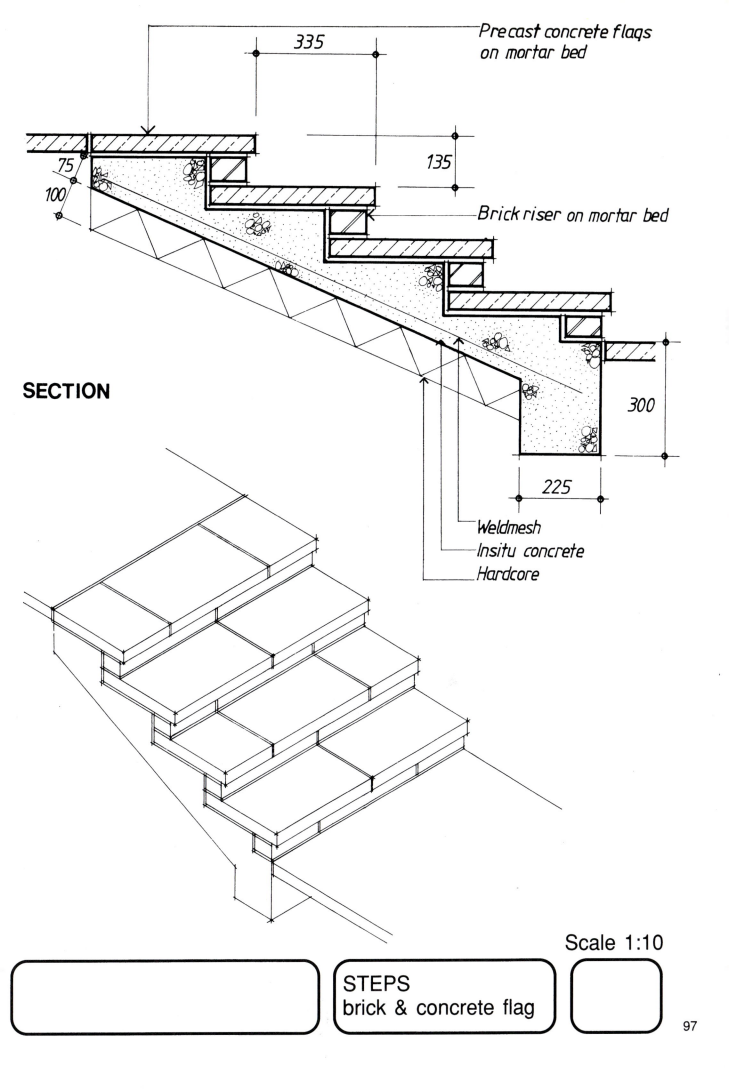

SECTION

335

135

75

100

Precast concrete flags
on mortar bed

Brick riser on mortar bed

300

225

Weldmesh

Insitu concrete

Hardcore

Scale 1:10

STEPS
brick & concrete flag

97

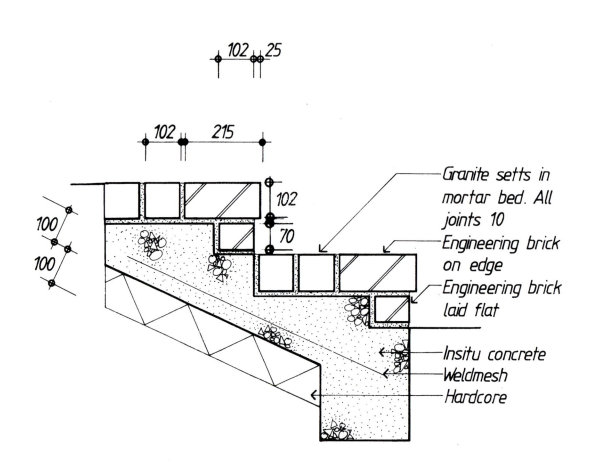

102 25

102 215

100

100

102

70

Granite setts in mortar bed. All joints 10

Engineering brick on edge

Engineering brick laid flat

Insitu concrete

Weldmesh

Hardcore

Scale 1:10

STEPS
brick & granite sett

98

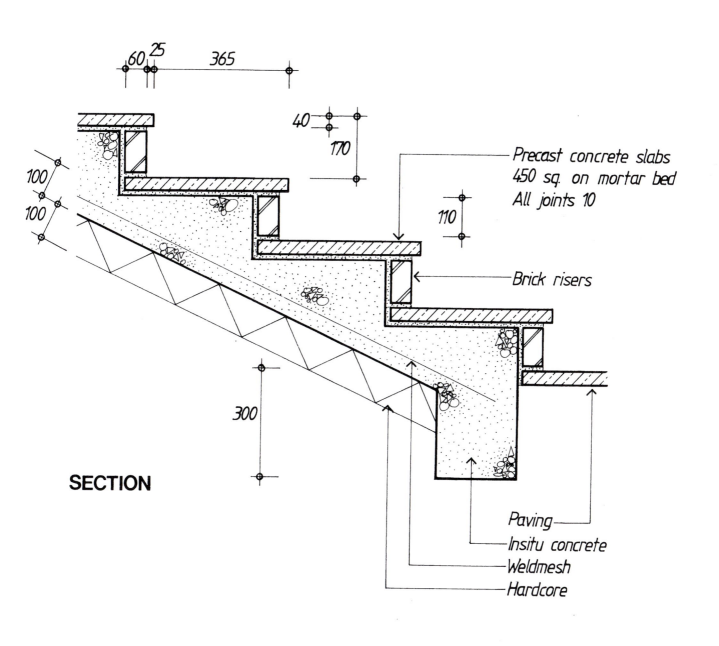

60 25 365

40

170

Precast concrete slabs
450 sq. on mortar bed
All joints 10

100

100

110

Brick risers

300

SECTION

Paving
Insitu concrete
Weldmesh
Hardcore

Scale 1:10

STEPS
brick & paving slab

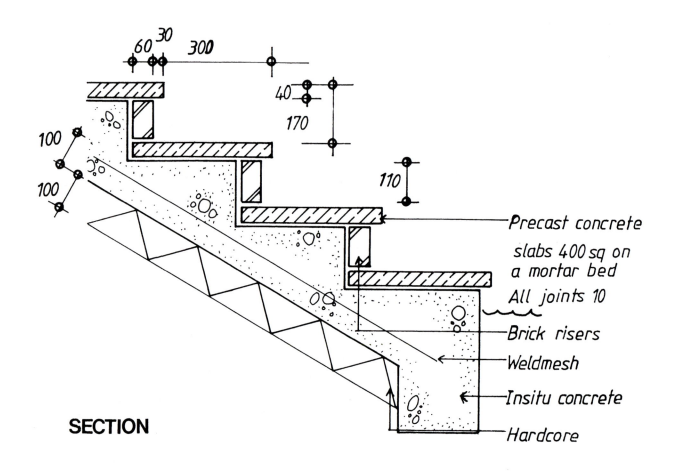

60 30 300

40

170

100

100

110

SECTION

Precast concrete
slabs 400 sq on
a mortar bed

All joints 10

Brick risers

Weldmesh

Insitu concrete

Hardcore

Scale 1:10

STEPS
brick & paving slab

100

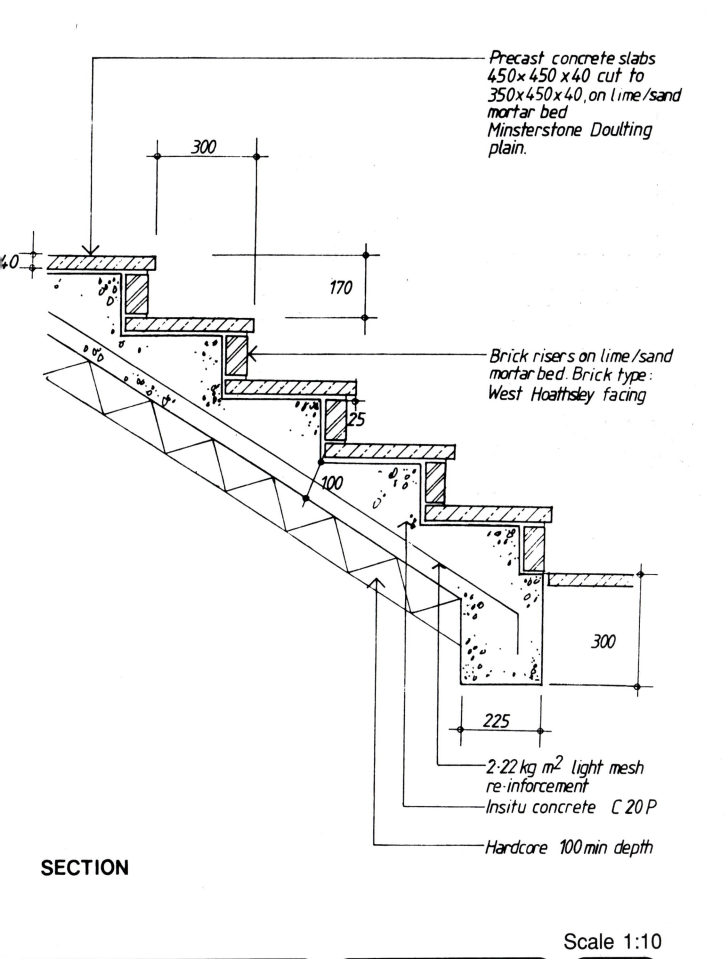

Precast concrete slabs
450 x 450 x 40 cut to
350 x 450 x 40, on lime/sand
mortar bed
Minsterstone Doulting
plain.

300

40

170

Brick risers on lime/sand
mortar bed. Brick type:
West Hoathsley facing

25

100

300

225

2·22 kg m² light mesh
re·inforcement

Insitu concrete C 20 P

Hardcore 100 min depth

SECTION

Scale 1:10

STEPS
brick & paving slab

101

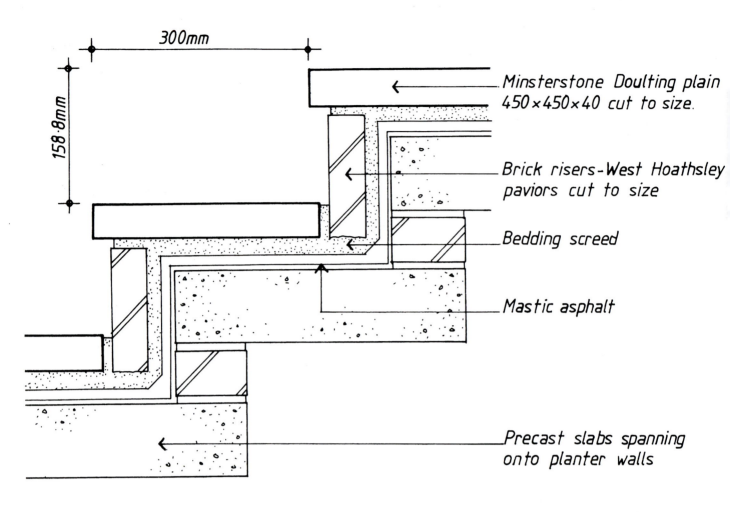

300mm

158·8mm

Minsterstone Doulting plain
450×450×40 cut to size.

Brick risers–West Hoathsley
paviors cut to size

Bedding screed

Mastic asphalt

Precast slabs spanning
onto planter walls

Note:–
to be read in conjunction
with architects' drawings
nos 629 / 333 and 315

Scale 1:5

STEPS
brick & paving slab

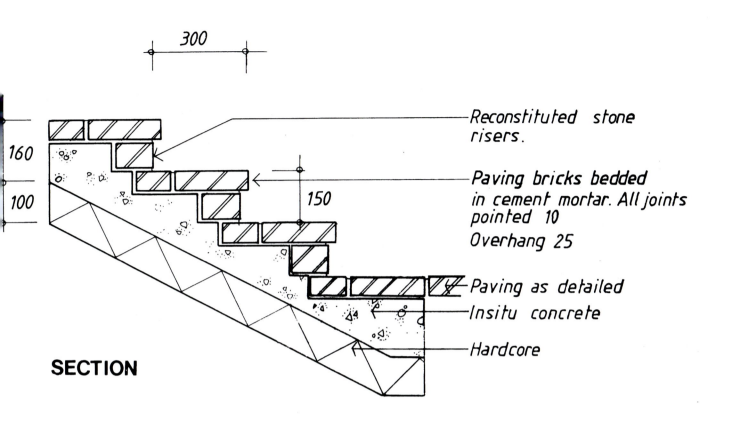

300

160

100

150

Reconstituted stone risers.

Paving bricks bedded in cement mortar. All joints pointed 10
Overhang 25

Paving as detailed

Insitu concrete

Hardcore

SECTION

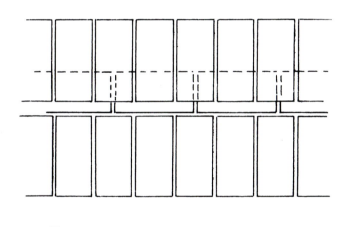

PLAN

Scale 1:10

STEPS
brick & stone

103

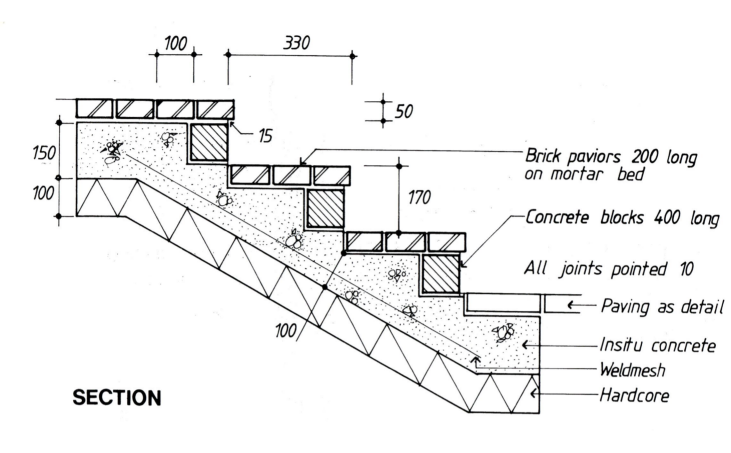

SECTION

100

330

50

150

100

15

Brick paviors 200 long
on mortar bed

170

Concrete blocks 400 long

All joints pointed 10

Paving as detail

Insitu concrete

Weldmesh

Hardcore

100

Scale 1:10

STEPS
brick/block

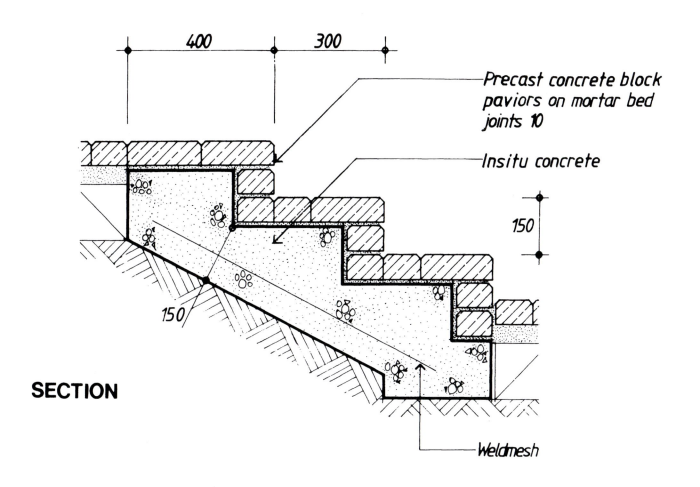

400 | 300

SECTION

Precast concrete block
paviors on mortar bed
joints 10

Insitu concrete

150

150

Weldmesh

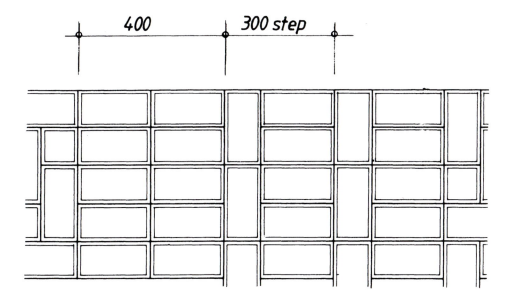

400 | 300 step

PLAN

Scale 1:10

STEPS
concrete block paviors

105

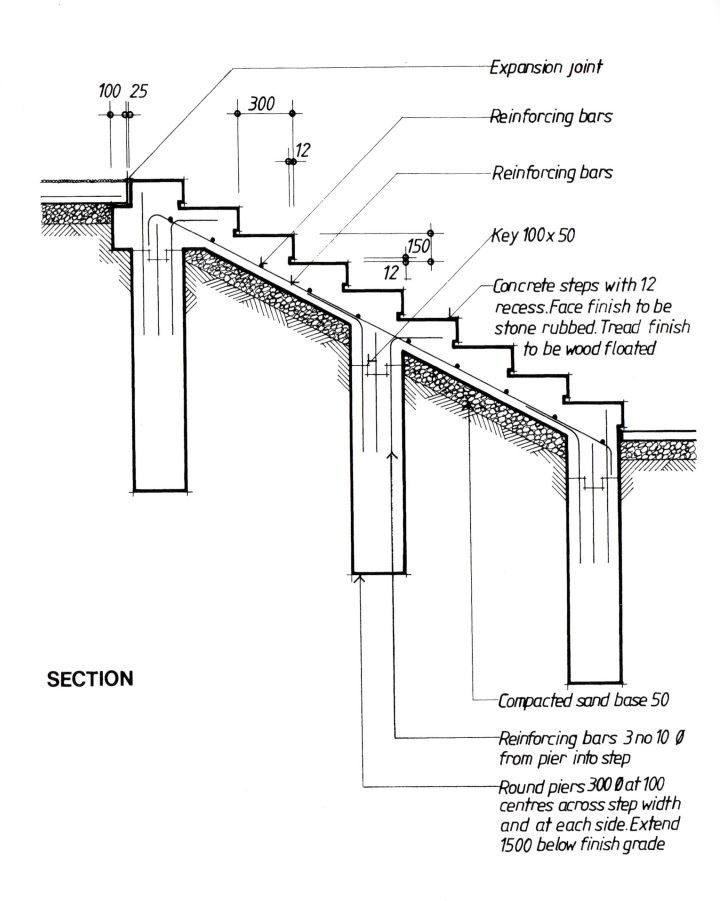

100 25

300

12

Expansion joint

Reinforcing bars

Reinforcing bars

150

12

Key 100 x 50

Concrete steps with 12 recess. Face finish to be stone rubbed. Tread finish to be wood floated

SECTION

Compacted sand base 50

Reinforcing bars 3 no 10 Ø from pier into step

Round piers 300 Ø at 100 centres across step width and at each side. Extend 1500 below finish grade

Scale 1:20

STEPS
concrete in-situ

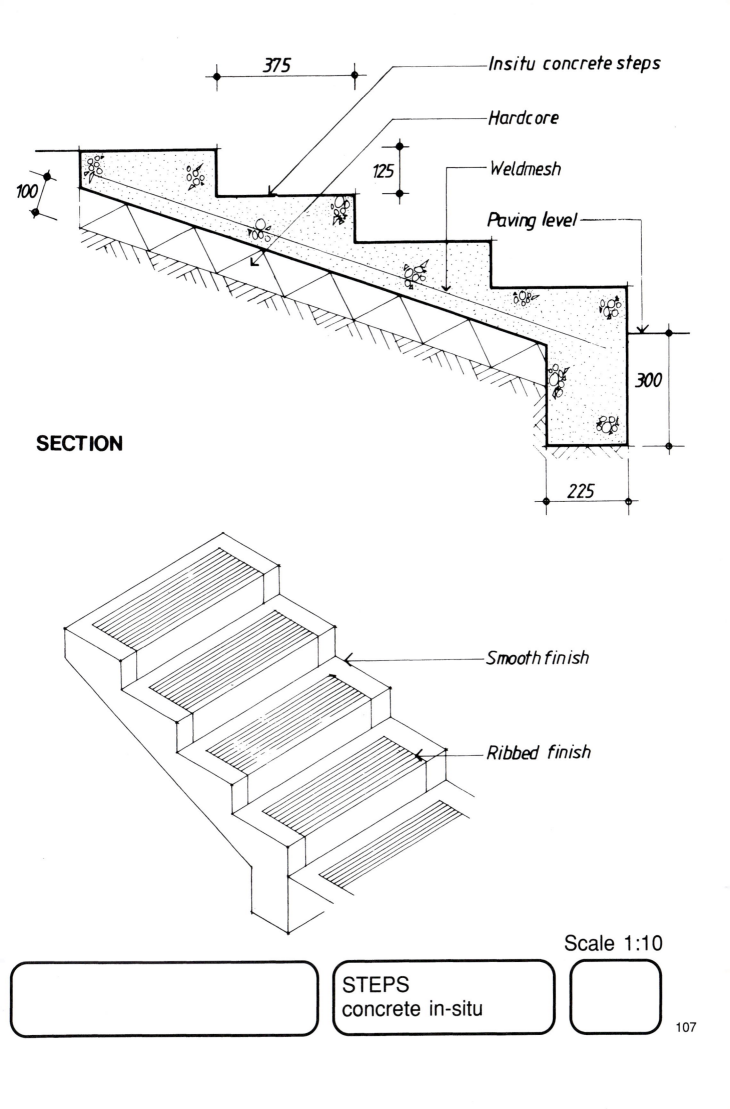

375

Insitu concrete steps

Hardcore

125

Weldmesh

Paving level

100

300

SECTION

225

Smooth finish

Ribbed finish

Scale 1:10

STEPS
concrete in-situ

107

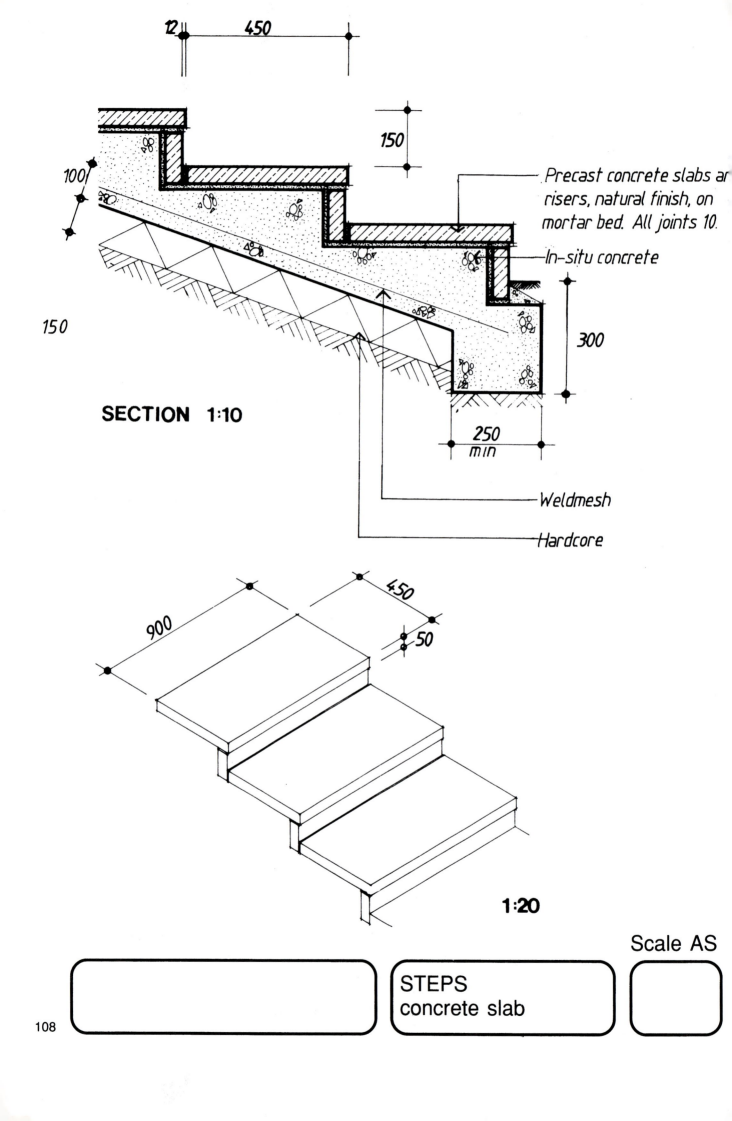

12 | 450

150

100|

150

SECTION 1:10

Precast concrete slabs ar risers, natural finish, on mortar bed. All joints 10.

In-situ concrete

300

250
min

Weldmesh

Hardcore

900

450

50

1:20

Scale AS

STEPS
concrete slab

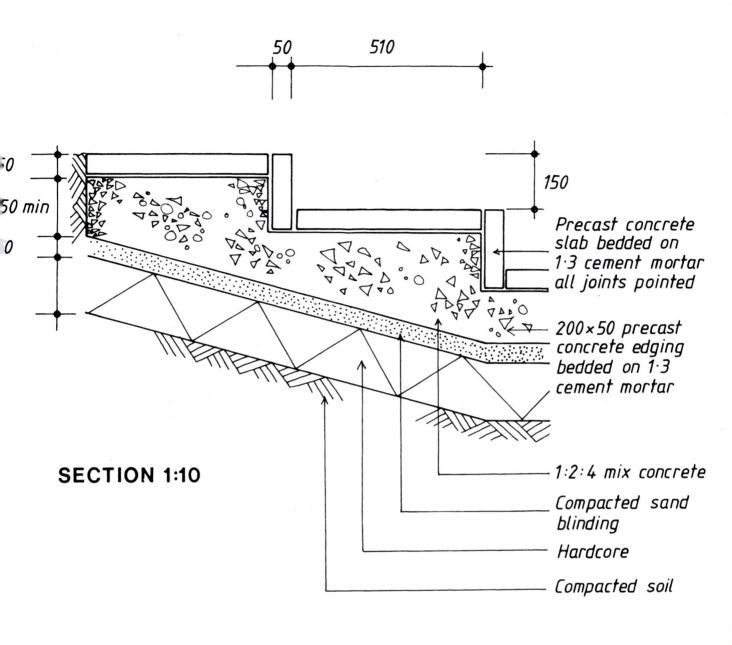

50   510

50

50 min

0

150

SECTION 1:10

Precast concrete
slab bedded on
1·3 cement mortar
all joints pointed

200×50 precast
concrete edging
bedded on 1·3
cement mortar

1:2:4 mix concrete

Compacted sand
blinding

Hardcore

Compacted soil

Scale 1:10

STEPS
concrete slab

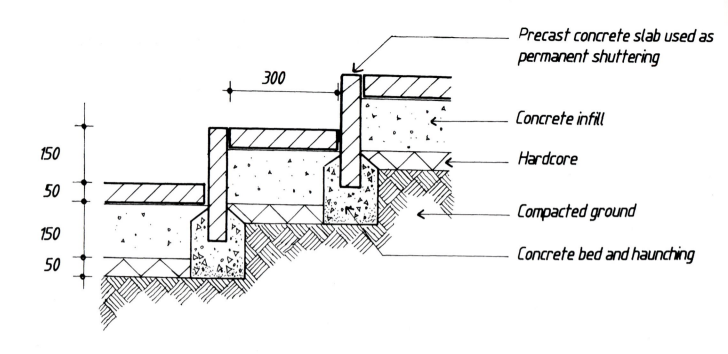

Precast concrete slab used as permanent shuttering

Concrete infill

Hardcore

Compacted ground

Concrete bed and haunching

300

150

50

150

50

SECTION

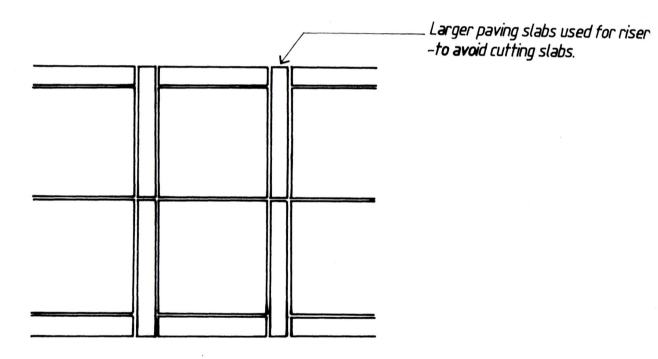

Larger paving slabs used for riser —to avoid cutting slabs.

PLAN

Scale 1:10

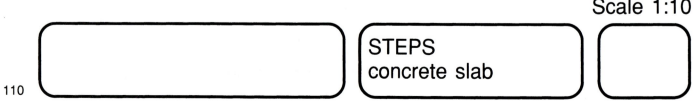

STEPS
concrete slab

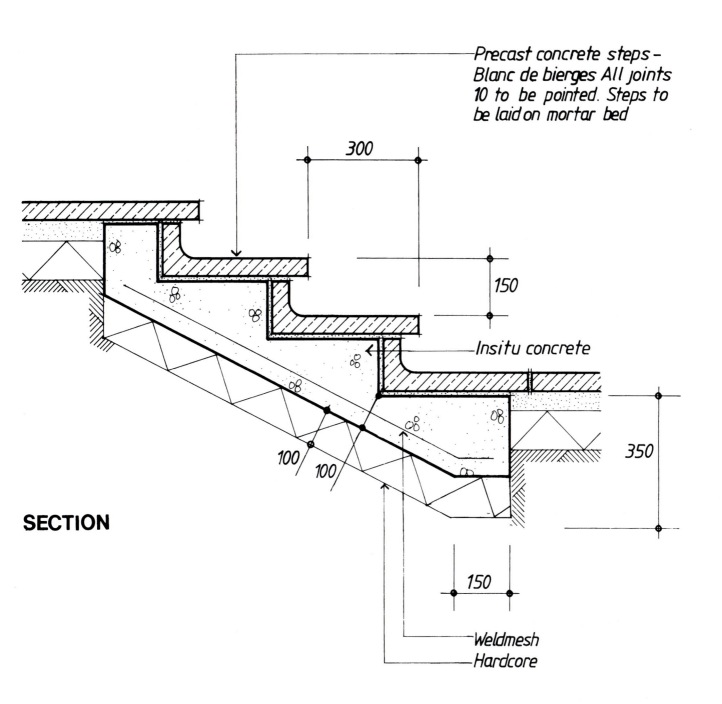

Precast concrete steps –
Blanc de bierges All joints
10 to be pointed. Steps to
be laid on mortar bed

300

150

Insitu concrete

SECTION

350

100   100

150

Weldmesh
Hardcore

Scale 1:10

STEPS
concrete units

111

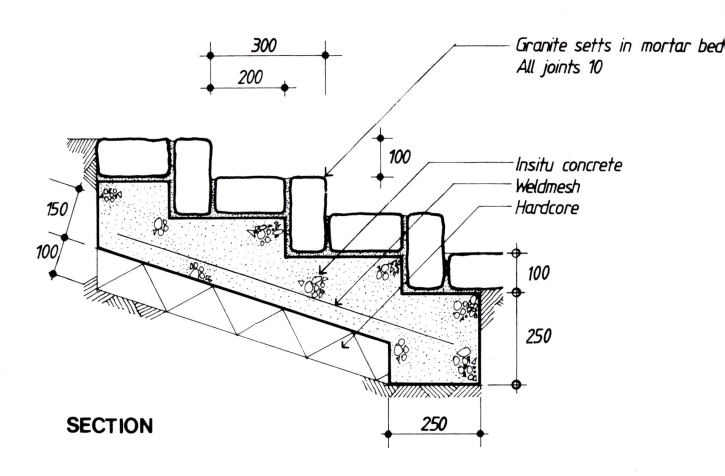

300

200

Granite setts in mortar bed
All joints 10

100

Insitu concrete
Weldmesh
Hardcore

150

100

100

250

SECTION

250

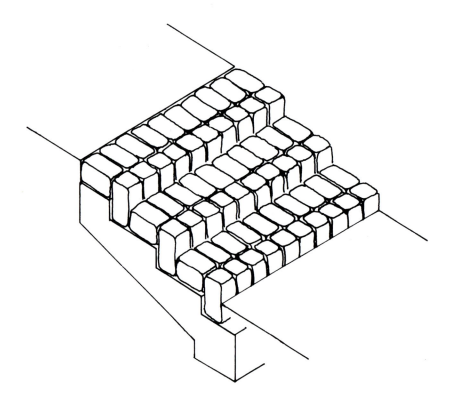

Scale 1:10

| | STEPS
granite sett | |

112

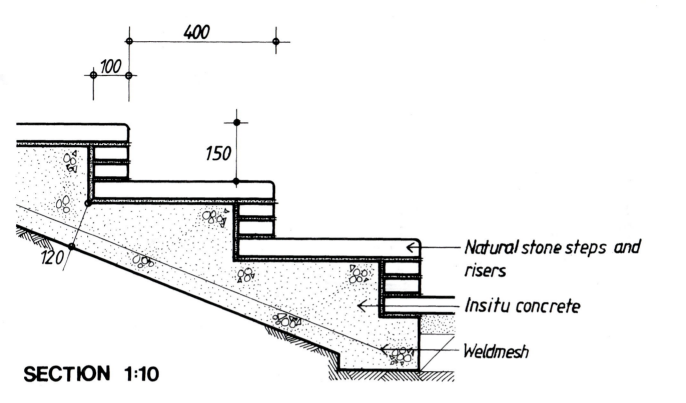

400

100

150

120

SECTION 1:10

Natural stone steps and risers

Insitu concrete

Weldmesh

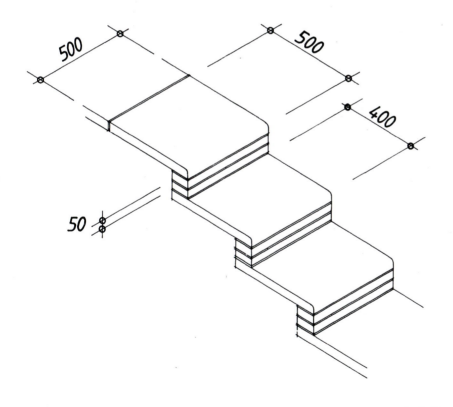

500

500

400

50

1:20

Scale AS

STEPS
natural stone

113

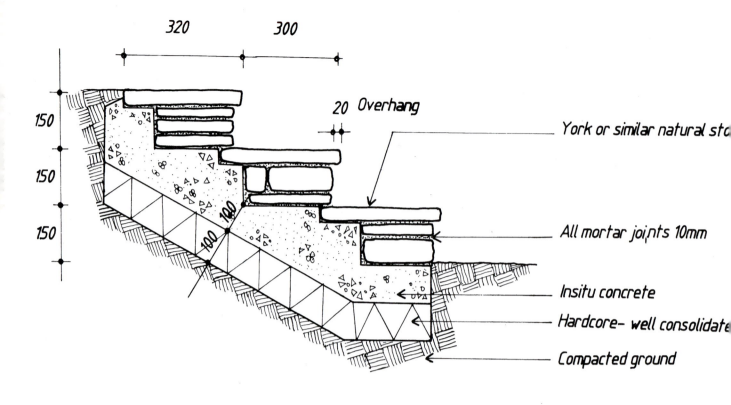

320   300

150

150

150

20 Overhang

100 100

SECTION

York or similar natural sto

All mortar joints 10mm

Insitu concrete

Hardcore- well consolidate

Compacted ground

Scale 1:10

STEPS
natural york stone

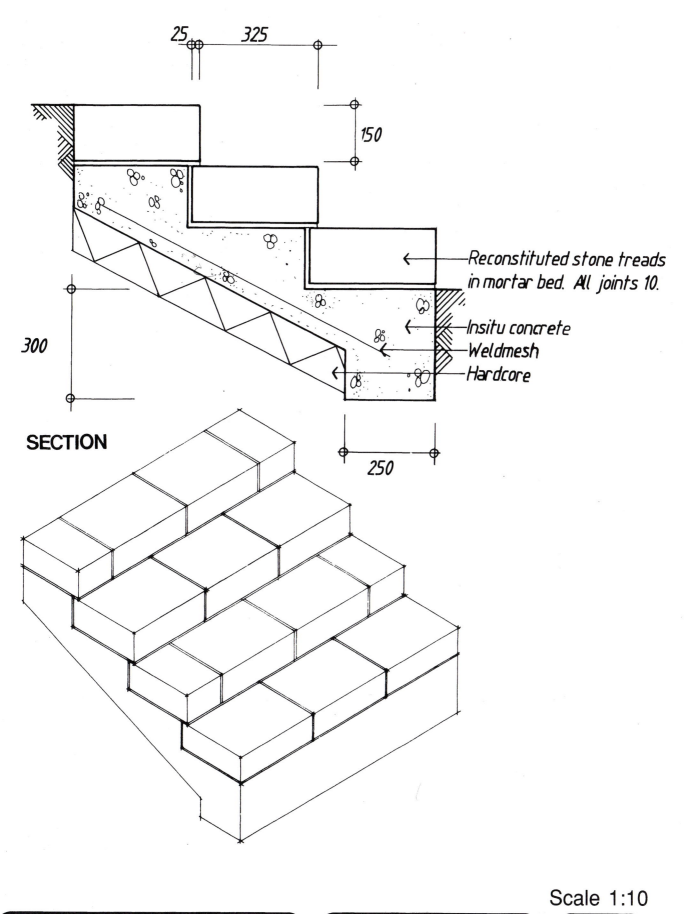

25   325

150

Reconstituted stone treads
in mortar bed. All joints 10.

Insitu concrete

Weldmesh

Hardcore

300

SECTION

250

Scale 1:10

STEPS
reconstituted stone

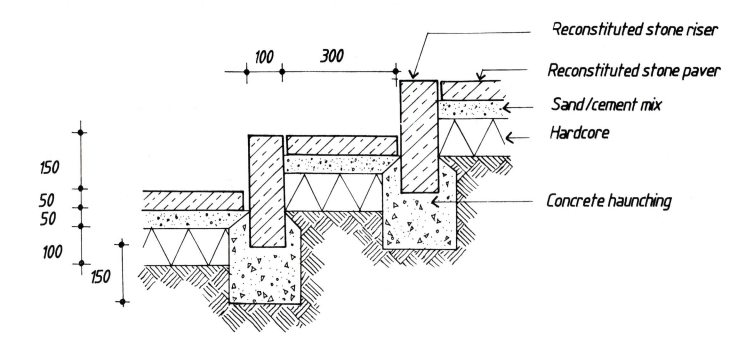

100 300

Reconstituted stone riser

Reconstituted stone paver

Sand/cement mix

Hardcore

Concrete haunching

150

50

50

100

150

SECTION

Scale 1:10

STEPS
reconstituted stone

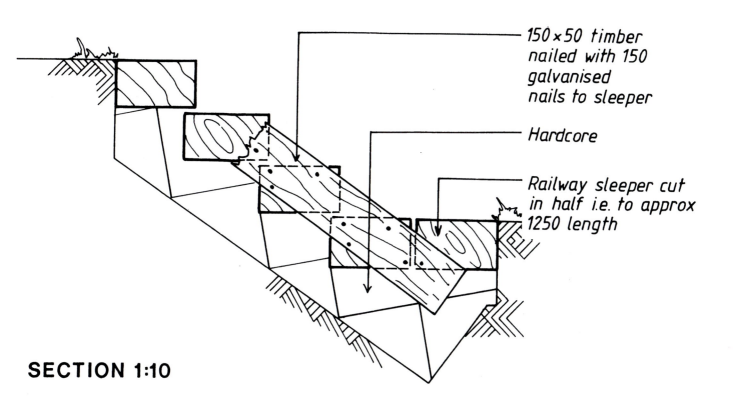

150 × 50 timber
nailed with 150
galvanised
nails to sleeper

Hardcore

Railway sleeper cut
in half i.e. to approx
1250 length

SECTION 1:10

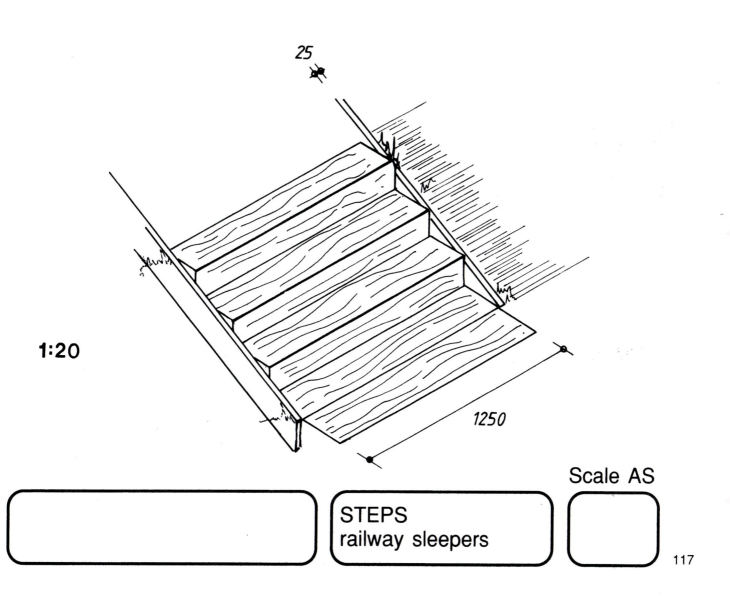

25

1:20

1250

Scale AS

STEPS
railway sleepers

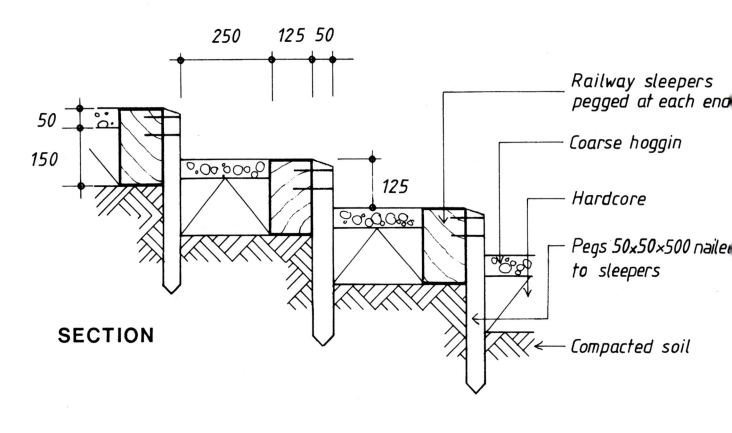

250   125   50

50

150

125

SECTION

Railway sleepers
pegged at each end

Coarse hoggin

Hardcore

Pegs 50×50×500 nailed
to sleepers

Compacted soil

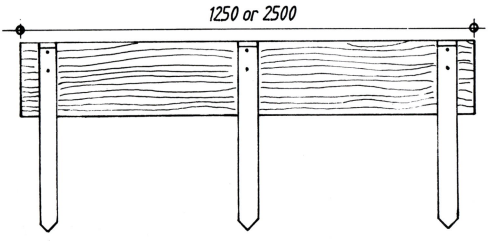

1250 or 2500

ELEVATION

Scale 1:10

STEPS
railway sleepers
and hoggin

118

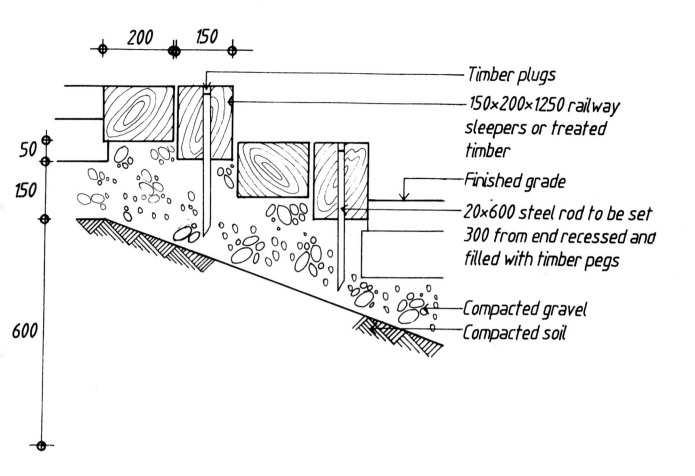

- Timber plugs
- 150×200×1250 railway sleepers or treated timber
- Finished grade
- 20×600 steel rod to be set 300 from end recessed and filled with timber pegs
- Compacted gravel
- Compacted soil

200
150
50
150
600

SECTION

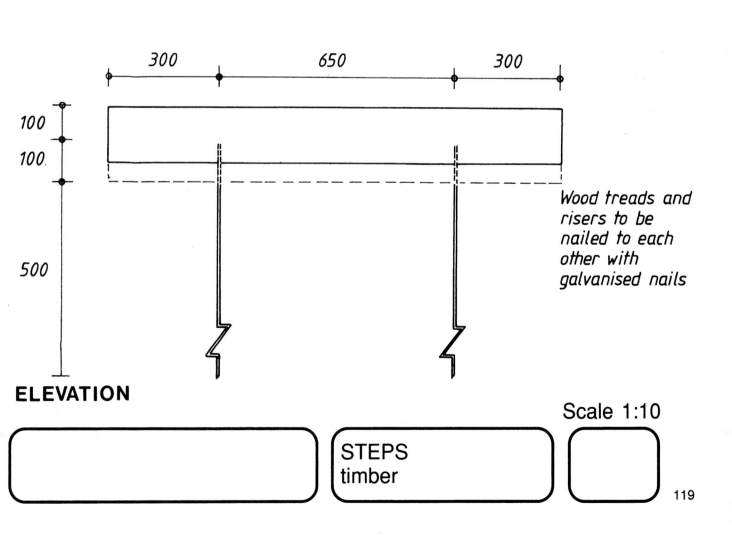

300
650
300

100
100
500

Wood treads and risers to be nailed to each other with galvanised nails

ELEVATION

Scale 1:10

STEPS
timber

119

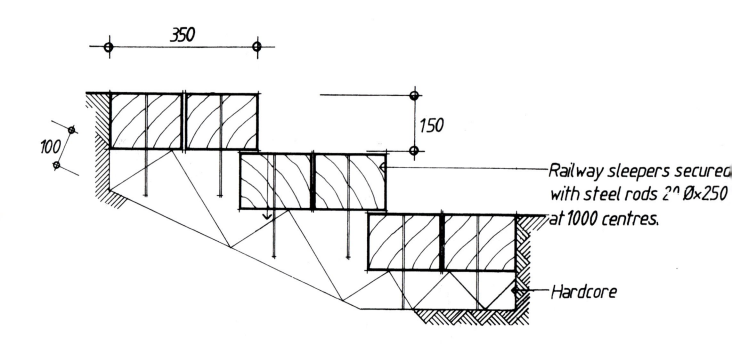

350

100

150

Railway sleepers secured
with steel rods 2" Ø×250
at 1000 centres.

Hardcore

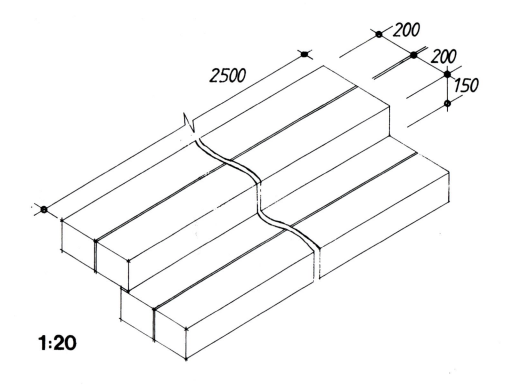

2500

200

200

150

1:20

Scale AS

STEPS
timber

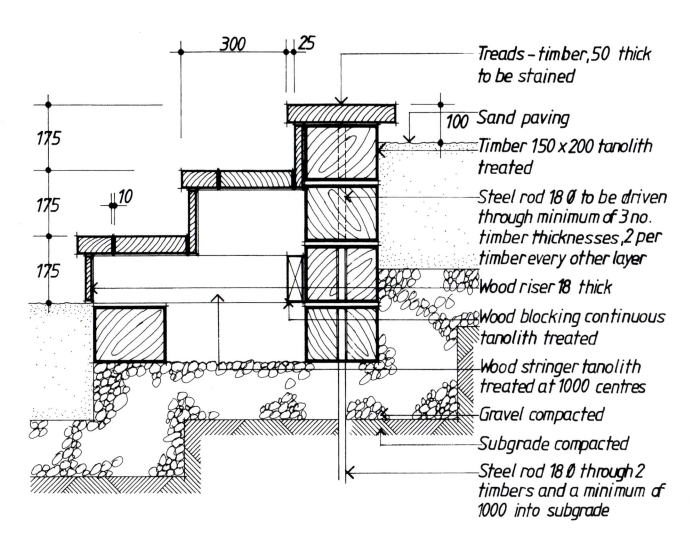

300 | **25**

175

175 | **10**

175

Treads – timber, 50 thick
to be stained

100 Sand paving

Timber 150 x 200 tanolith
treated

Steel rod 18 Ø to be driven
through minimum of 3 no.
timber thicknesses, 2 per
timber every other layer

Wood riser 18 thick

Wood blocking continuous
tanolith treated

Wood stringer tanolith
treated at 1000 centres

Gravel compacted

Subgrade compacted

Steel rod 18 Ø through 2
timbers and a minimum of
1000 into subgrade

SECTION

Scale 1:10

STEPS
timber

121

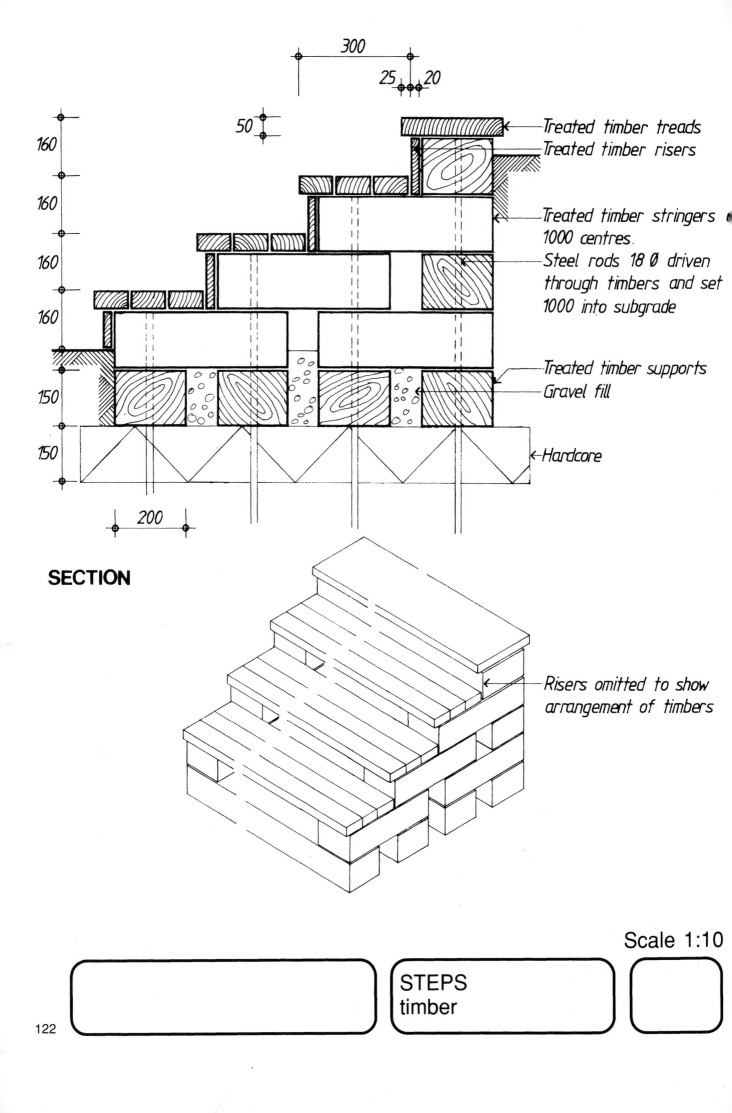

300

25 20

50

160

160

160

160

150

150

Treated timber treads
Treated timber risers

Treated timber stringers
1000 centres.
Steel rods 18 Ø driven
through timbers and set
1000 into subgrade

Treated timber supports
Gravel fill

←Hardcore

SECTION

200

Risers omitted to show
arrangement of timbers

Scale 1:10

STEPS
timber

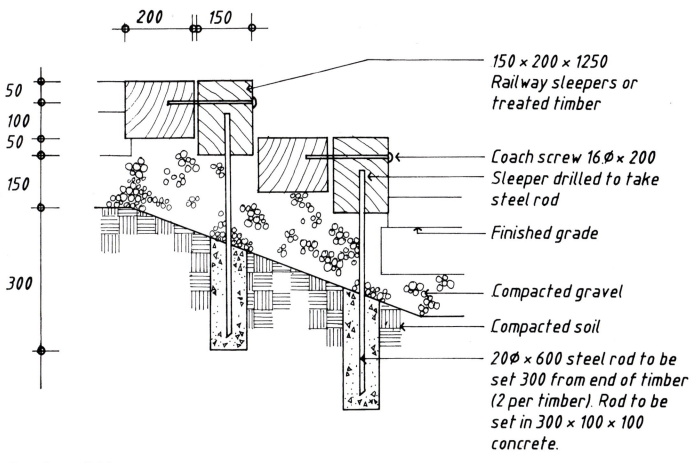

| | 200 | 150 | |

50	
100	
50	
150	
300	

150 × 200 × 1250
Railway sleepers or
treated timber

Coach screw 16.Ø × 200

Sleeper drilled to take
steel rod

Finished grade

Compacted gravel

Compacted soil

20Ø × 600 steel rod to be
set 300 from end of timber
(2 per timber). Rod to be
set in 300 × 100 × 100
concrete.

SECTION

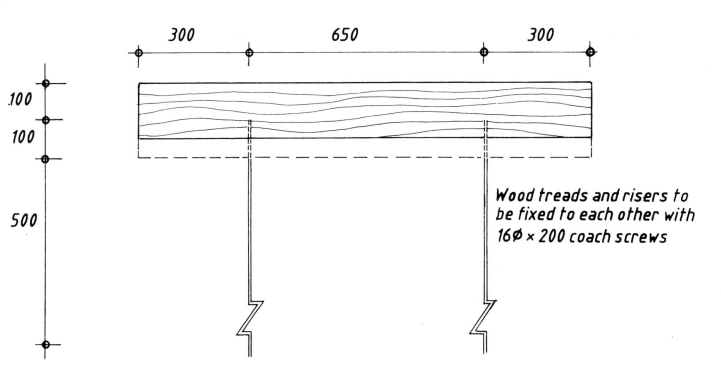

| 300 | 650 | 300 |

100	
100	
500	

Wood treads and risers to
be fixed to each other with
16Ø × 200 coach screws

ELEVATION

Scale 1:10

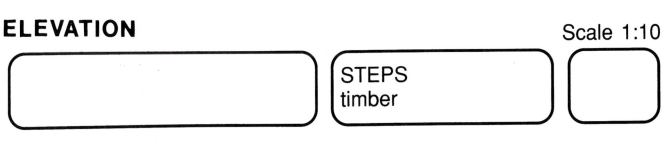

STEPS
timber

123

200

Finished grade of bark

Railway sleeper

150

150

Shredded bark surface

150

Hardcore or Hoggin

Compacted soil

Reinforcement bar

SECTION 1:10

200 | 1500

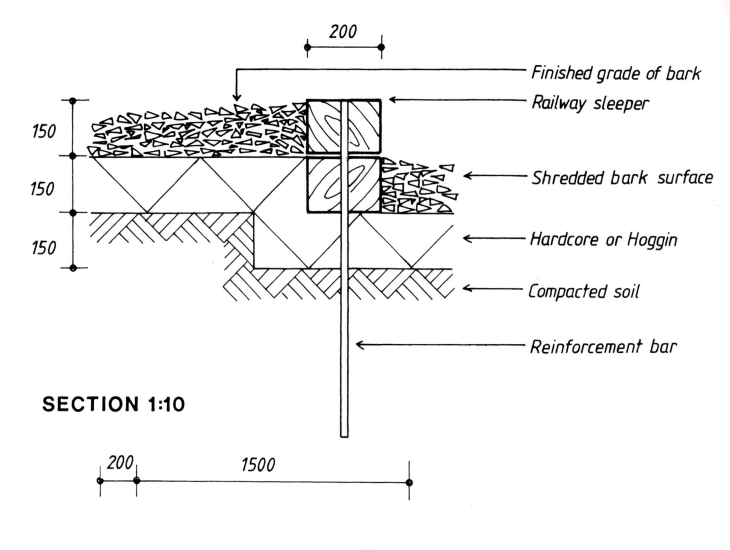

200

1150

PLAN 1:20

Scale AS

STEPS
timber & aggregate

124

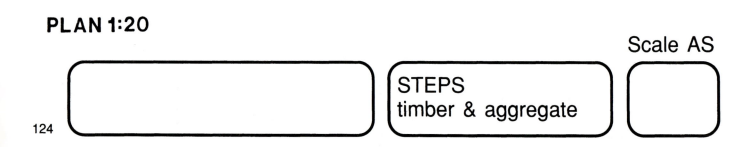

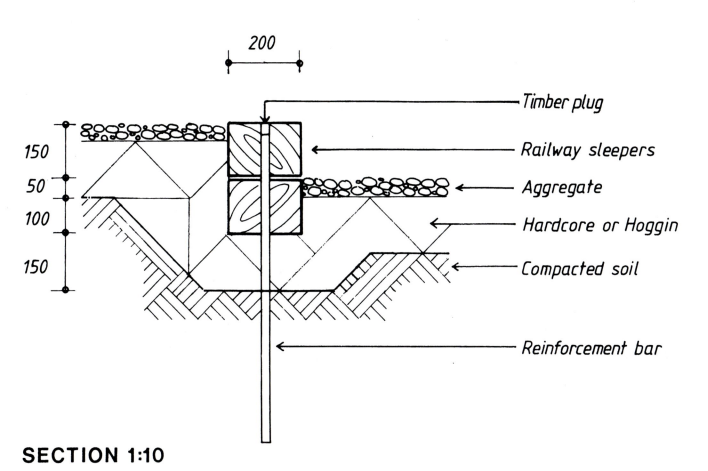

200

Timber plug

150

Railway sleepers

50

Aggregate

100

Hardcore or Hoggin

150

Compacted soil

Reinforcement bar

SECTION 1:10

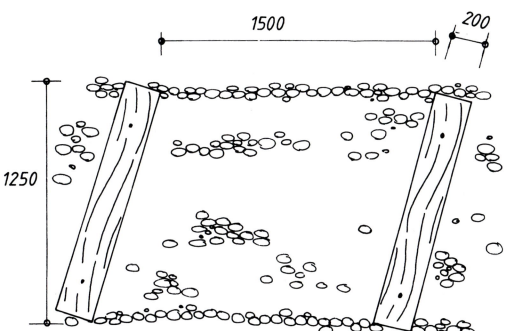

1500

200

1250

PLAN 1:20

Scale AS

STEPS
timber & aggregate

125

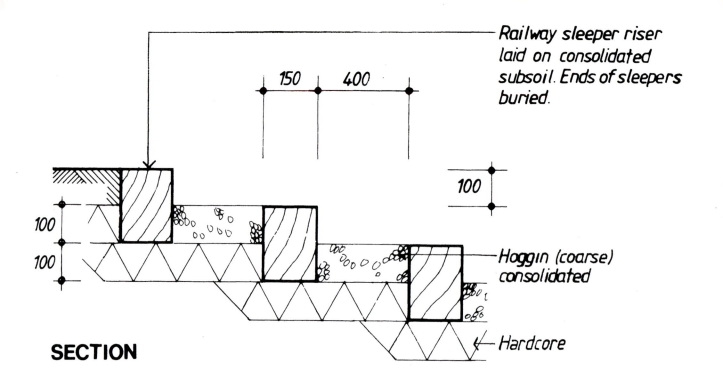

Railway sleeper riser laid on consolidated subsoil. Ends of sleepers buried.

150 400

100

100

100

Hoggin (coarse) consolidated

Hardcore

SECTION

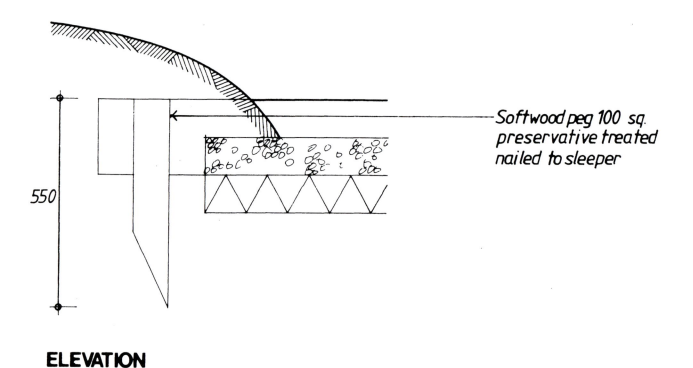

Softwood peg 100 sq. preservative treated nailed to sleeper

550

ELEVATION

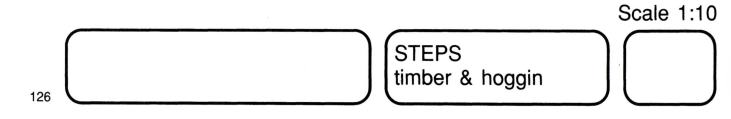

Scale 1:10

STEPS
timber & hoggin

126

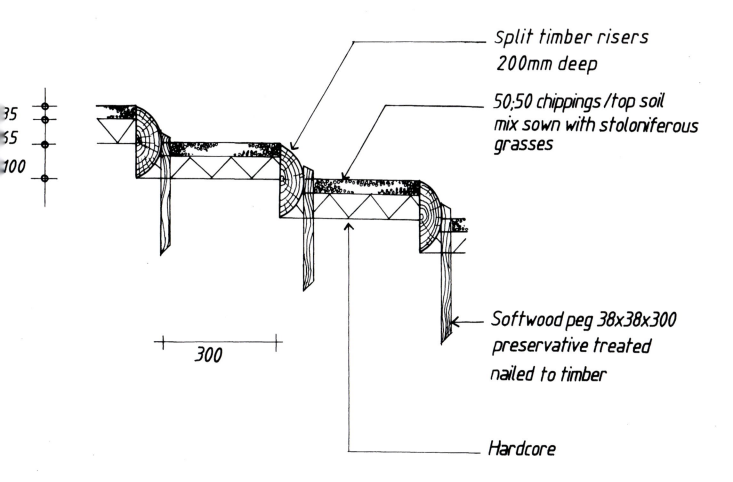

35

55

100

Split timber risers
200mm deep

50:50 chippings / top soil
mix sown with stoloniferous
grasses

300

Softwood peg 38x38x300
preservative treated
nailed to timber

Hardcore

SECTION

Scale 1:10

STEPS
split timber
and chippings

127

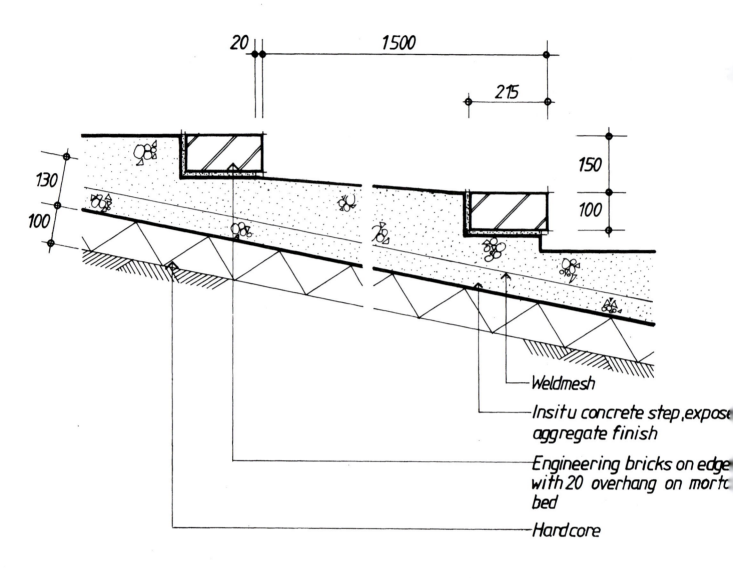

20 1500

215

130

100

150

100

Weldmesh

Insitu concrete step, expose aggregate finish

Engineering bricks on edge with 20 overhang on mortc bed

Hardcore

SECTION

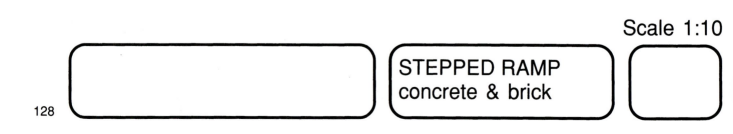

Scale 1:10

STEPPED RAMP
concrete & brick

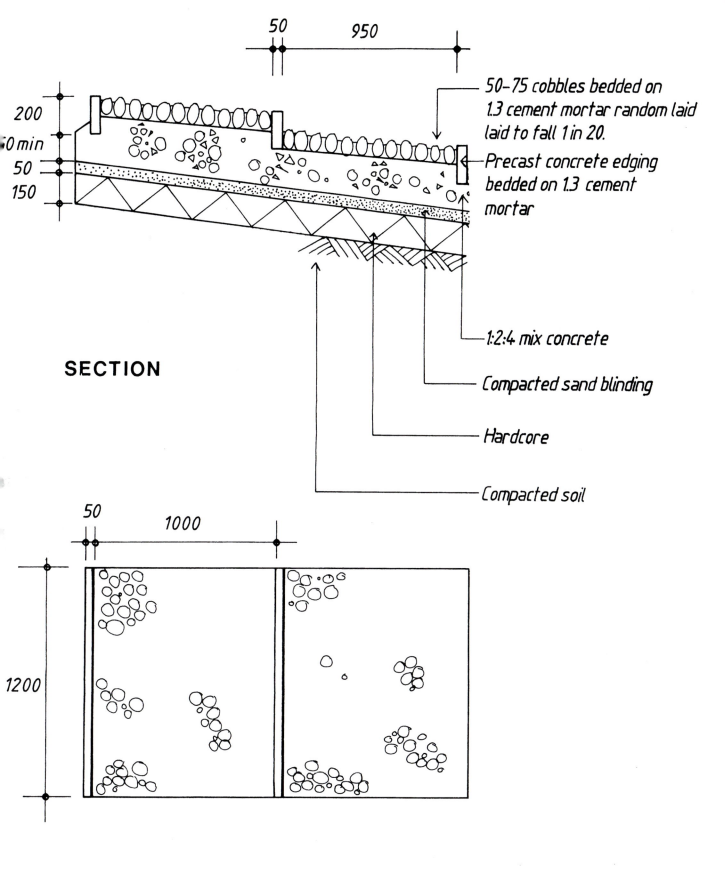

50 950

50-75 cobbles bedded on
1.3 cement mortar random laid
laid to fall 1 in 20.

200

50 min

50

150

Precast concrete edging
bedded on 1.3 cement
mortar

SECTION

1:2:4 mix concrete

Compacted sand blinding

Hardcore

Compacted soil

50 1000

1200

PLAN

Scale 1:20

STEPS
cobbled stepped ramp

129

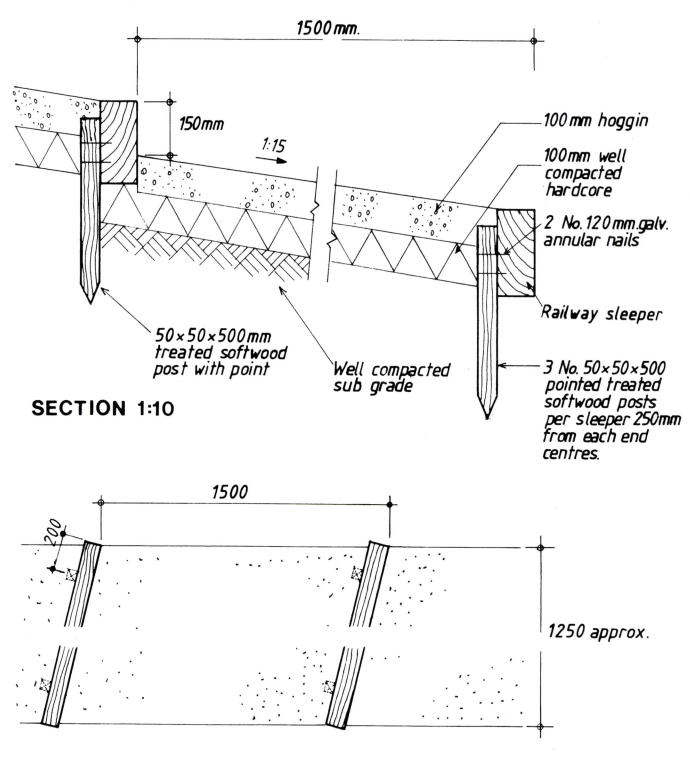

1500 mm.

150mm

1:15

100 mm hoggin

100mm well compacted hardcore

2 No. 120 mm galv. annular nails

Railway sleeper

3 No. 50×50×500 pointed treated softwood posts per sleeper 250mm from each end centres.

50×50×500mm treated softwood post with point

Well compacted sub grade

SECTION 1:10

1500

200

1250 approx.

PLAN 1:20

Scale AS

STEP RAMP
railway sleeper

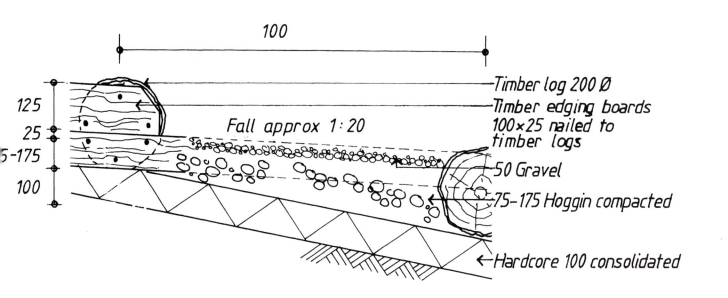

100

125

25

5-175

100

Timber log 200 Ø
Timber edging boards
100×25 nailed to
timber logs
50 Gravel
75-175 Hoggin compacted

Fall approx 1:20

←Hardcore 100 consolidated

SECTION 1:10

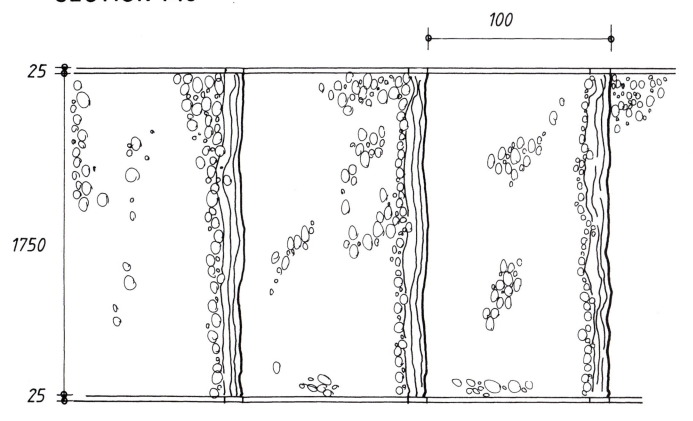

100

25

1750

25

PLAN 1:20

Scale AS

STEPPED RAMP
timber log

131

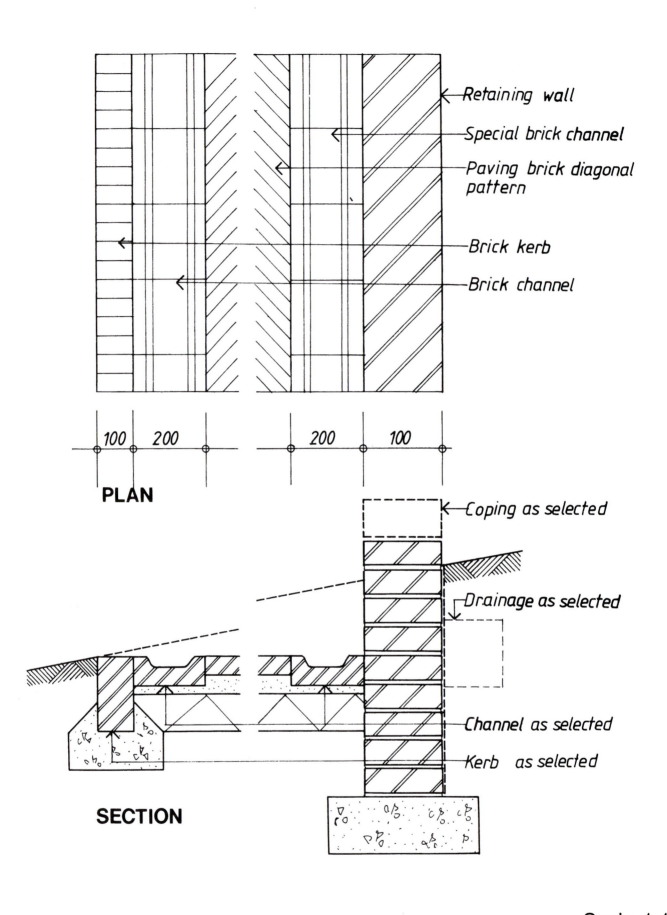

← Retaining wall

← Special brick channel

Paving brick diagonal pattern

Brick kerb

Brick channel

| 100 | 200 | | 200 | 100 |

PLAN

← Coping as selected

Drainage as selected

Channel as selected

Kerb as selected

SECTION

Scale 1:10

RAMP
brick pavior

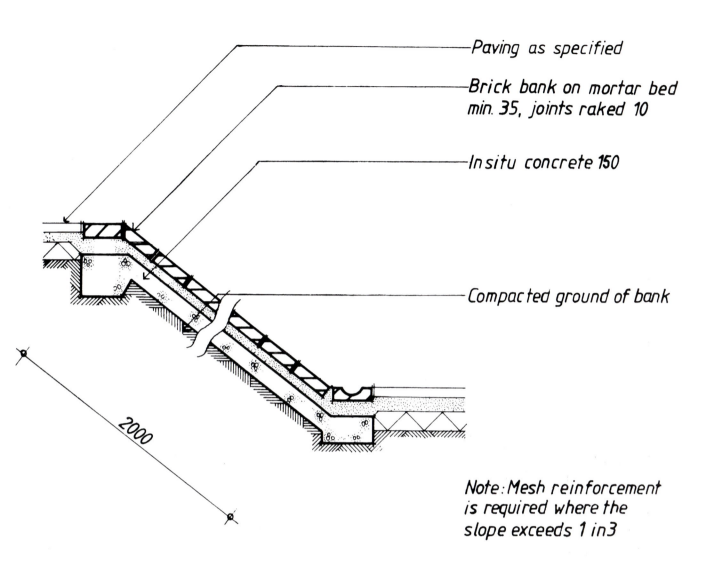

Paving as specified

Brick bank on mortar bed min. 35, joints raked 10

In situ concrete 150

Compacted ground of bank

2000

Note: Mesh reinforcement is required where the slope exceeds 1 in 3

SECTION

Scale 1:10

EMBANKMENT
brick

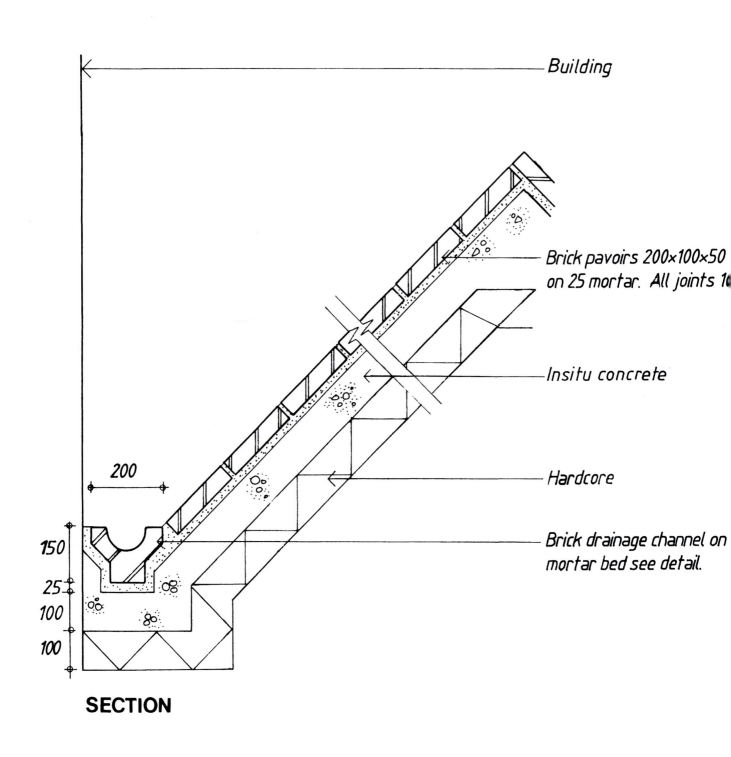

Building

Brick pavoirs 200×100×50
on 25 mortar. All joints 1[

Insitu concrete

Hardcore

Brick drainage channel on
mortar bed see detail.

200

150

25

100

100

SECTION

Scale 1:10

EMBANKMENT
brick

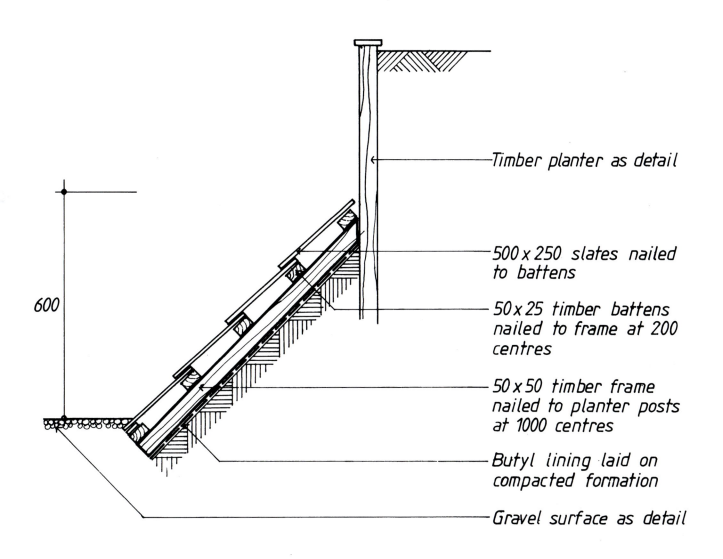

600

Timber planter as detail

500 x 250 slates nailed to battens

50 x 25 timber battens nailed to frame at 200 centres

50 x 50 timber frame nailed to planter posts at 1000 centres

Butyl lining laid on compacted formation

Gravel surface as detail

SECTION

Scale 1:10

EMBANKMENT
slate

MARGINS, EDGES AND TRIMS

GUIDANCE NOTES

Mowing margins

An important aim in the detailing of grass areas is the elimination of edge trimming. Grass edges should be kept at least 225 mm away from walls and other obstructions, and should abut a hard edge. The infill can be of any material that will not support plant growth. Loose gravel and hoggin should be used with discretion, because they require a high standard of maintenance. Mowing strips can also be used around planted areas.

Edges

Edges are necessary to retain the substrata of paving and to prevent the edges breaking away. They should be retained by a concrete foundation and haunching, except where timber has been used. They are also used to mark limits of ownership or to sub-divide areas of concrete paving. Edges also establish the character of a road or lane, especially in rural areas where a kerb would not be in sympathy with the overall landscape. In urban areas edges would not generally be used on the sides of main roads but could be found in small-scale roads on housing estates, driveways or pedestrian walkways. Edges also provide a neat finish to any paved surface and provide visual demarcation, but again they should be chosen with care to reflect the surroundings of the area, be it city, town or village.

Timber edging

The use of timber for edging is usually limited to gravel, hoggin or bound surfaces which are used for light vehicle or pedestrian traffic. The surfaces are kept flush with the edge.

Concrete edging

Precast concrete units are usually available 450 mm long, but their length severely limits the radius to which they can be laid in order to produce a smooth curved edge.

SPECIFICATION CHECK LIST

General

Exact location and extent of each type of margin or edge should be shown on drawings. A separate specification clause for each main type of unit will permit their separate referencing on the drawn details.

Materials

Concrete for foundations
State concrete mix, reference and size of foundations.

Mortar bedding
State mortar mix, reference and thickness.

Precast concrete units
To BS 7263: Part 1: where units will be subjected to the application of de-icing salts it is preferable to specify that they are hydraulically pressed.
Specify details of units. Give either BS profile figure number or the manufacturer's reference and size (width × height). Most manufacturers will supply alternative sizes and/or profiles to the range of units given in BS 7263: Part 1 including 600 mm lengths in the most commonly used profiles. Length of units range from 450 mm to 915 mm in BS 7263: Part 1. List any special shapes required and specify finish and colour.

Stone
Specify the type of stone and the quarry or source if known and the surface finish. BS

435 specifies and gives illustrations for three types of finish:

A – Fine picked
B – Fair picked and single axed or ridged
C – Rough punched.
Obtain advice from supplier before selecting finish. Existing margins and edges which have been redressed or reshaped and redressed to BS 435 may be supplied as new.

Paving bricks
This clause is for ordinary walling bricks which are often used for paving bedded frog down if frogged bricks are used. Note that the terms 'pavers', 'paviours' and 'paving bricks' are all common uses. Engineering bricks to BS 3921 are frequently used for pavings.
Select class A or B as appropriate, class A having the higher compressive strength and lesser absorption rating. State colour, precise selection of bricks for pavings, manufacturer and reference.

Clay pavers
To comply with BS 6677: solid bricks with durability designation FL, work size and manufacturer's reference.

Calcium silicate pavers
To BS 6371: Part 1: type PA calcium silicate bricks: solid (no voids) bricks to BS 187 with a strength class of 5 or better should be specified. State manufacturer's name and reference.

Granite setts
To BS 435: size 100 × 100 × 100 mm/100 × 100 mm in 150 to 250 mm lengths.
New setts: other sizes specified in the BS are 75 × 125 and 150 mm, 100 × 125 and 150 mm. The BS is not restricted to granite; other igneous rocks are suitable. State if stone other than granite is required along with supplier's name and reference. Second-hand setts: specify size, type of stone, etc., along with name of supplier.

Concrete blocks (small element paving)
To BS 7263: Part 1: state manufacturer's name and reference. Edges are normally

chamfered and blocks are available in textured finish and coloured.

Cobbles
Hard water-smoothed stones of similar oval shape. Size with the smallest diameter in the 30 to 50 mm/50 to 75 mm/175 to 100 mm range. State size, colour range and supplier's name and reference.

Workmanship

General
BS 7263, Part 2: Code of practice for laying (PC flags, kerbs, etc.). This reflects common practice but more detailed advice could be obtained from the BCA and the NPKA for flags and the BDA for bricks.

Control samples
The specification of control samples should be related to the size and importance of the job. It may be difficult to justify control samples on small jobs. Include information on type of paving, minimum size of control sample and any features to be included in the sample area.

Bases under pavings
See chapter on Foundations. Specify details of thickness and method of compaction. This will depend upon the bearing capacity of the sub-grade.
If the sub-base is used extensively by site traffic, damage is bound to occur and this should be made good prior to laying paving, including any excavation through the sub-base for drainage runs.
The bedding should not be used for blinding or levelling the sub-base if it is outside the specified tolerances.
The drainage of paved areas should be designed in accordance with BS 6367: Code of practice for drainage of roofs and paved areas: Section 3, Part 9. All gradients must be formed in the sub-base and not in the bedding course, which must be of constant thickness.

Levels of paving
Paving should be set above drainage outlets to allow for future settlement under trafficking.

Concrete slabs

On sand: An economical method of providing paving for light foot traffic. Normally laid on a fill material such as hoggin or hardcore. Sand joints tend to get washed out or grow weeds; weak mortar joints prevent this but still enable the slabs to be easily lifted for access or re-use.

On mortar dabs: This is a commonly used method that facilitates laying and levelling. Joints are dry butted.

Bedded solid: This method is normally used to support vehicular traffic and, given a well-compacted adequate base, should not crack or move, particularly if the thicker (63 mm) flags to BS 7263: Part 1 are used.

Stone flags

Solid rather than spot bedding should be specified. Specify joint widths suited to the type of stone. Riven sandstone laid random pattern may need joints up to 20 mm wide while accurately sized stone may lend itself to narrow joints and poured grout.

Bricks

On sand: This is for walling-type bricks (not paviours as described) laid on sand, and must not be confused with the block pavings. Bricks laid on sand, either with distinct sand joints or laid close butted with sand brushed into the unavoidable spaces, make a simple but effective constructed paving for pedestrian traffic.

On mortar: This paving uses bricks as stated above. The bricks can be jointed as the work proceeds but the method of brushing completely dry or very dry mortar into open joints as a separate operation overcomes the risks of unsightly mortar stains on the pavings.

Block/brick pavers

Small element units are usually laid as for interlocking block/brick pavers. If pavers are required to be jointed with acid-resisting mortar or grout, this is specialist work and needs careful specification.

Granite setts

On sand: Specify details as for bricks. If it is required to lay these to an interlocking pattern to receive vehicular traffic, specify them as for interlocking block pavings.

Cobble paving

Specify height above ground level, type of bedding, size and type of joints. If being specified in renovation, the pavings are best specified as 'to match existing'.

Mortar bedding

For very firm bonding to the base, it might be advisable to specify dusting the compacted and levelled bedding with cement finely sieved and coating the backs of slabs with a cement slurry at time of laying. A form of bedding, strongly recommended for block, tile and slab flooring, is the semi-dry or 'thick bed' method.

Jointing and grouting

The jointing methods should be written into the descriptions of the methods of laying the paving followed by details of protection of the work. State either dry mortar or mortar-pointed or sand-filled joints along with size of joints.

Dry mortar joints: This method of jointing is recommended for any type of absorbent paving (e.g. brick or concrete) from which it is very difficult to remove the marks of mortar or grout. It can be applied quite dry or mixed almost dry, which facilitates compaction to form a very dense joint.

Mortar-pointed joints: Due to relative movement and frost, mortar-pointed joints tend to deteriorate in time, and repointing may be necessary every few years. The use of a fairly coarse sand (rather than an ordinary building sand) will improve durability of the joints.

Sand-filled joints: Sand-filled joints will allow the development of moss and other plant growth, which may be considered desirable. For narrow (3 mm) joints a grade F sand will be appropriate, but for wider joints grade C (coarse) may be preferred.

Movement joints

Specify any movement joints required.

Sealant

For general guidance on selection of sealants see BS 6213. Insert details.

Protection
Specify methods of protection of work from
both inclement weather and any traffic.

DETAIL SHEETS

Margins
Brick
Brick/gravel
Concrete (2)
Concrete sett
Concrete/cobbles (2)
Timber/cobbles
Timber/gravel
Paving slab
Paving block
Hoggin
Granite sett
Gravel
Edges
BDC kerb sett
BDC kerb sett high
Brick
Paving brick
Brick edge restraint
Edge/channel paving bricks
Edge kerb and channel engineering brick
Paving brick on end
Concrete (2)
Concrete *in-situ*
Precast concrete
Precast concrete unit
Trims
Brick (3)
Cobbles
Concrete *in-situ*
Granite sett (4)

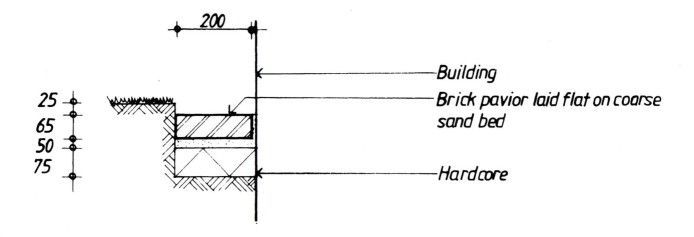

200

25
65
50
75

Building

Brick pavior laid flat on coarse sand bed

Hardcore

SECTION

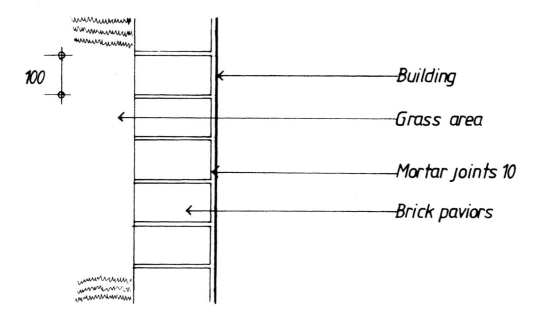

100

Building

Grass area

Mortar joints 10

Brick paviors

PLAN

Scale 1:10

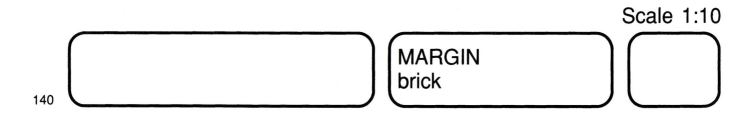

MARGIN
brick

140

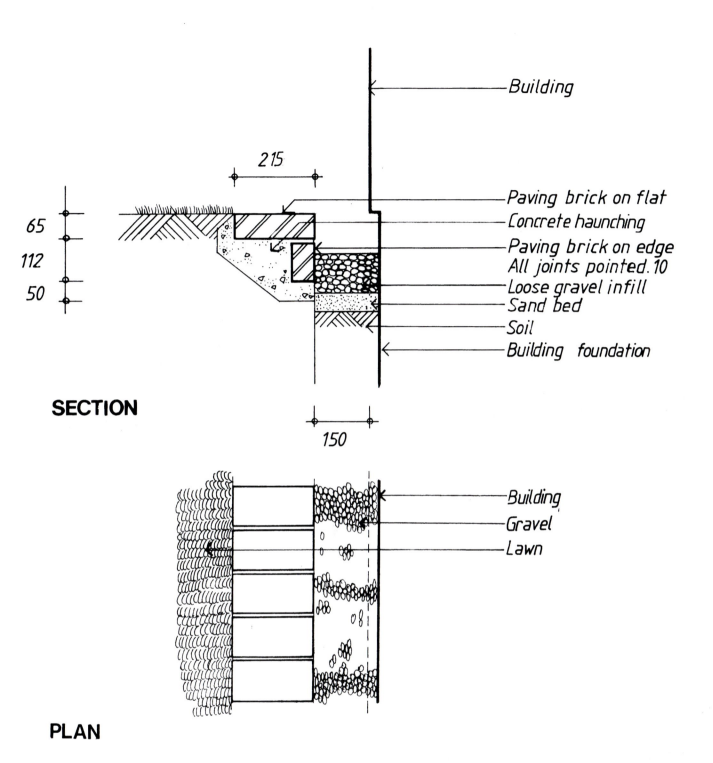

SECTION

215

65
112
50

150

Building

Paving brick on flat

Concrete haunching

Paving brick on edge
All joints pointed. 10

Loose gravel infill

Sand bed

Soil

Building foundation

PLAN

Building

Gravel

Lawn

Scale 1:10

MARGIN
brick/gravel

141

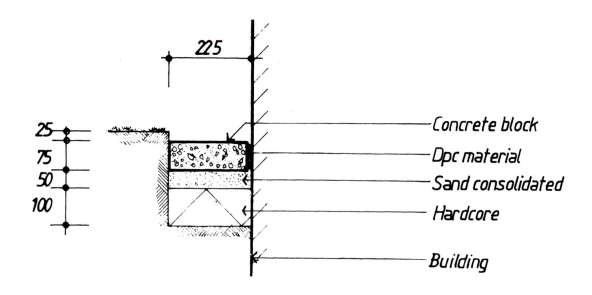

225

25
75
50
100

Concrete block

Dpc material

Sand consolidated

Hardcore

Building

SECTION

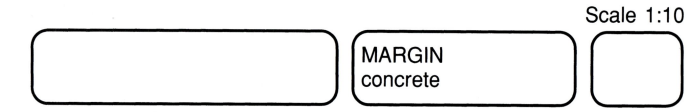

Scale 1:10

	MARGIN concrete	

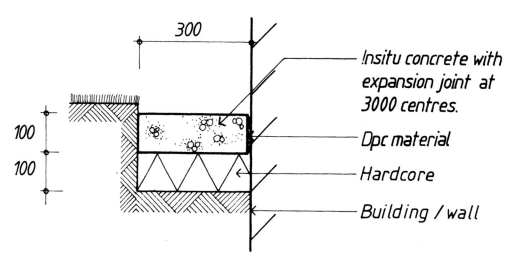

300

100

100

!nsitu concrete with
expansion joint at
3000 centres.

Dpc material

Hardcore

Building / wall

SECTION

Scale 1:10

	MARGIN concrete	

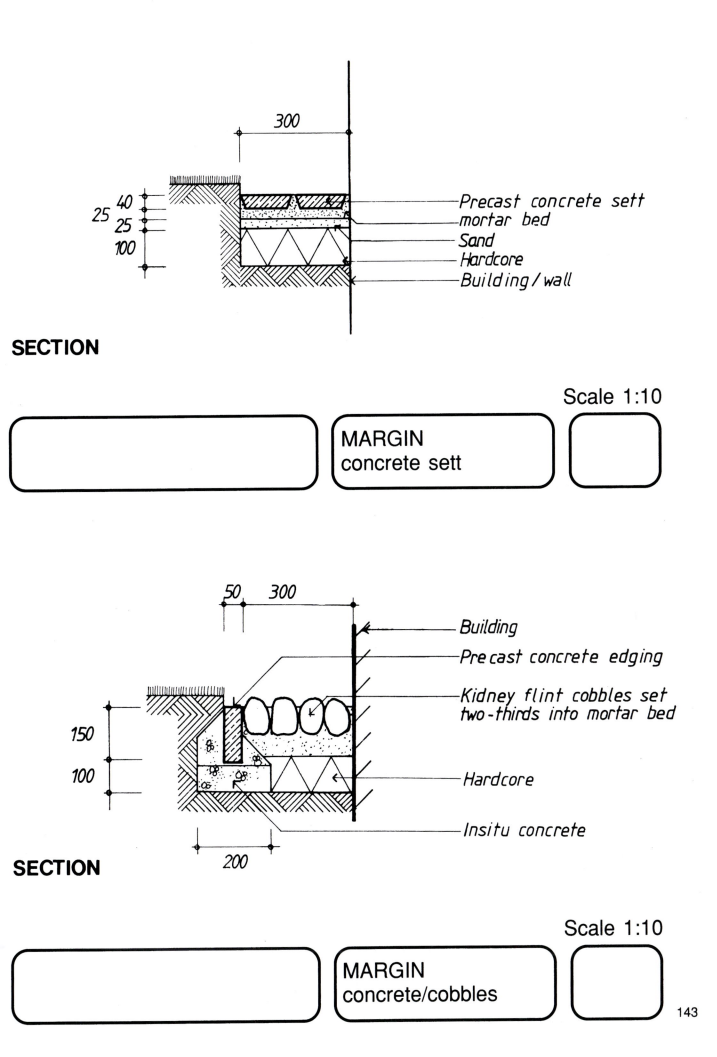

SECTION

300

25 40
25
100

— Precast concrete sett
— mortar bed
— Sand
— Hardcore
— Building / wall

Scale 1:10

MARGIN
concrete sett

SECTION

50   300

150

100

200

— Building
— Precast concrete edging
— Kidney flint cobbles set two-thirds into mortar bed
— Hardcore
— Insitu concrete

Scale 1:10

MARGIN
concrete/cobbles

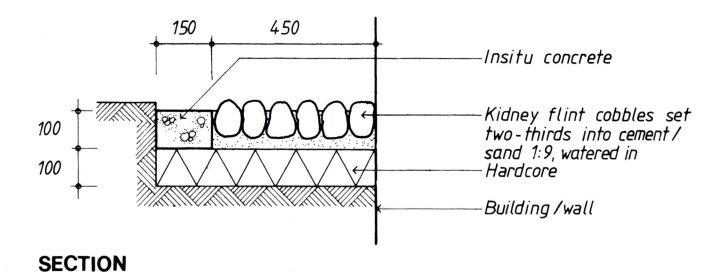

150 450

Insitu concrete

100

100

Kidney flint cobbles set
two-thirds into cement/
sand 1:9, watered in

Hardcore

Building/wall

SECTION

Scale 1:10

MARGIN
concrete/cobbles

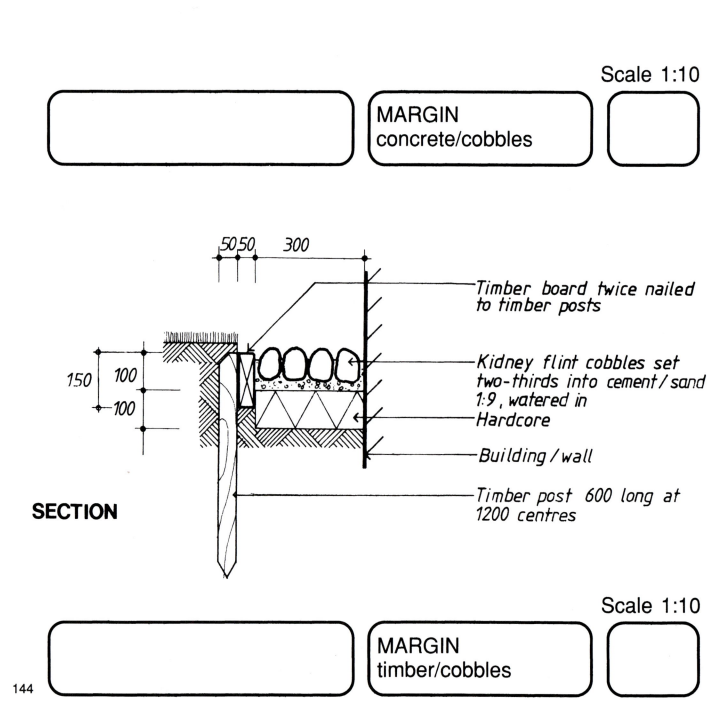

50 50 300

Timber board twice nailed
to timber posts

150 100

100

Kidney flint cobbles set
two-thirds into cement/sand
1:9, watered in

Hardcore

Building/wall

Timber post 600 long at
1200 centres

SECTION

Scale 1:10

MARGIN
timber/cobbles

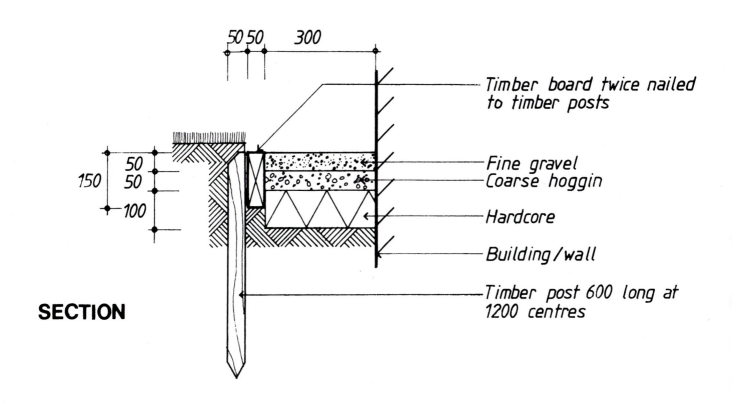

50 50   300

150   50
       50
       100

SECTION

Timber board twice nailed
to timber posts

Fine gravel
Coarse hoggin

Hardcore

Building / wall

Timber post 600 long at
1200 centres

Scale 1:10

MARGIN
timber/gravel

145

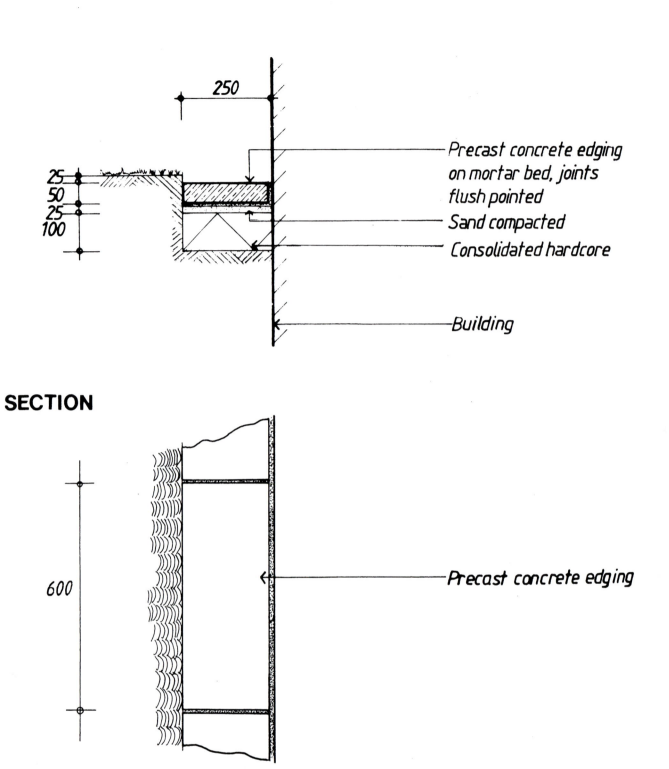

250

25
50
25
100

Precast concrete edging
on mortar bed, joints
flush pointed

Sand compacted

Consolidated hardcore

Building

SECTION

600

Precast concrete edging

PLAN

Scale 1:10

MARGIN
paving slab

146

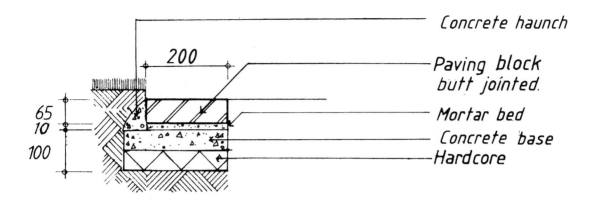

Concrete haunch

Paving block
butt jointed.

Mortar bed

Concrete base

Hardcore

200

65
10
100

SECTION

Scale 1:10

| | EDGE
paving block | |

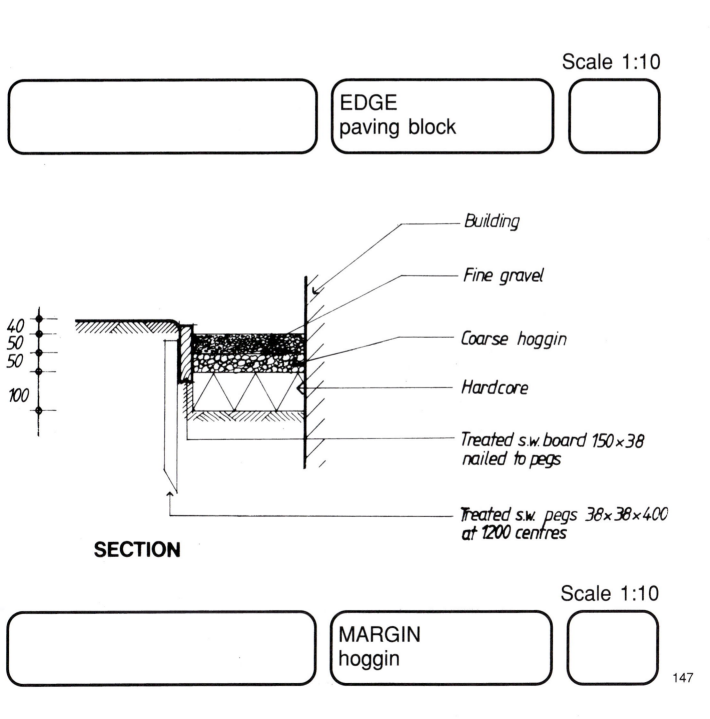

Building

Fine gravel

Coarse hoggin

Hardcore

Treated s.w. board 150 × 38
nailed to pegs

Treated s.w. pegs 38 × 38 × 400
at 1200 centres

40
50
50
100

SECTION

Scale 1:10

| | MARGIN
hoggin | |

147

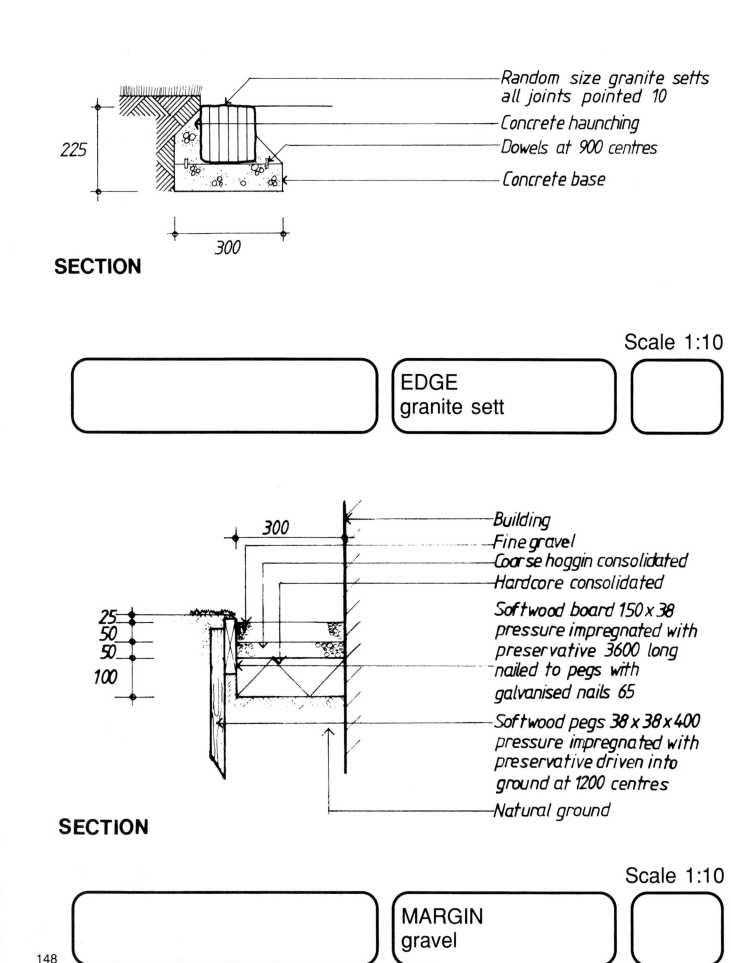

225

300

SECTION

Random size granite setts
all joints pointed 10

Concrete haunching

Dowels at 900 centres

Concrete base

Scale 1:10

| EDGE |
| granite sett |

300

25
50
50
100

SECTION

Building
Fine gravel
Coarse hoggin consolidated
Hardcore consolidated

Softwood board 150 x 38
pressure impregnated with
preservative 3600 long
nailed to pegs with
galvanised nails 65

Softwood pegs 38 x 38 x 400
pressure impregnated with
preservative driven into
ground at 1200 centres

Natural ground

Scale 1:10

| MARGIN |
| gravel |

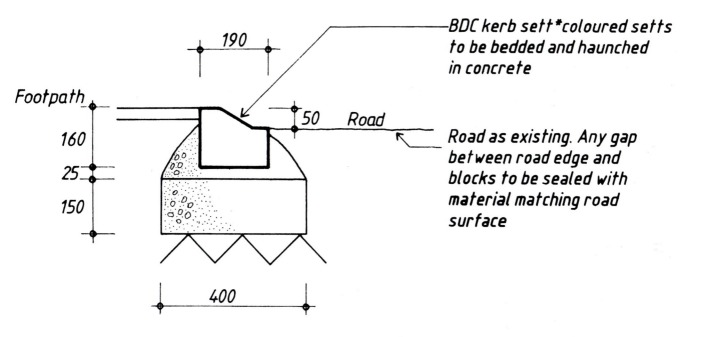

190

BDC kerb sett* coloured setts to be bedded and haunched in concrete

Footpath

50 Road

160

25

150

Road as existing. Any gap between road edge and blocks to be sealed with material matching road surface

400

* Available from:
BDC Concrete Products Ltd.
Corporation Road,
Newport,
Gwent NPT OWT

Scale 1:10

BDC
kerb sett

149

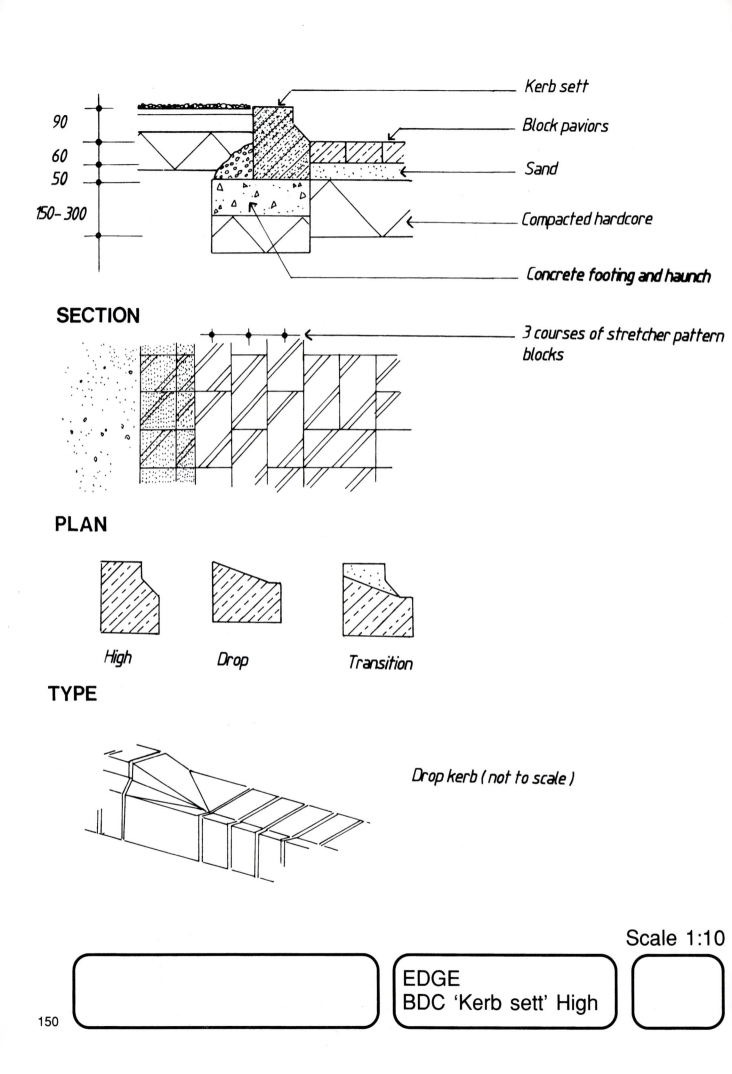

SECTION

- Kerb sett
- Block paviors
- Sand
- Compacted hardcore
- Concrete footing and haunch

90
60
50
150–300

3 courses of stretcher pattern blocks

PLAN

High   Drop   Transition

TYPE

Drop kerb (not to scale)

Scale 1:10

EDGE
BDC 'Kerb sett' High

150

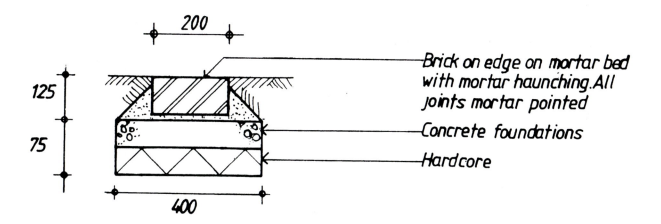

200

125

75

400

Brick on edge on mortar bed
with mortar haunching. All
joints mortar pointed

Concrete foundations

Hardcore

SECTION

Scale 1:10

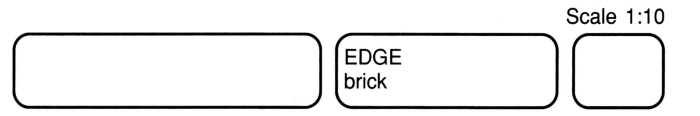

| | EDGE brick | |

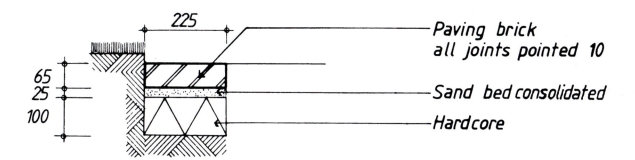

225

65
25
100

Paving brick
all joints pointed 10

Sand bed consolidated

Hardcore

SECTION

Scale 1:10

| | EDGE paving brick | |

151

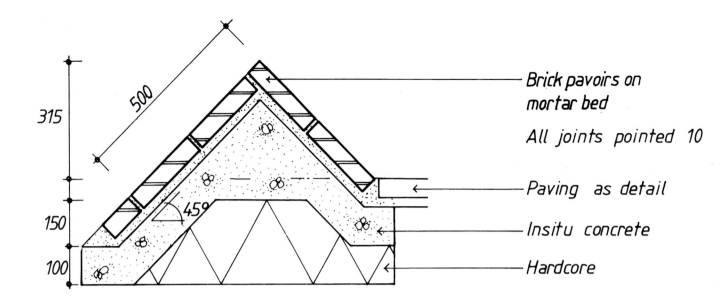

315

500

150

100

45°

Brick pavoirs on
mortar bed

All joints pointed 10

Paving as detail

Insitu concrete

Hardcore

SECTION

Scale 1:10

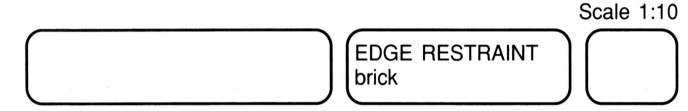

EDGE RESTRAINT
brick

65   225

225

25
75

350

Paving brick on end

Paving brick on edge
all joints pointed 10

Mortar bed

Hardcore

Concrete haunching

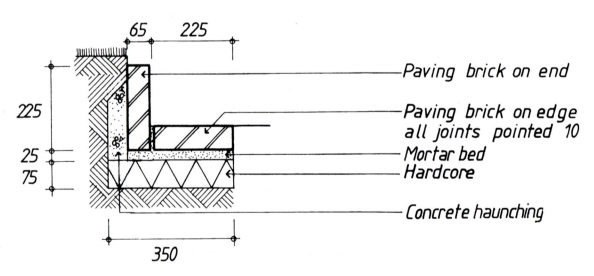

SECTION

Scale 1:10

EDGE/CHANNEL
paving bricks

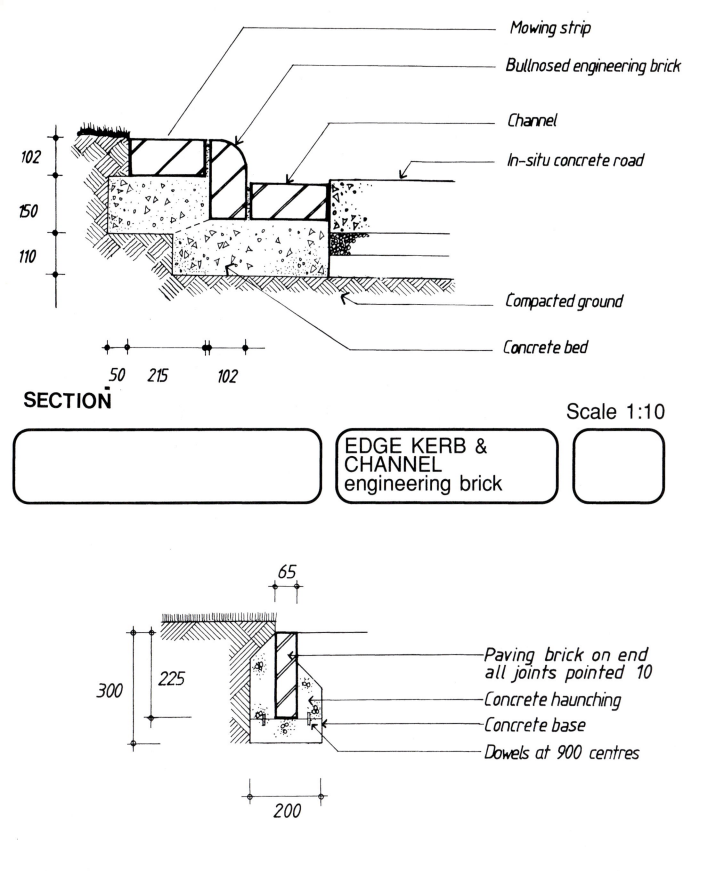

102

150

110

50 215 102

Mowing strip

Bullnosed engineering brick

Channel

In-situ concrete road

Compacted ground

Concrete bed

SECTION

Scale 1:10

EDGE KERB &
CHANNEL
engineering brick

65

300 225

200

Paving brick on end
all joints pointed 10

Concrete haunching

Concrete base

Dowels at 900 centres

SECTION

Scale 1:10

EDGE
paving brick on end

153

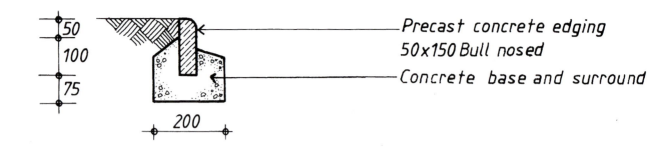

SECTION

Scale 1:10

| | EDGE concrete | |

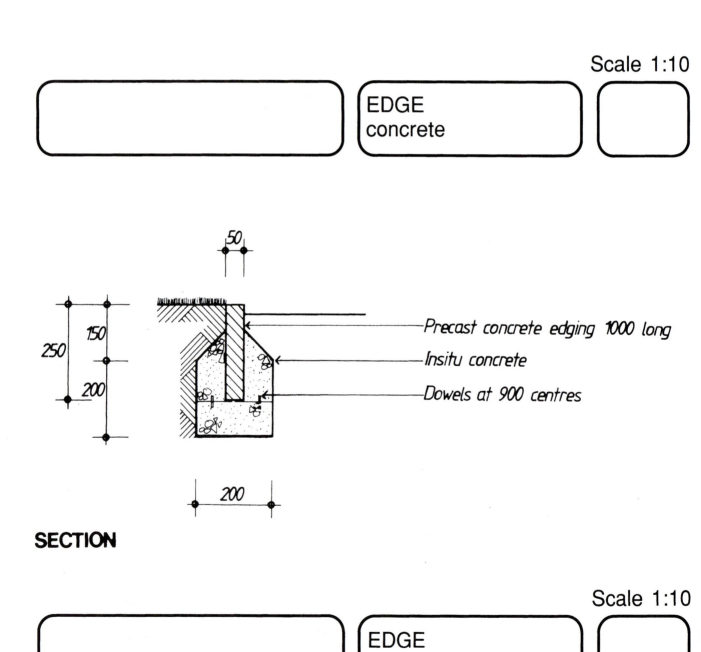

SECTION

Scale 1:10

| | EDGE concrete | |

154

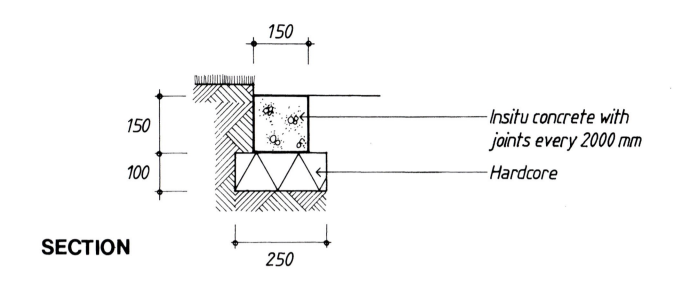

SECTION

150

150

100

250

Insitu concrete with joints every 2000 mm

Hardcore

Scale 1:10

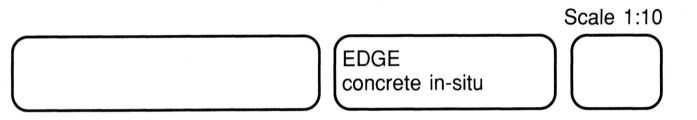

| | EDGE
concrete in-situ | |

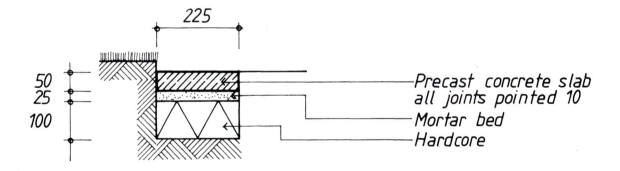

225

50
25
100

Precast concrete slab all joints pointed 10

Mortar bed

Hardcore

SECTION

Scale 1:10

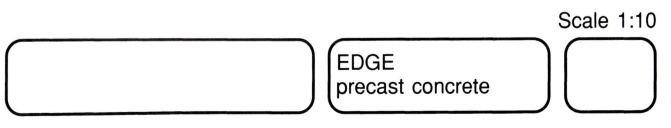

| | EDGE
precast concrete | |

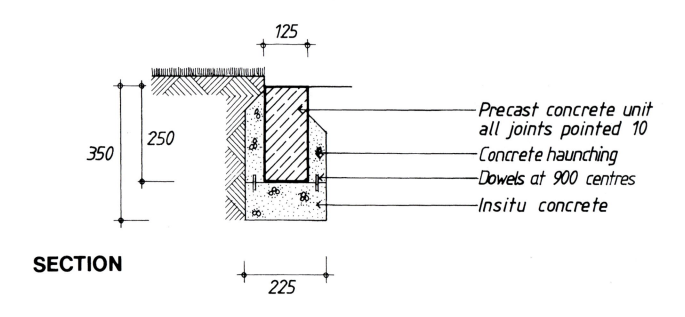

125

250

350

225

SECTION

Precast concrete unit
all joints pointed 10

Concrete haunching

Dowels at 900 centres

Insitu concrete

Scale 1:10

EDGE
precast concrete unit

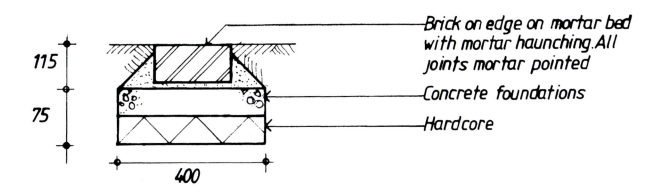

115

75

400

SECTION

Brick on edge on mortar bed
with mortar haunching. All
joints mortar pointed

Concrete foundations

Hardcore

Scale 1:10

TRIM
brick

157

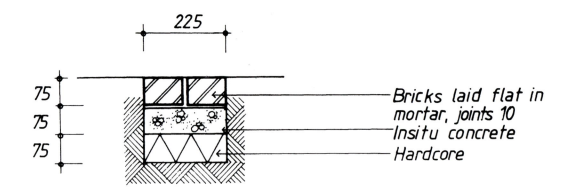

225

75
75
75

Bricks laid flat in
mortar, joints 10
Insitu concrete
Hardcore

SECTION

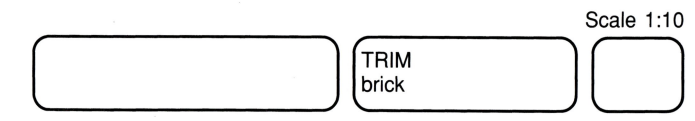

Scale 1:10

| | TRIM brick | |

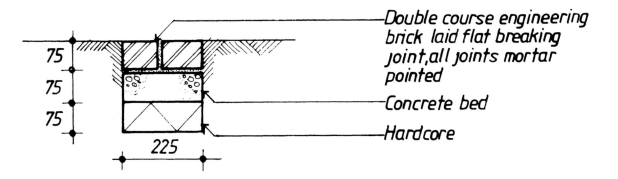

75
75
75

225

Double course engineering
brick laid flat breaking
joint, all joints mortar
pointed

Concrete bed

Hardcore

SECTION

Scale 1:10

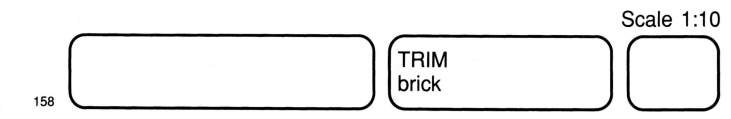

| | TRIM brick | |

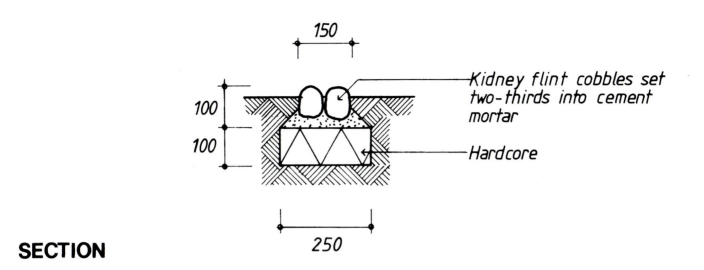

SECTION

150

100

100

250

Kidney flint cobbles set
two-thirds into cement
mortar

Hardcore

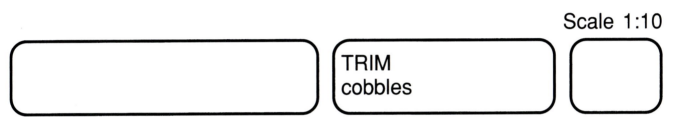

Scale 1:10

TRIM
cobbles

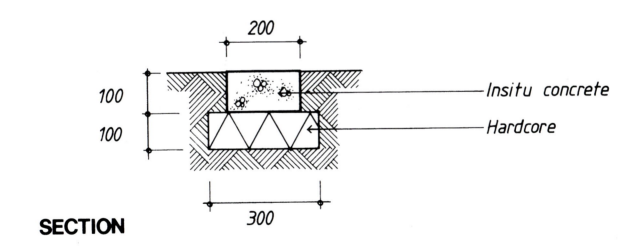

200

100

100

300

Insitu concrete

Hardcore

SECTION

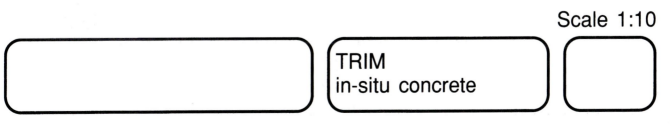

Scale 1:10

TRIM
in-situ concrete

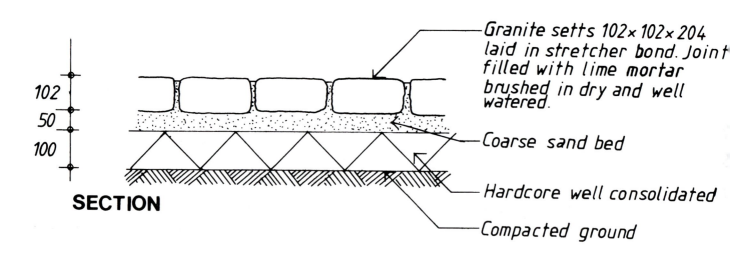

SECTION

102
50
100

Granite setts 102×102×204 laid in stretcher bond. Joint filled with lime mortar brushed in dry and well watered.

Coarse sand bed

Hardcore well consolidated

Compacted ground

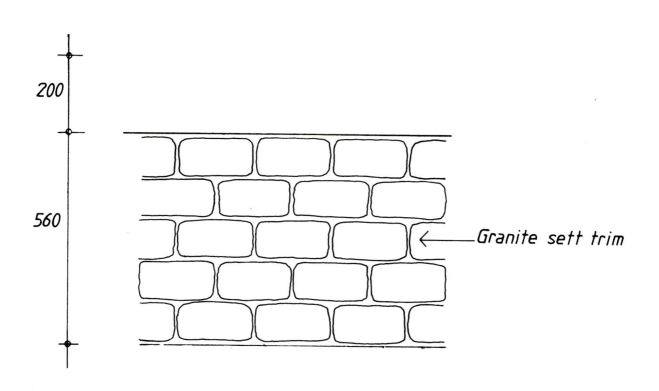

200

560

Granite sett trim

PLAN

Scale 1:10

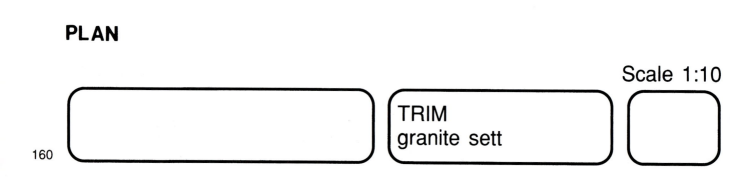

TRIM
granite sett

160

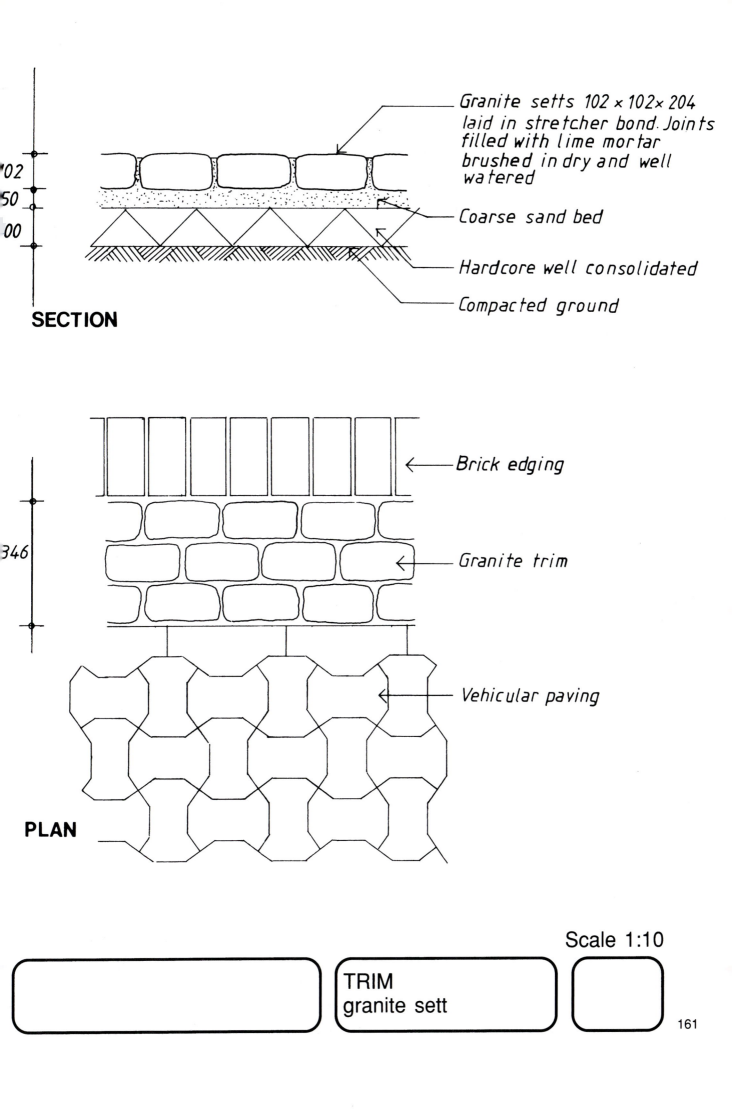

SECTION

Granite setts 102 × 102× 204 laid in stretcher bond. Joints filled with lime mortar brushed in dry and well watered

Coarse sand bed

Hardcore well consolidated

Compacted ground

102
50
00

Brick edging

346

Granite trim

Vehicular paving

PLAN

Scale 1:10

TRIM
granite sett

161

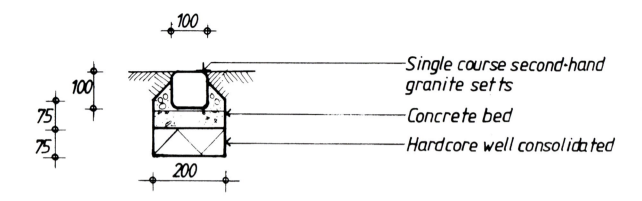

Single course second-hand granite setts

Concrete bed

Hardcore well consolidated

SECTION

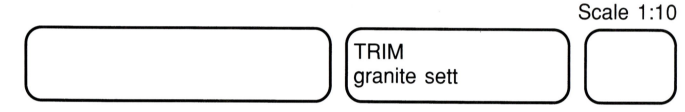

TRIM
granite sett

Scale 1:10

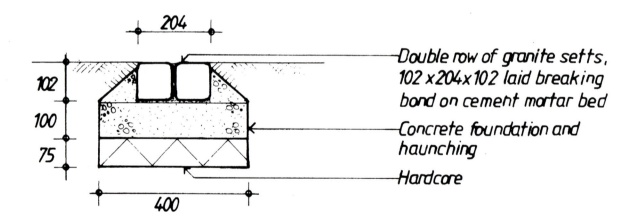

Double row of granite setts, 102 x 204 x 102 laid breaking bond on cement mortar bed

Concrete foundation and haunching

Hardcore

SECTION

TRIM
granite sett

Scale 1:10

162

KERBS

GUIDANCE NOTES

Appearance

Kerbs are necessary to prevent the lateral spread of the road, to control surface water drainage from the road, and to discourage the encroachment of vehicles on to footpaths or grass verges. In certain situations the character of an area could be spoilt by edging roads with upstanding kerbs, and they can be dangerous where fast-moving traffic is prevalent. In such circumstances flush kerbs (usually of 125–250 mm precast concrete) are used. There is no reason other materials or other design approaches should not be considered, particularly where the preservation of a rural character is desirable. Any road kerb detail will have to be agreed with the adopting authority.

Material

A wide variety of materials are available, from granite to concrete block and precast concrete. Granite, while very expensive, is ideal for rural areas and is tough and durable. Reconstituted granite kerbs are also available; they are considerably cheaper and there are many places where they would be preferable to smooth precast concrete kerbs. Bricks and large blocks of timber such as railway sleepers are also used for kerbs in certain small-scale schemes.

Setting of kerbs

Kerbs should be laid before the base and surfacing of the road and are usually on a 100–150 mm bed of concrete (dry mix of 1:3:6). The concrete should be well haunched up at the back of the kerb. Joints should be formed with cement and sand mortar (1:3). Expansion joints to *in-situ* concrete kerbs for flexible roads should be at 20-metre intervals. With concrete roads the expansion joints should coincide with the joints in the road slab. A flexible filler should be placed between the kerbs as between the road slabs.

Types

Precast concrete kerbs can be obtained with a bull nose, a raked top or a chamfered face and are often smooth-surfaced and grey/white in colour. Granite kerbs, especially reconstituted types, are only made in rectangular sections. Special coloured concrete brick units are also now available. An upstand kerb to a concrete slab should sit on the slab, as it is not its function to prevent it from spreading. The kerb is haunched up with concrete at the back. An upstand kerb to a flexible road or pavement should prevent the road from spreading, so it is placed where it will retain the layers of granular material. At the junctions of paths and soft areas, sometimes a kerb is necessary to prevent the spilling of soil or the breaking of a grassed edge. A low brick kerb or similar small unit is more appropriate than standard concrete units.

A stepped kerb is a much more interesting detail because the pedestrian is given an advantage over the vehicle by being quite separate. It is seen in many older towns and is very useful where there are distinct changes in level.

SPECIFICATION CHECK LIST

General

Exact location and extent of each type should be shown on drawings. A separate clause for each main type of unit will permit their separate referencing on the drawn detail.

Materials

Sub-base
State concrete mix reference and size for foundations and haunching.

Precast concrete
Where precast concrete kerbs will be subjected to the application of de-icing salts it is preferable to specify that they are hydraulically pressed, otherwise they may be made by any process.
Insert manufacturer and brand or range name along with any reference.
Insert details of main unit. Associated components such as quadrants and dropper kerbs should be listed as special shapes. Give either BS profile figure

number or the manufacturer's reference and size (width × height).
BS 340 specifies products by figure number according to profile as follows:

Kerbs: Figures 1 to 9 (single size given for each figure)
Quadrants: Figure 14 (two sizes given)
Radius kerbs: Figure 15 (method of sizing given)
Dropper kerbs: Figure 16 (for use with figures 2a and 7 kerb profiles)

Lengths of units are given as 915 mm.
List associated components such as transition or dropper kerbs, radius channels, internal and external angle kerbs, etc.
Finish/colour. This item can be used where specification is by reference to BS 340 only, or to specify proprietary options which are not implicit in the appropriate reference. Obtain advice from supplier before selecting finish. Existing kerbs, channels and quadrants which have been redressed or reshaped and redressed to BS 435 may be supplied as-new.
Miscellaneous: Specify items such as steel dowels for haunching, etc.

Stone
Insert type of stone (e.g. granite setts), the name of supplier and, where appropriate, name of quarry. If choice of supplier is left to contractor delete the sub-item or insert 'to be approved'.
BS 435 specifies the following standard sizes (width × height):

- Edge kerbs: 200/150 × 300 mm
  150 × 250/200 mm
  125 × 250 mm
- Flat kerbs: 300 × 200/150 mm
  250 × 125/150 mm

Minimum length of kerbs is given as 600 mm unless otherwise specified or stipulated by the supplier. List associated components such as radius kerbs and quadrants. BS 435 specifies and gives illustrations for three types of finish:

A – fine picked
B – fair picked and single axed or ridged
C – rough punched.

Brick/block kerbs
Insert manufacturer and brand or range name.
Clay bricks: solid bricks with a durability designation FL to BS 3921 should be specified for kerbs.
Calcium silicate bricks: solid (no voids) bricks with a BS 187 strength class of 5 or better should be specified. Concrete blocks to BS 6717: Part 1 should be specified. Specify size of bricks or blocks required and colour.
Concrete block units are available with textured and exposed aggregate finishes. List associated components such as 90° internal/external angles, radius units, crossover units, transition units, etc. Include manufacturer's references where appropriate.

Workmanship

Bases
Describe methods of ground excavation and compaction: ground preparation followed by the backfilling material and compaction.

Inclement weather
Describe type of protection of the work required during inclement weather.

Laying units
Give information on the laying of the units, their cutting, levels and haunching.
Dowels: Kerb dowels (for use with 'holes' kerbs) and haunching dowels are for use where kerbs and edgings are liable to be displaced by wheel impact, e.g. roads next to landscaped areas or where the adjacent paving will not provide good lateral support. State steel bars centres.
Radius and angle kerbs: Provide details on these special kerbs if necessary.

Accuracy
State tolerance allowed.

Joints
Insert one of the following:

Dry, thickness of trowel blade.
Narrow filled, tooled.

Dry joints with a small gap will take up thermal movement in long runs of concrete kerbs.

For stone/bricks insert:
Tooled or tooled coloured.

For concrete blocks insert:
Dry, tightly butted or tooled or tooled coloured.

Movement joints: Brick kerbs depend on good adhesion of the mortar bed – this may fail if thermal, etc., stresses are allowed to accumulate. For general guidance on selection of sealants see BS 6213. Sealant must not be oil based. Silicone has less onerous requirements for preparation of the joint compared with polysulphides. State proprietary name, reference and colour.

Protection
State time required for the protection of the work before it can be used by traffic.

DETAIL SHEETS

Typical kerbs: precast concrete (2)
Brick (3)
Continental
Countryside
Kerb stepped granite
Granite stepped
Granite sett
Granite
Stone and cobblestone gutter
Timber
Timber log
Kerb and channel – brick and concrete
Concrete (2)
Drop
Concrete and granite sett
Kerb/wheel stop
Railway sleeper (2)

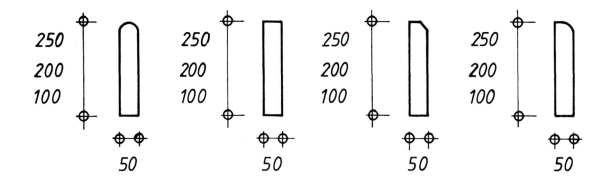

250
200
100

50

250
200
100

50

250
200
100

50

250
200
100

50

*Edgings manufactured in
915mm lengths.
Range of heights available
as shown.*

Scale 1:10

TYPICAL EDGES
precast concrete

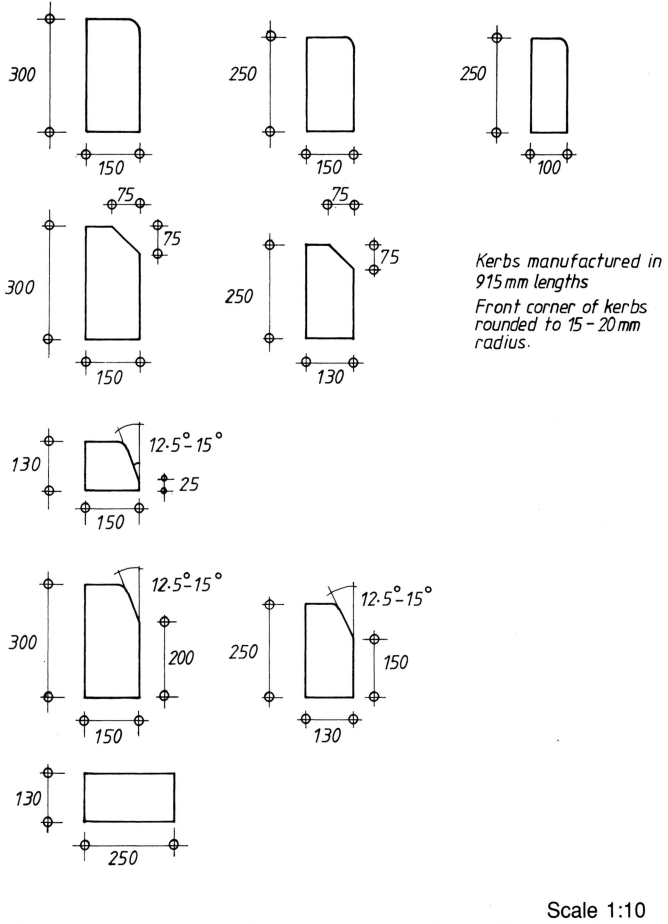

300　150

250　150

250　100

75　75

300　150

250　130

Kerbs manufactured in
915 mm lengths

Front corner of kerbs
rounded to 15 – 20 mm
radius.

130　12.5°– 15°　25　150

300　12.5°– 15°　200　150

250　12.5°– 15°　150　130

130　250

Scale 1:10

TYPICAL EDGES
precast concrete

167

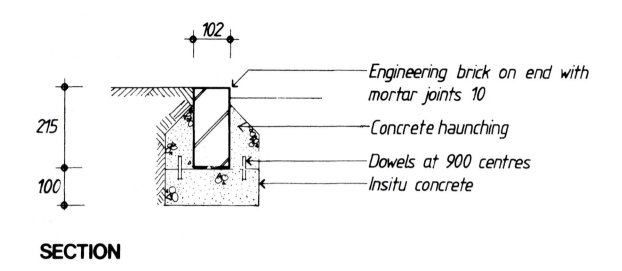

- Engineering brick on end with mortar joints 10
- Concrete haunching
- Dowels at 900 centres
- Insitu concrete

102

215

100

SECTION

Scale 1:10

	KERB brick

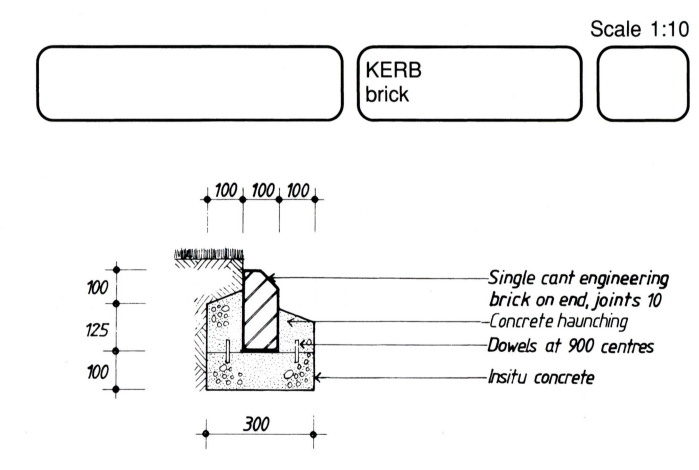

- Single cant engineering brick on end, joints 10
- Concrete haunching
- Dowels at 900 centres
- Insitu concrete

100 | 100 | 100

100

125

100

300

SECTION

Scale 1:10

	KERB brick

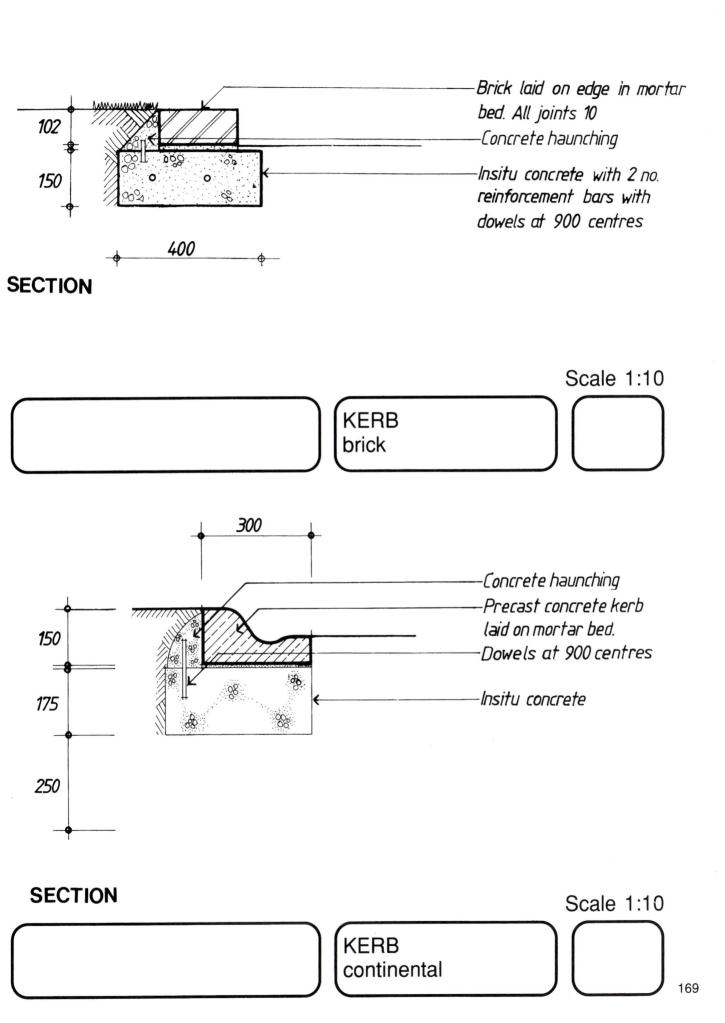

SECTION

Brick laid on edge in mortar bed. All joints 10

Concrete haunching

Insitu concrete with 2 no. reinforcement bars with dowels at 900 centres

102

150

400

Scale 1:10

KERB
brick

300

Concrete haunching

Precast concrete kerb laid on mortar bed.

Dowels at 900 centres

Insitu concrete

150

175

250

SECTION

Scale 1:10

KERB
continental

169

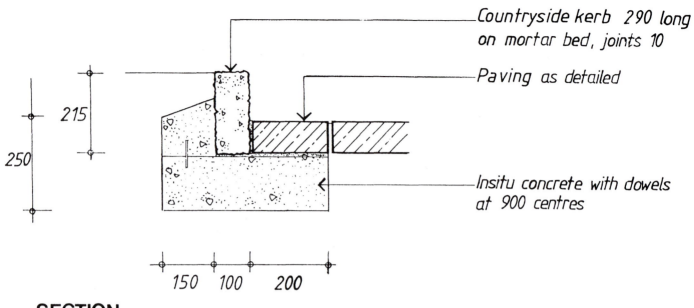

Countryside kerb 290 long
on mortar bed, joints 10

Paving as detailed

Insitu concrete with dowels
at 900 centres

215

250

150   100   200

SECTION

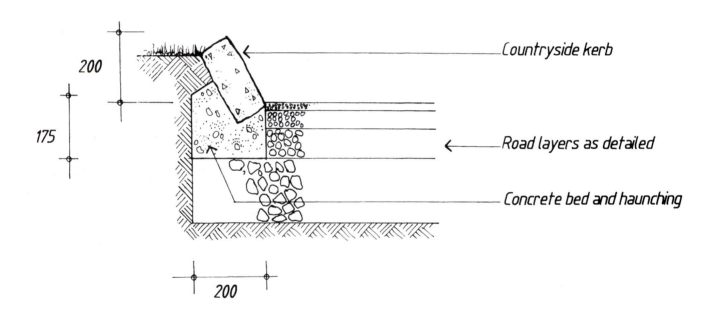

Countryside kerb

Road layers as detailed

Concrete bed and haunching

200

175

200

SECTION

Scale 1:10

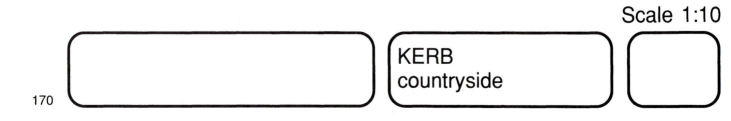

KERB
countryside

170

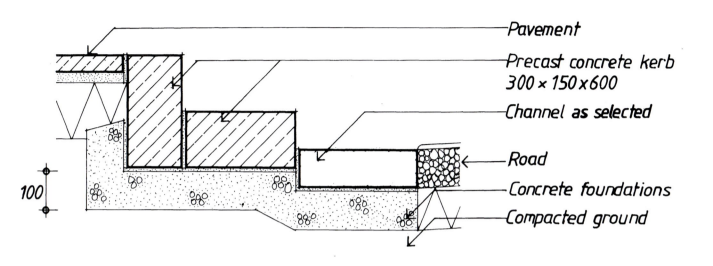

Pavement

Precast concrete kerb
300 × 150 × 600

Channel as selected

Road

Concrete foundations

Compacted ground

100

SECTION

Scale 1:10

KERB
stepped

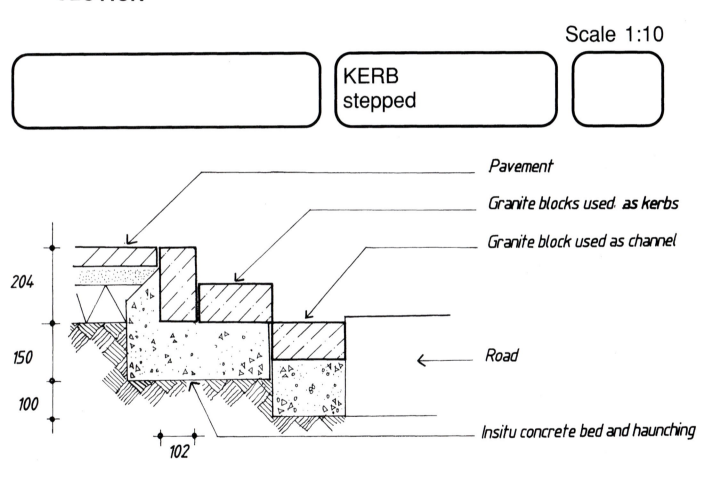

Pavement

Granite blocks used as kerbs

Granite block used as channel

Road

Insitu concrete bed and haunching

204

150

100

102

SECTION

Scale 1:10

KERB STEPPED
granite

171

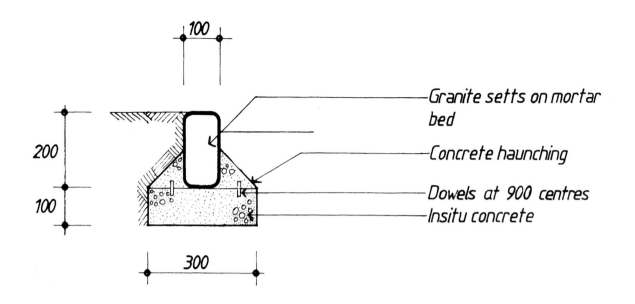

100

200

100

300

Granite setts on mortar
bed

Concrete haunching

Dowels at 900 centres

Insitu concrete

SECTION   Scale 1:10

| | KERB
granite sett | |

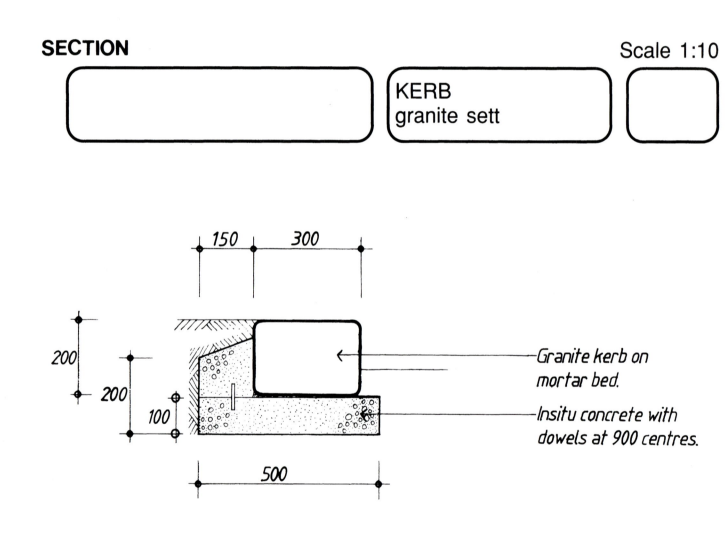

150   300

200

200

100

500

Granite kerb on
mortar bed.

Insitu concrete with
dowels at 900 centres.

SECTION   Scale 1:10

| | KERB
granite | |

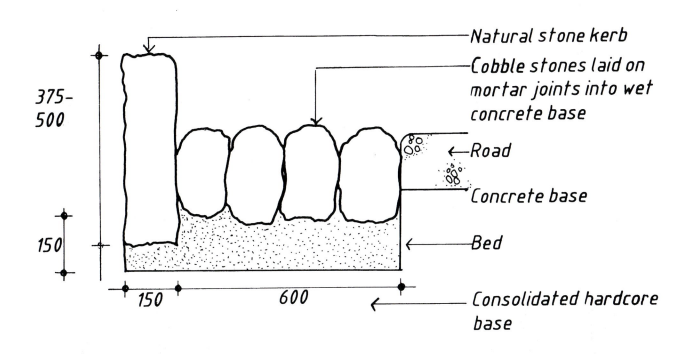

375-
500

150

150   600

Natural stone kerb

Cobble stones laid on
mortar joints into wet
concrete base

←Road

Concrete base

Bed

Consolidated hardcore
base

SECTION   Scale 1:10

KERB – stone &
cobblestone gutter

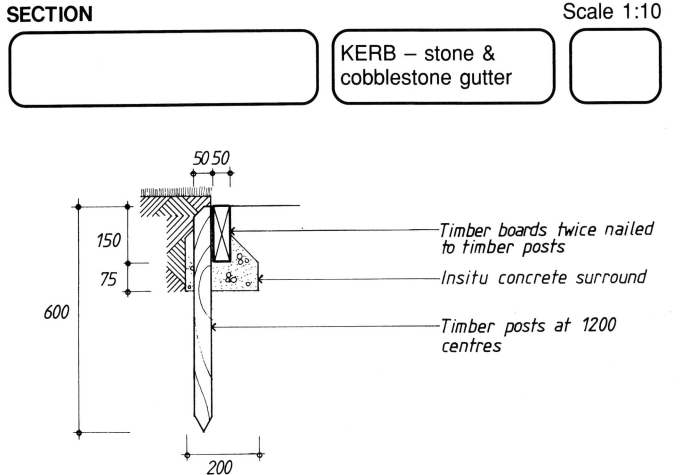

50 50

150

75

600

200

Timber boards twice nailed
to timber posts

Insitu concrete surround

Timber posts at 1200
centres

SECTION   Scale 1:10

KERB
timber

173

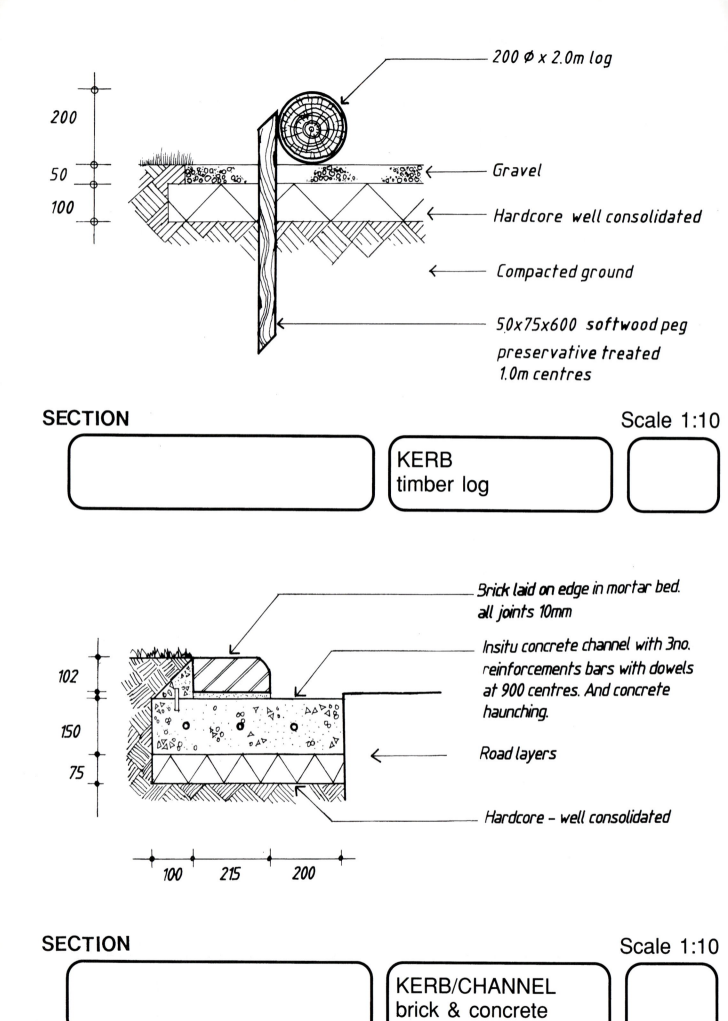

200 Ø x 2.0m log

200

50 ← Gravel

100 ← Hardcore well consolidated

← Compacted ground

50x75x600 softwood peg
preservative treated
1.0m centres

SECTION
Scale 1:10

KERB
timber log

Brick laid on edge in mortar bed.
all joints 10mm

Insitu concrete channel with 3no.
reinforcements bars with dowels
at 900 centres. And concrete
haunching.

102

150 ← Road layers

75

← Hardcore – well consolidated

100   215   200

SECTION
Scale 1:10

KERB/CHANNEL
brick & concrete

174

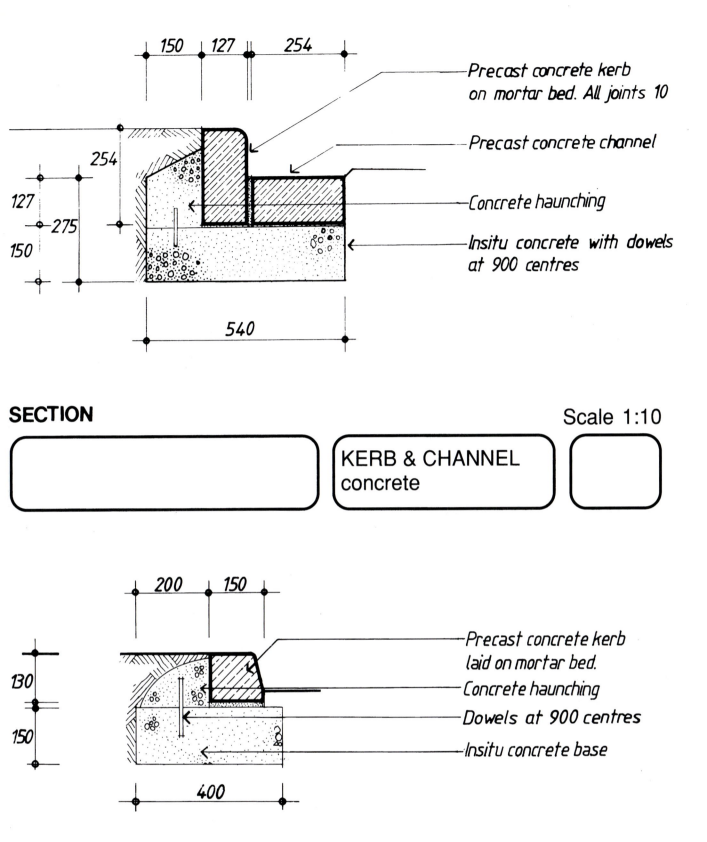

150 | 127 | 254

254

127

—275

150

540

Precast concrete kerb on mortar bed. All joints 10

Precast concrete channel

Concrete haunching

Insitu concrete with dowels at 900 centres

SECTION   Scale 1:10

KERB & CHANNEL
concrete

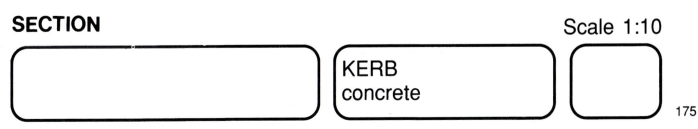

200 | 150

130

150

400

Precast concrete kerb laid on mortar bed.

Concrete haunching

Dowels at 900 centres

Insitu concrete base

SECTION   Scale 1:10

KERB
concrete

175

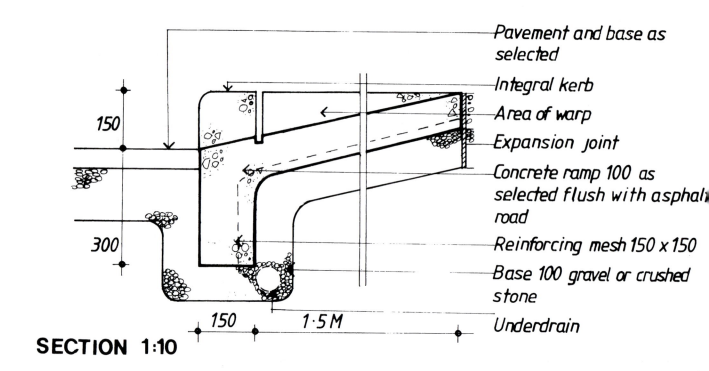

150

300

150   1·5 M

SECTION 1:10

- Pavement and base as selected
- Integral kerb
- Area of warp
- Expansion joint
- Concrete ramp 100 as selected flush with asphalt road
- Reinforcing mesh 150 x 150
- Base 100 gravel or crushed stone
- Underdrain

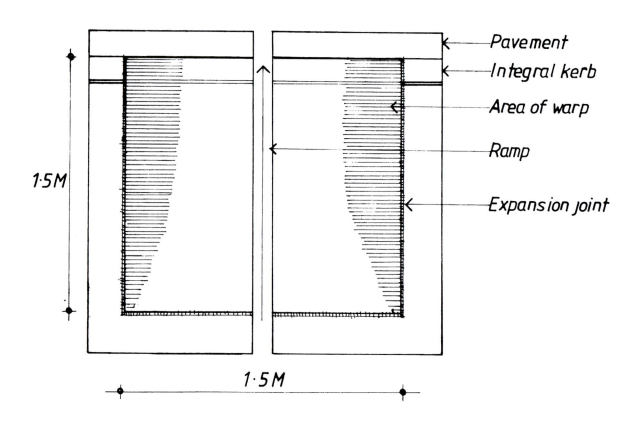

1·5 M

1·5 M

PLAN 1:20

- Pavement
- Integral kerb
- Area of warp
- Ramp
- Expansion joint

Scale AS

KERB
drop

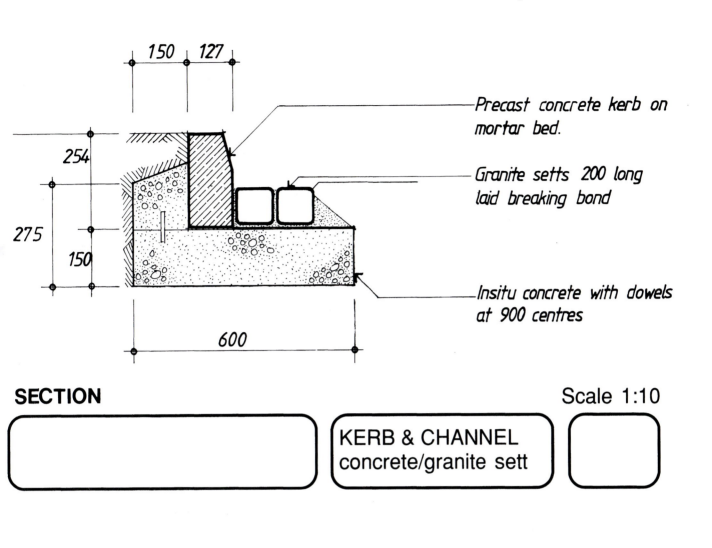

150 127

254

275

150

600

Precast concrete kerb on
mortar bed.

Granite setts 200 long
laid breaking bond

Insitu concrete with dowels
at 900 centres

SECTION

Scale 1:10

KERB & CHANNEL
concrete/granite sett

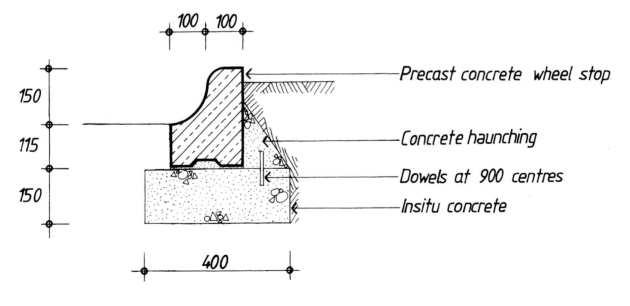

100 100

150

115

150

400

Precast concrete wheel stop

Concrete haunching

Dowels at 900 centres

Insitu concrete

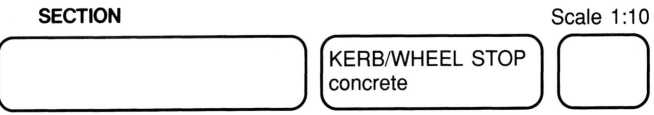

SECTION

Scale 1:10

KERB/WHEEL STOP
concrete

177

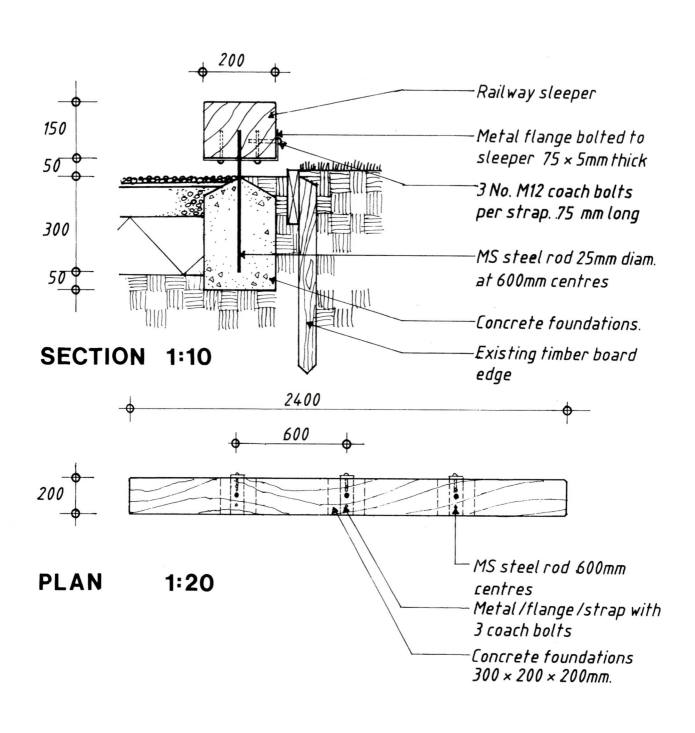

200

150

50

300

50

SECTION 1:10

Railway sleeper

Metal flange bolted to
sleeper 75 × 5mm thick

3 No. M12 coach bolts
per strap. 75 mm long

MS steel rod 25mm diam.
at 600mm centres

Concrete foundations.

Existing timber board
edge

2400

600

200

PLAN   1:20

MS steel rod 600mm
centres

Metal /flange /strap with
3 coach bolts

Concrete foundations
300 × 200 × 200mm.

Scale AS

WHEEL STOP
railway sleeper

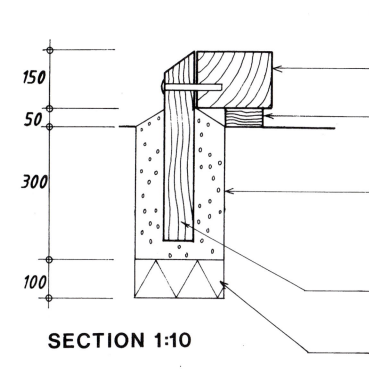

SECTION 1:10

150

50

300

100

Rail sleeper 150×200×2500 bolted to support post with 150×16mm galvanised coach screws.

100×50×100 pressure treated softwood bearer.

Concrete foundation 300×225× 350 shaped at top. Insert Malthoid paper between support posts and concrete at top.

100×75×500 pressure treated softwood support post, single weathered.

Hardcore.

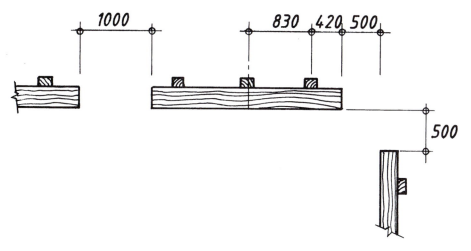

1000   830 420 500

500

PLAN 1:50

WHEEL STOP
railway sleepers

DRAINAGE CHANNELS

GUIDANCE NOTES

Appearance

Drainage channels are used for draining large areas of paving and ramps or paths contained between walls. The width of the channel must be related to the size of the gully grating. They can also be used alongside roads and drives, offering an interesting design solution and creating their own character, as can be seen in many conservation areas. They should be made part of the paving pattern. As well as channelling water run-off they also act as a trim, especially useful on rolled surfaces where the roller cannot get up to the edge.

Types

Channels can be dished or flat and can be made of a wide variety of materials, such as *in-situ* concrete, precast concrete, granite, stone and bricks.
Sandstone is seldom used, granite setts and cobblestones provide a texture change, but the latter slows the flow of water, due to the rough surface. This may be very useful in some circumstances. The type of channel selected must be in keeping with the surrounding area and the style of architecture, especially where new schemes link up with older ones. This is not always easy because of economic factors, especially where an area adjoins a conservation area. Dished channels are usually of precast concrete or stone; the latter are expensive. Flat channels should have the surface sufficiently shaped to ensure the flow of water to the drainage gully.

Falls

Falls should be between 1:2000 for precast concrete materials and 1:60 for brick and granite setts. See References for more detailed information.
An alternative to surface channels is the use of a 'Safeticurb' section of a glazed half-round channel with a cast-iron grating. Both types need a high degree of maintenance to prevent silting up. Gratings are removable to provide access for cleaning, but because they are tough they will withstand traffic and corrosion.

SPECIFICATION CHECK LIST

Channels

Specifiers are advised to complete the detailing of paving junctions and edges before completing this section of the specification. Such assembly drawings can be cross-referenced to the clauses in this section.

General

Exact location and extent of each type of drainage channel should be shown on drawings. A separate clause for each main type of unit will permit their separate referencing on the drawn details.

Materials

Bases
State concrete mix reference and size for foundations and haunching.

Precast concrete
BS 340: where concrete channels will be subjected to the application of de-icing salts it is preferable to specify that they are hydraulically pressed, otherwise they may be made by any process.
Insert manufacturer and brand or range name along with any reference. Insert details of main unit. Give either BS profile figure number or the manufacturer's reference and size (width × height).
BS 340 specifies products by figure number according to profile as follows:

Channels figures 1 to 9 (single size given for each figure)

Channels figure 15 (method of sizing given).

Length of units are given as 915 mm. Most manufacturers will supply alternative sizes and/or profiles to the range of units given in BS 340 including 600 mm lengths in the most commonly used profiles. List any special shapes required.
Finish/colour. This sub-item can be used where specification is by reference to BS 340 only, or to specify proprietary options. Insert details.

Stone
Insert type of stone, name of supplier and, where appropriate, name of quarry. If choice of supplier is left to the contractor delete the sub-item or insert 'to be approved'.
BS 435 specifies the following standard sizes (width × height): 300/250 × 150 mm. Minimum length of channels is given as 600 mm unless otherwise specified by the purchaser or stipulated by the supplier. List any requirements for special shapes. BS 435 specifies and gives illustrations for three types of finish:

A – fine picked
B – fair picked and single axed or ridged
C – rough punched.

Obtain advice from supplier before selecting finish. Existing channels which have been redressed or reshaped and redressed to BS 435 may be supplied as-new.
Draw attention to any special or unusual features of the work (e.g. work around gullies, etc.).

Brick/block channel
Insert manufacturer and brand or range name.
Clay bricks: solid bricks with a durability designation FL to BS 3921 should be specified for channels.
Calcium silicate bricks: solid (no voids) bricks with a BS 187 strength class of 5 or better should be specified. Concrete blocks to BS 6717: Part 1 should be specified. Specify size of bricks or blocks required and colour.

Concrete block units are available with textured and exposed aggregate finishes. List associated components such as 90° internal/external angles, radius units, crossover units, transition units, etc. Include manufacturer's references where appropriate.

Drainage channel systems
These are available in precast concrete, polyester concrete, GRV, cast iron and galvanised steel.
Insert manufacturer and brand or range name. The phrase 'or equivalent approved' may be included. Insert size of channel where not implicit in the manufacturer's reference. For Accessories insert manufacturer's reference(s) and finish where appropriate. Typical accessories are gratings, access covers, rodding eyes, silt boxes, end caps, outlets, transition units, etc.

Workmanship

Bases
Describe methods of ground excavation and compaction; ground preparation followed by the backfilling material and compaction.

Laying units
Give information on the laying of the units, their cutting levels and haunching. Set out to an even gradient to ensure no ponding or backfall. Lowest points of channels to be 6 mm above drainage outlets. Channels should be set higher than drainage outlets to allow for settlement.

Inclement weather
Describe type of protection of the work required during inclement weather.

Drainage channel system
Lay to an even gradient to ensure no ponding or backfall. Insert method of laying. Remove all silt and debris before handing over.

Radius and angle channels
Provide details where necessary.

Accuracy
State tolerance and maximum deviations allowed.

Joints
Specify types of mortar joints, colour and size. Insert one of the following:
Dry, thickness of trowel blade, narrow filled, tooled or tooled coloured. Dry joints with a small gap will take up thermal movement in long runs of concrete channels.

For stone/bricks insert:
Tooled or tooled coloured.

For concrete blocks insert:
Dry, tightly butted or tooled or tooled coloured.

Movement joints
Brick channels depend on good adhesion of the mortar bed – this may fail if thermal, etc., stresses are allowed to accumulate. For general guidance on selection of sealants see BS 6231. Sealant must not be oil based. Silicone has less onerous requirements for preparation of the joint compared with polysulphides.

Protection
State time required for the protection of the work before it can be used by traffic.

Detail sheets

Brick(4)
Precast concrete (3)
Concrete units
Precast concrete deep unit
Precast concrete wide unit
Precast concrete edge channel
Precast concrete safeticurb
Precast concrete safeticurb and granite setts
Cobblestones
Granite setts
Gravel
Metal and cobbles
Metal
Sand play area underdrain

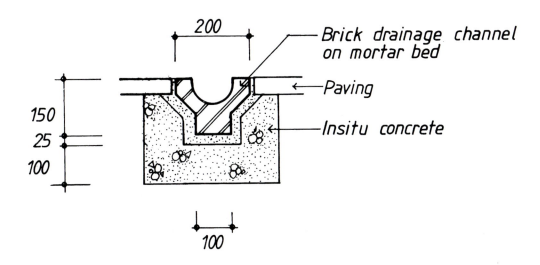

200

Brick drainage channel
on mortar bed

150
25
100

Paving

Insitu concrete

100

SECTION

Scale 1:10

	DRAINAGE CHANNEL brick	

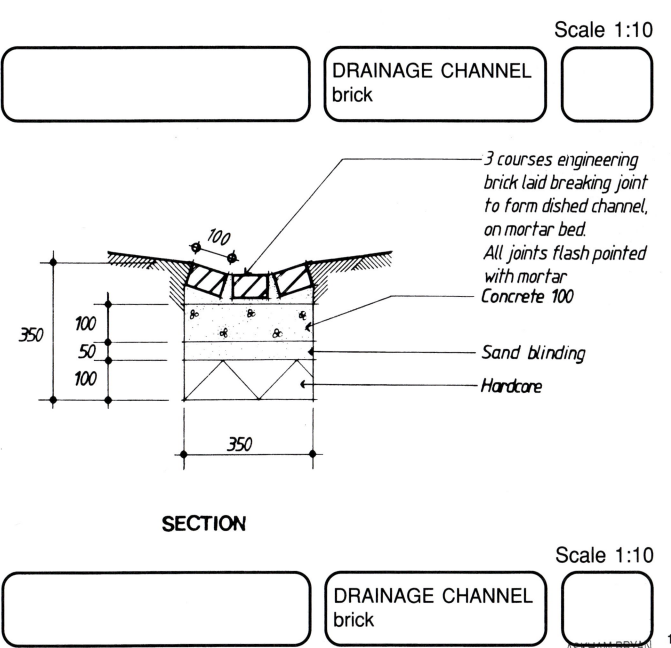

100

3 courses engineering
brick laid breaking joint
to form dished channel,
on mortar bed.
All joints flash pointed
with mortar

Concrete 100

Sand blinding

Hardcore

350

100
50
100

350

SECTION

Scale 1:10

	DRAINAGE CHANNEL brick	

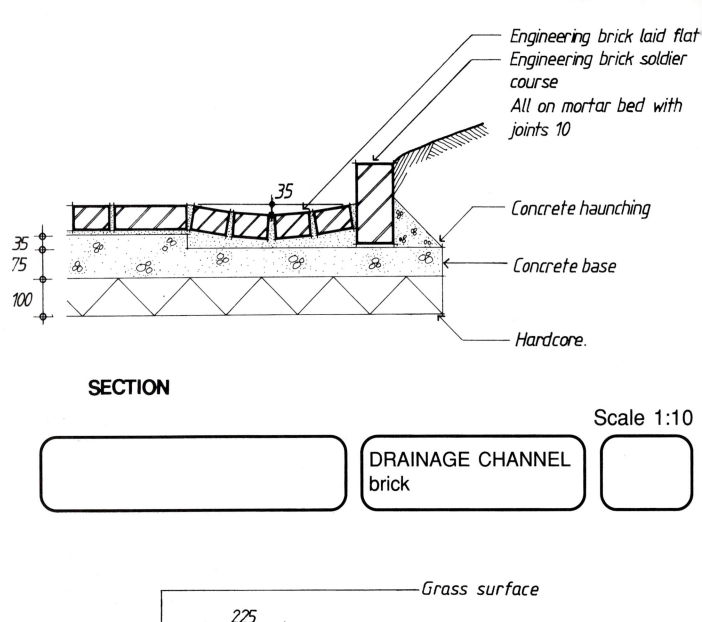

Engineering brick laid flat

Engineering brick soldier course

All on mortar bed with joints 10

Concrete haunching

Concrete base

Hardcore.

35

35
75
100

SECTION

Scale 1:10

DRAINAGE CHANNEL
brick

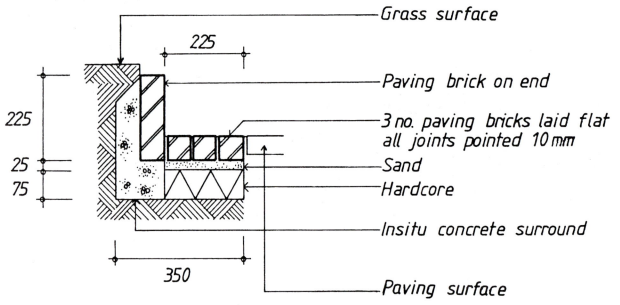

Grass surface

Paving brick on end

3 no. paving bricks laid flat all joints pointed 10 mm

Sand

Hardcore

Insitu concrete surround

Paving surface

225

225

25
75

350

Scale 1:10

CHANNEL
brick

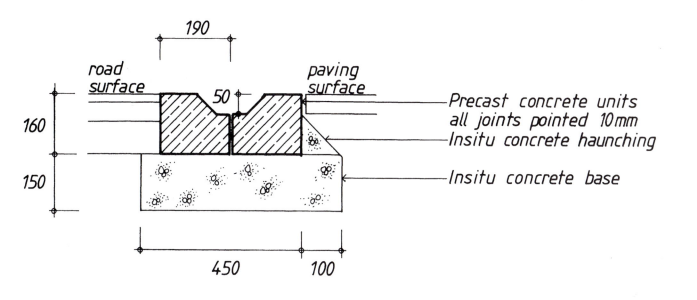

road surface

paving surface

190

50

160

150

450   100

Precast concrete units
all joints pointed 10mm

Insitu concrete haunching

Insitu concrete base

Scale 1:10

DRAINAGE CHANNEL
precast concrete

Precast concrete dished
channel 250×125 bedded
on mortar
all joints pointed

250

375   100
       50
       100

400

Conrete haunching

Concrete base

Sand blinding

Hardcore

SECTION

Scale 1:10

DRAINAGE CHANNEL
precast concrete

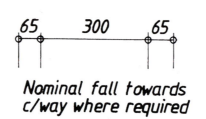

Nominal fall towards
c/way where required

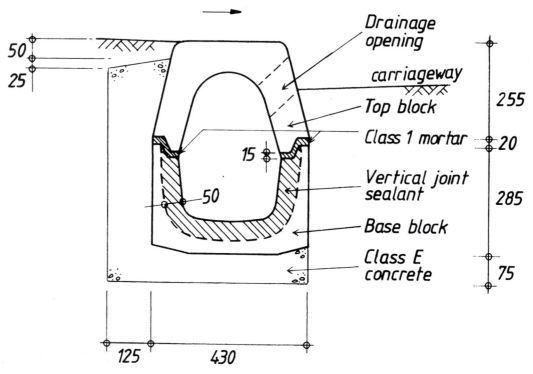

50
25

Drainage
opening

carriageway

255

Top block

Class 1 mortar   20

15

Vertical joint
sealant

285

50

Base block

Class E
concrete

75

125   430

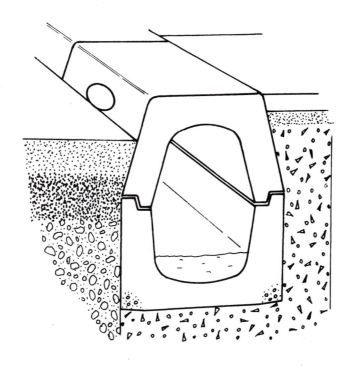

DRAINAGE CHANNEL
precast concrete

186

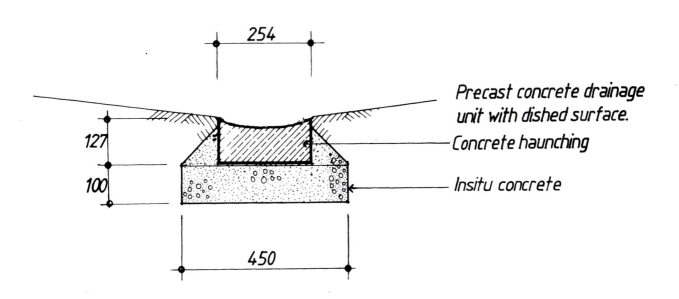

Precast concrete drainage unit with dished surface.

Concrete haunching

Insitu concrete

254

127

100

450

SECTION

Scale 1:10

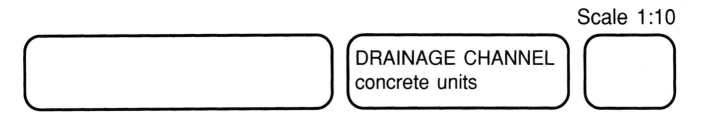

DRAINAGE CHANNEL
concrete units

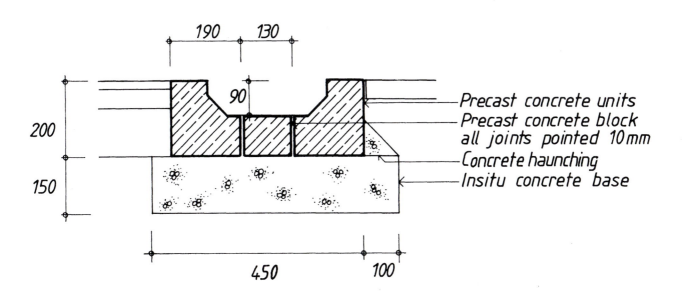

190 130

90

200

150

450 100

Precast concrete units
Precast concrete block all joints pointed 10 mm
Concrete haunching
Insitu concrete base

Scale 1:10

DRAINAGE CHANNEL
deeper unit

187

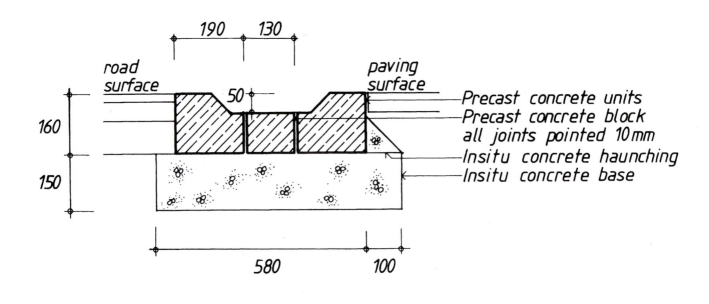

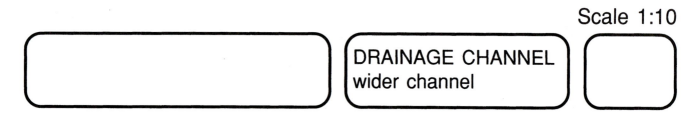

road
surface

paving
surface

Precast concrete units
Precast concrete block
all joints pointed 10mm
Insitu concrete haunching
Insitu concrete base

190   130

50

160

150

580   100

Scale 1:10

DRAINAGE CHANNEL
wider channel

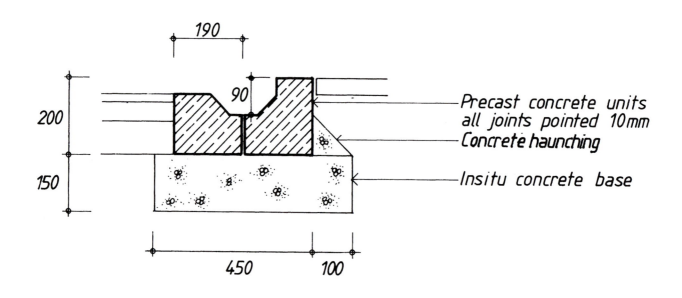

190

90

200

150

Precast concrete units
all joints pointed 10mm
Concrete haunching

Insitu concrete base

450   100

Scale 1:10

DRAINAGE CHANNEL
edge channel

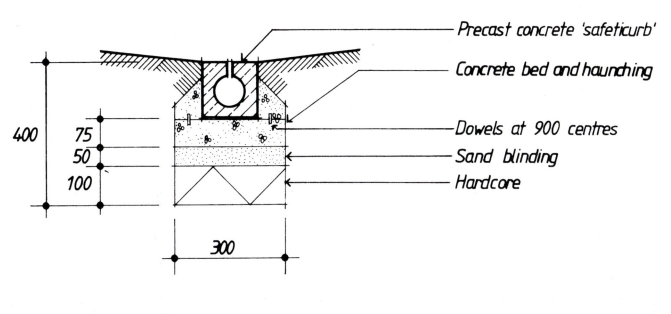

Precast concrete 'safeticurb'

Concrete bed and haunching

Dowels at 900 centres

Sand blinding

Hardcore

400

75

50

100

300

SECTION

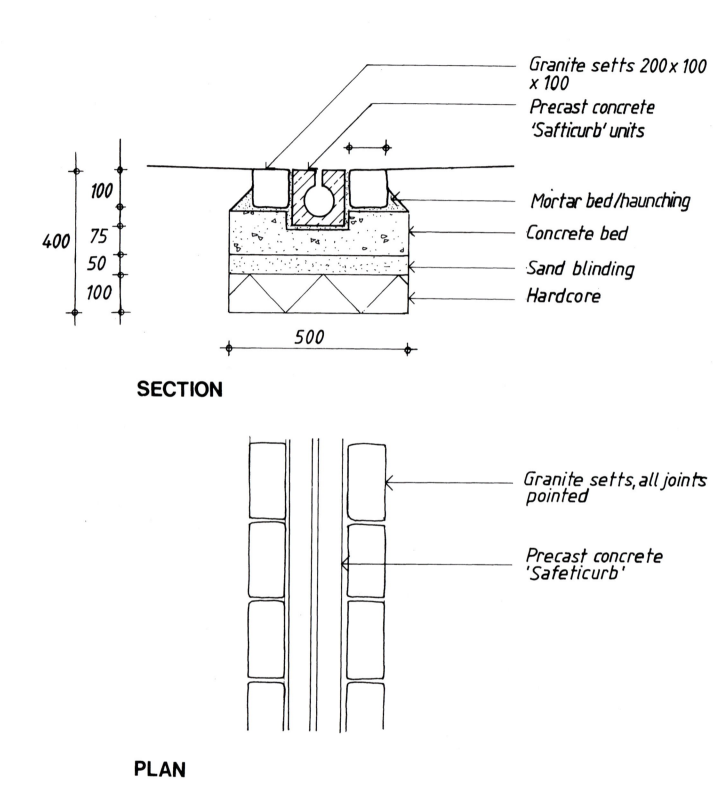

SECTION

Granite setts 200 x 100 x 100

Precast concrete 'Safticurb' units

Mortar bed/haunching

Concrete bed

Sand blinding

Hardcore

100
75
50
100

400

500

PLAN

Granite setts, all joints pointed

Precast concrete 'Safeticurb'

Scale 1:10

DRAINAGE CHANNEL
safeticurb/setts

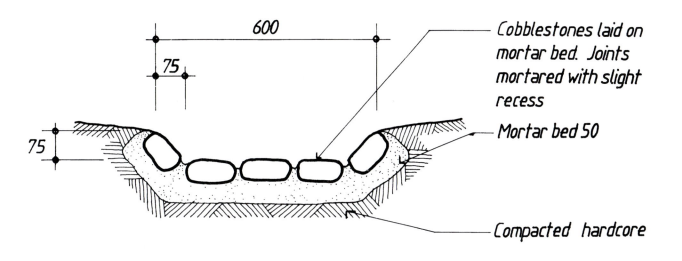

600

75

75

Cobblestones laid on mortar bed. Joints mortared with slight recess

Mortar bed 50

Compacted hardcore

SECTION

Scale 1:10

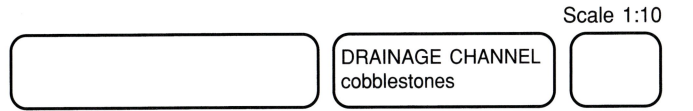

DRAINAGE CHANNEL
cobblestones

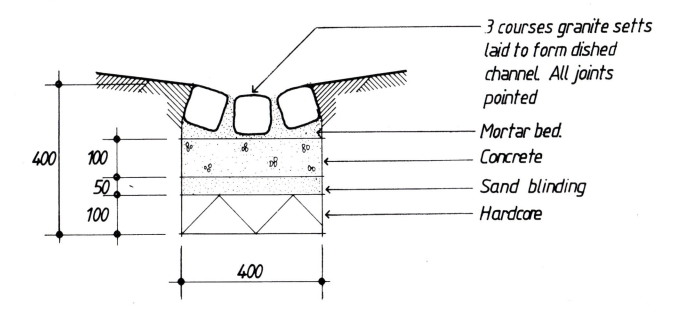

3 courses granite setts laid to form dished channel. All joints pointed

Mortar bed.

Concrete

Sand blinding

Hardcore

400

100

50

100

400

SECTION

Scale 1:10

DRAINAGE CHANNEL
granite setts

191

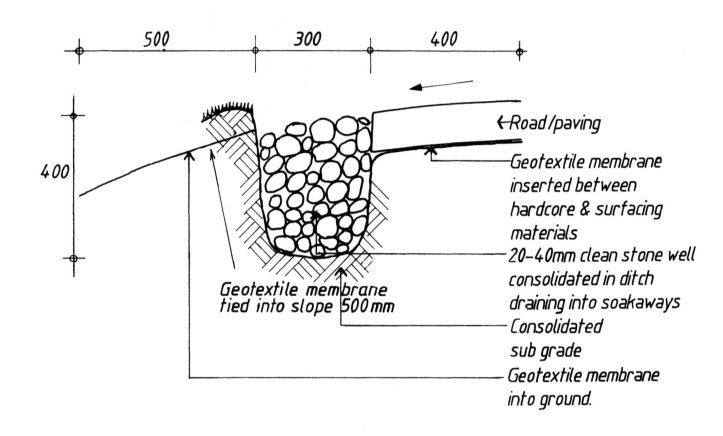

500   300   400

400

←Road/paving

Geotextile membrane
inserted between
hardcore & surfacing
materials

20–40mm clean stone well
consolidated in ditch
draining into soakaways

Geotextile membrane
tied into slope 500mm

Consolidated
sub grade

Geotextile membrane
into ground.

Scale 1:10

DRAINAGE CHANNEL
gravel

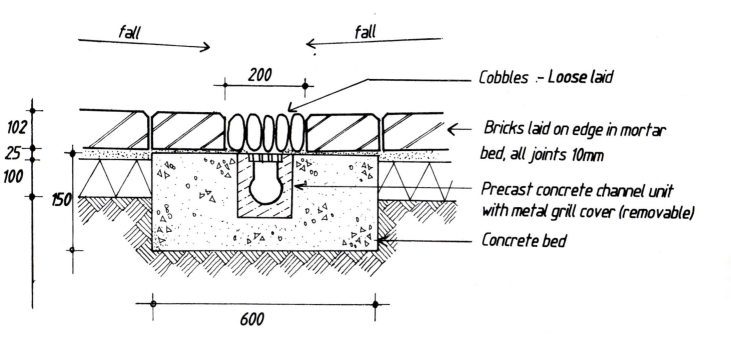

fall →   ← *fall*

200

102

25

100

150

600

Cobbles :- Loose laid

Bricks laid on edge in mortar
bed, all joints 10mm

Precast concrete channel unit
with metal grill cover (removable)

Concrete bed

SECTION

Product guide– Charcon

Scale 1:10

DRAINAGE CHANNEL
metal

193

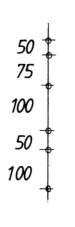

50
75
100
50
100

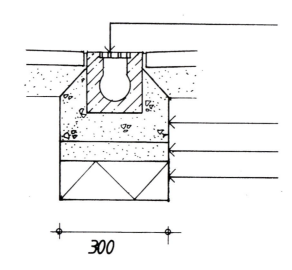

Precast concrete
channel unit with
metal grill cover
(removable)

Concrete bed and
haunching
Sand blinding

Hardcore

300

SECTION

Product guide
Charcon

Scale 1:10

DRAINAGE CHANNEL
metal

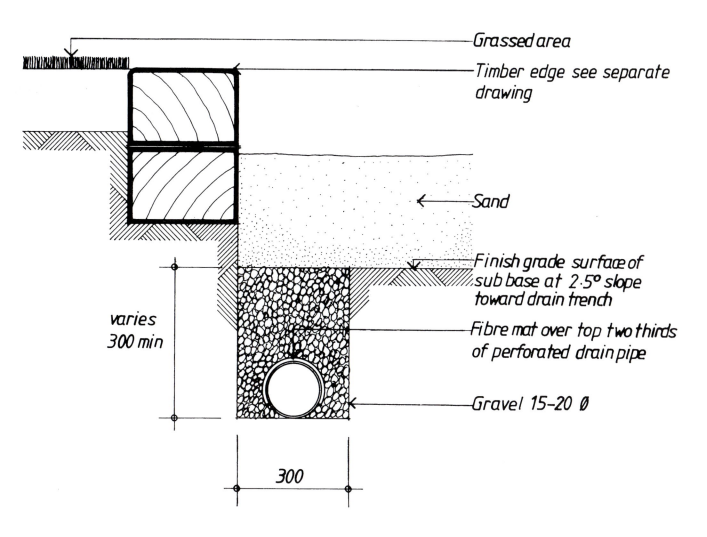

Grassed area

Timber edge see separate drawing

Sand

Finish grade surface of sub base at 2·5° slope toward drain trench

Fibre mat over top two thirds of perforated drain pipe

Gravel 15–20 Ø

varies 300 min

300

SECTION

Scale 1:10

UNDERDRAIN
sand play area

REFERENCES

APPENDIX A

Flexible paving

Asphalt and Coated Macadam Association
What's in a road? 1985
Construction and surfacing of parking areas for medium and heavyweight vehicles, 1985
Decorative and coloured finishes for bituminous surfacings, 1986
BACMI guide, 1986
Modern Flexible Road Construction
The Types and Scope of Coated Macadam
NBA 'Building' Commodity File,
Component File (90), Section 03

Transport and Road Research Laboratory
Road Note No. 29 (3rd edition), *A Guide to the Structural Design of Pavements for New Roads*, HMSO, 1970
Road Note No. 39 (2nd edition), *Recommendations for Road Surface Dressing*, HMSO, 1981
Laboratory Report 1132, *The Structural Design of Bituminous Roads* 1984

HMSO
D. Croney, *The Design and Performance of Road Pavements*, 1977
TRRL, *Sources of White and Coloured Aggregates in Great Britain*, 1966 (Now out of print but copies may be found in libraries. Its content is covered in part by *The BACMI Guide*.)
TRRL, *Protection of Sub-grades and Granular Sub-bases*, 1968
TRRL, *Recommendations for Road Surface Dressing*, 1981

Soil-cement bases

W.P. Andrews, *Soil-cement Roads*, The Cement and Concrete Association
Soil-cement roads. *Fixed Equipment of the Farm*, No. 19, HMSO
Specification for the construction of housing estate roads using soil-cement, HMSO
Note: All the above were published in the 1950s and copies might be difficult to find.

Rigid paving

Cement and Concrete Association
Farm Construction series: *Laying Roads with Ready-Mixed Concrete*, 6th edition, 1979
W. Monks, *Appearance Matters; Visual concrete*, 1984
W. Monks, *Appearance Matters; Tooled concrete finishes*, 1985
W. Monks, *Appearance Matters; Exposed aggregate concrete finishes*, 1985
A. Pink, *Winter Concreting*, 1978
D.E. Shirley, *Concreting in Hot Water*, 1980
D.E. Shirley, *Sulphate Resistance of Concrete*, 1984
D.E. Shirley, *Introduction to Concrete*, 1985
D.C. Teychenne *et al.*, *Design of Normal Concrete Mixes*, 1975

British Aggregate Construction Materials Industry
Anon., *The BACMI Guide*, 1986
Building Research Establishment/Transport and Road Research Laboratory/Cement and Concrete Association
D.C. Teychenne *et al.*, *Design of Normal Concrete Mixes* (joint publication to replace Road Note 4)

Interlocking block paving

Concrete Block Paving Association (Interpave)
List of members and product guide, 1986
Concrete block paving – Structural design of the pavement, 1986
Concrete block paving – Surface design consideration, 1986
Concrete block paving – Detailing, 1986
Concrete block paving – Laying, 1986

Cement and Concrete Association
Anon., *Specification for precast concrete paving blocks*, 1980
Anon., *Code of practice for laying precast concrete block pavements*, 1983
J. Knapton, *The Design of Concrete Block Roads*, 1976

A.A. Lilley and A.J. Clark, *Concrete Block Paving for Lightly Trafficked Roads and Paved Areas*, 1980

HMSO
A guide for the structural design of pavements for new roads, 1970
The Brick Development Association
Publishes information specific to clay pavers.

Unit paving

Various publications are available from the Cement and Concrete Association, the Decorative Paving and Walling Association, the Concrete Block Paving Association (Interpave), the National Paving and Kerb Association, the Stone Federation, the British Precast Concrete Federation, the Concrete Brick Federation of Clay Industries. Ultimately, individual manufacturers' literature must be consulted and samples inspected.
BCA Publication 48.033, *Laying pre-cast concrete paving flags*
BDS Design Note 8, *Rigid paving with clay and calcium silicate pavers*
Specification for pre-cast paving blocks, Cement and Concrete Association, September 1980

Trim to pavings

Roads and pavements intended for vehicular use are normally designed by a road engineer, and even when the landscape designer is specifying lightly trafficked pavements it is advisable to consult an engineer when the site is on unstable or made-up ground.

General

British Precast Concrete Federation
R. Cartwright (ed.), *Design of urban space: a GLC manual*, Architectural Press, 1980

Countryside Commission
Surfaces of Rural Car Parks
Department of the Environment
Design Bulletin 5 *Landscaping for Flats*
Circular 79/72 *Children's playspace*, HMSO, 1972

Design Bulletin 27 *Children at play*, HMSO, 1973
Design Bulletin 32 *Residential roads and footpaths: Layout considerations*, HMSO, 1980
Landscape: Guide to sources of information, HMSO, 1978
Building Regulations 1985: Access for disabled people, HMSO, 1987

Department of Education and Science
Building Bulletin 28 *Playing fields and hard surface areas*, HMSO, 1982
Specification for outdoor sports and recreation facilities, National Playing Fields Association, 1980

Department of Transport/Department of the Environment
Specification for Road and Bridge Works (5th edn), Reprinted 1980
Schedule of Rates for Minor Works and Maintenance of Roads and Pavings, 3rd edn, HMSO, 1981
Roads in Urban Areas, 3rd impression 1973, reprinted 1980
Metric Supplement, 1974
Design Bulletin DB 12: *Cars in Housing 2*, HMSO, 1971
Design Bulletin DB 32: *Residential Roads and Footpaths: Layout consideration*, HMSO, 1977

Department of Transport (DTp)
Specification for Highway Works, 1986
The National Paving and Kerb Association
Data Sheet 4: Paving flags – techniques for laying
Data Sheet 6: Precast concrete kerbs, channels and edgings. Model specification clauses for kerbs and footways
D.C. Teychenne *et al: Design of Normal Concrete Mixes*, Prepared jointly by BRE, TRRL and the Cement and Concrete Association to replace Road Note No 4
Guide to Concrete Road Construction, HMSO, 1987
Soil Mechanics for Road Engineers, HMSO, 1952

BIBLIOGRAPHY

APPENDIX B

AJ Technical Studies, Landscape Brickwork. *Architects' Journal*

AJ Technical Studies, Concrete Paving Blocks Residential Roads. *Architects' Journal*, 25.2.76, p. 399

AJ Technical Studies, Hard Landscape in Stone. *Architects' Journal*, 19.5.76, p. 1005

AJ Technical Studies, Products in Practice. Supplement 30.11.83, p. 3

AJ Technical Studies, Designing with Plants. *Architects' Journal*, 1984

AJ Technical Studies, Consultants: Landscape Architect. *Architects' Journal*, 18.4.84, p. 65

AJ Technical Studies, Landscape Contracts. *Architects' Journal*, 20.6.84, p. 87

J. Ashurst and F.G. Dimes. *Stone in Building*, 1977

E. Beazley, *Design and Detail of the Space between Buildings*, 1960

R.M. Cartwright, *Design of Urban Space*, 1980

M.F. Downing, *Landscape Construction*, 1977

M. Gage and T. Kirkbride, *Design in Blockwork*, 2nd edition, Architectural Press, 1976

M. Gage and M. Vandenberg, *Hard Landscape in Concrete*, Architectural Press, 1975

C.C. Handisyde, *Hard Landscape in Brick*, Architectural Press, 1976

G. John and H. Heard, *Handbook of Sports and Recreational Building Design*, Architectural Press, 1981

A.A. Lilley and A.J. Clark, *Concrete Blocks Paving for Lightly Trafficked Roads and Paved Areas*

A.A. Lilley and J.R. Collins, *Laying Concrete for Block Paving: Specification for Pre-Cast Paving Blocks*, September 1980

A.A. Lilley and A.J. Clark, *Concrete Blocks Paving for Lightly Trafficked Roads and Paved Areas*

A.A. Lilley and J.R. Collins, Laying Concrete for Block Paving: Specification for Pre-Cast Paving Blocks, September 1980

A.A. Lilley and A.J. Clark, *Concrete Blocks Paving for Lightly Trafficked Roads and Paved Areas*

A.A. Lilley and J.R. Collins, *Laying Concrete for Block Paving: Specification for Pre-Cast Paving Blocks*, September 1980

A.A. Lilley and J. Knapton, *Concrete Block Paving for Roads*, January 1976

W.M. Littlewood, *Tree Detailing*

D. Lovejoy & Partners, *Spon's Landscape Handbook*, E & F N Spon, 1983

A. Pinder and A. Pinder, *Beazley's Design and Detail of the Space between Buildings*, E & F N Spon, 1990

C. Tandy, *Handbook of Urban Landscape*, Architectural Press, 1972

G.S. Thomas, *Plants for Ground Cover*, Dent, 1970

A.E. Weddle (ed.), *Techniques of Landscape Architecture*, Heinemann, 1967

A.E. Weddle, *Landscape Techniques*, William Heinemann, 1979

BRITISH STANDARDS

APPENDIX C

Flexible paving

BS 63: Part 1: 1987 and Part 2: 1987 Single sized roadstone and chippings

BS 76: 1986 Tars for road purposes

BS 434: 1984 Bitumen for road emulsions

BS 435: 1975 Dressed natural stone kerbs, channels, quadrants and setts

BS 497: 1976 Cast manhole covers, road gully gratings and frames for drainage purposes
Part 1: Cast iron and cast steel

BS 594: 1985 Rolled asphalt for roads and other paved areas

BS 1446: 1973 Mastic asphalt (natural rock asphalt fine aggregate) for roads and footways

BS 1447: 1973 Mastic asphalt (limestone fines aggregate) for roads and footways

BS 1984: 1967 Gravel aggregate for surface treatment (including surface dressings) on roads

BS 3690: Bitumens for building and civil engineering
Part 1: 1982 Bitumens for road purposes
Part 2: 1983 Bitumen mixtures
Part 3: 1983 Bitumen for building and civil engineering

BS 4987: 1973 Coated macadams for roads and other paved areas

BS 5273: 1985 Dense tar surfacing for roads and other paved areas

Rigid paving

BS 12: 1978 Ordinary and rapid hardening Portland cement

BS 146: Part 2: 1973 Portland blastfurnace cement

BS 812: 1975/1985 Sampling and testing aggregates, sands and fillers

BS 882: 1983 Aggregates from natural sources for concrete.

BS 1881: 1970/1984 Method of testing concrete (This has many parts and some have no application in concrete pavements.)

BS 2499: 1973 Hot applied joint sealants for concrete pavements

BS 4483: 1985 Steel fabric for the reinforcement of concrete

BS 4550: 1970/1978 Methods of testing cement (Again with many parts.)

BS 3148: 1980 Methods of testing water for concrete

BS 5075: Part 1: 1982 Concrete mixtures; accelerating, retarding, water reducing (use of admixtures)

BS 5212: 1975 Cold poured joint sealants for concrete pavements

BS 5328: 1981 Methods for specifying concrete including ready-mixed concrete

BS 6044: 1987 Pavement marking paints

BS 6367: 1983 Code of Practice for drainage or roofs and paved areas

BS 6543: 1985 Industrial by-products and waste materials

Interlocking block paving

BS 6717: Part 1:1986 Precast concrete paving blocks (Covers manufacturer of the blocks.)

BS 6717: Part 2 (in preparation). (Will cover construction of pavements using the blocks.)

Unit paving

BS 368: 1970 Precast concrete flags

BS 435: 1975 Dressed natural stone kerbs, channels, quadrants and setts

BS 1217: 1986 Cast stone

BS 1286: 1974 Clay tiles for flooring

BS 3921: 1985 Clay bricks and blocks

Trim to pavings

BS 340: 1979 Precast concrete kerbs, channels, edgings and quadrants

MANUFACTURERS AND SUPPLIERS

(PAVING, STEPS, MARGINS)

APPENDIX D

ACO Polymer Products Limited
Hitchin Road
Shefford
Bedfordshire SG17 5JS
(0462 816666)

Atlas Stone Products
Westington Quarry
Chipping Campden
Glos GL55 6EG
(0386 841104)

Abru Aluminium Ltd
Building Products Division
Pennygillam Industrial Estate
Launceston
Cornwall PL15 7ED
(0566 3535)

Aquapipes
Darlingscott Road
Shipston on Stour
Warwickshire CV36 4DZ
(0608 61347)

ARC Conbloc
Conbloc Divisional Office
Besselsleigh Road
Abingdon
Oxfordshire OX13 6LQ
(0865 730808)

W. Armes & Son
Cornard Road
Sudbury
Suffolk CO10 6XB
(0787 72988)

BDC Concrete Products Ltd
Corporation Road
Newport
Gwent NP9 0WT
(0633 244181)

Blue Circle Industries Ltd
Church Road
Murston
Sittingbourne
Kent ME10 3TN
(0795 21066)

Boral Edenhall Concrete Products
Barbary Plains
Edenhall
Penrith
Cumbria CA11 8SP
(076881 731)

Breedon plc
Breedon-on-the-Hill
Derby DE7 1AP
(0332 862254)

Brickhouse Dudley Manufacturing
Co
Dudley Road West
Tipton
West Midlands DY4 7XD
(021 557 3922)

W. F. Broomfield
Afton Road
Freshwater
Isle of Wight PO40 9UH
(0983 752921)

Broxap and Corby Ltd
Walker Street
Radcliffe
Manchester M26 9JH
(061 796 5600)

BTR Landscaper
PO Box 3 Centurion
Farington
Preston
Lancashire PR5 2RE
(0722 421 711)

Burnham Signs Burnham & Co
(Onyx)
Kangley Bridge Road
London SE26 5AL
(081 659 1525)

Butterley Brick Limited
Wellington Street
Ripley
Derby DE5 3DZ
(0773 570570)

Charcon (ECC Quarries)
Hulland Ward
Derby DE6 3ET
(0335 70600)

Colas Products
Galvin Road
Slough
Berks SL1 4DL
(0753 71551)

Concrete Services
Ouse Acres
Boroughbridge Road
York YO2 5SR
(0904 79415)

Concrete Utilities
Lower Road
Great Amwell
Ware
Hertfordshire SG12 9TA
(0920 2272)

CU-Phosco Street Furniture
Charles House
Furlong Way
Great Amwell, Ware
Herts SG12 9TA
(0920 462272)

Dunhouse Quarry Co. Ltd
Onyx House
7 Church Road
Bishop Auckland
Durham DL14 7LB
(0388 602322)

DW Lighting
Stanstead Abbots
Ware
Hertfordshire SG12 8HE
(0920 870567)

ECC Building Products Ltd
Hulland Ward
Derby DE6 3ET
(0335 370600)

E.J. Elgood Ltd
Insulcrete Works
Yeoman Street
London SE8 5DU
(071 237 1144)

Emcol International Ltd
Royal London Buildings
42 Baldwin Street
Bristol BS1 1PN
(0272 290161)

Furnitubes International Ltd
Seager Buildings
Brookmill Road
London SE8 4HL
(081 694 9333)

Garden and Leisure Products
(ECC Quarries)
Okus
Swindon
Wiltshire SN1 4JJ
(0793 512288)

GEC (Street Lighting)
PO Box 17
East Lane
Wembley
Middlesex HA9 7PG
(081 904 4321)

Game and Playtime
Roddinglaw Works
Roddinglaw
Edinburgh EH12 9DB
(031 333 2222)
(048 675815)

Geometric Furniture
The Old Mill
Shepherd Street
Royton
Oldham OL2 5PB
(061 633 1119 and 061 620 2346)

George Fischer
46 Eagle Wharf Road
London N1 7EE
(071 253 1044)

Glasdon
Preston New Road
Blackpool FY4 4UL
(0253 696838)

Grass Concrete
Walker House
22 Bond Street
Wakefield
West Yorkshire WF1 2QP
(0924 375997)

Green Bros. (Geebro)
South Road
Hailsham
East Sussex BN27 3DT
(0323 840771)

Gush and Dent
New Road
Torrington
North Devon EX38 8EN
(080 52 2405)

Haddonstone Ltd
The Forge House
East Haddon
Northampton NN6 8DB
(0604 770711)

Hodkin and Jones (Sheffield)
Dunston House
Dunston Road
Sheepbridge
Chesterfield S41 9QD
(0246 455255)

Holton Builders
Holton cum Beckering
Lincoln LN3 5NG
(0673 858348)

Frederick Jones & Son
Whittington Road
Oswestry
Shropshire SY11 1HZ
(0691 653251)

Ibstock Building Products Ltd
Ibstock
Leicester LE6 1HS
(0530 60531)

ICI Fibres Geotextile Group
Pontypool
Gwent NP4 0YD
(049 55 57722)

Langley London
The Tile Centre
161-167 Borough High Street
London SE1 1HU
(071 407 4444)

M. Laurier & Sons Ltd
Unit 1
18 Marshgate Lane
London E15 2NH
(081 534 7211)

Lumitron
Chandos Road
London NW10 6PA
(081 965 0211)

Malcolm, Ogilvie & Co
31 Constitution Street
Dundee DD3 6NL
(0382 22974)

Marshalls Mono Ltd
Southowram
Halifax
W. Yorks HX3 9SY
(0422 366 666)

Mather & Smith Ltd
The Ashford Foundry
Brunswick Road
Ashford
Kent TN23 1ED
(0233 624911)

Mawrob Co. (Engineers)
121a–125a Sefton Street
Southport
Merseyside PR8 5DR
(0704 37408)

Metalliform
Chambers Road
Hoyland
Barnsley
South Yorkshire S74 0EZ
(0226 350555)

Milner Delaux Ltd
Eastrea Road
Whittlesey
Peterborough PE7 2AG
(0733 202566)

Minsterstone (Wharf Lane) Ltd
Ilminster
Somerset
(046 05 2277)

MMG Civil Engineering Systems
Vermuyden House
Wiggenhall St Germans
Kings Lynn
Norfolk PE34 3ES
(0553 85791)

Nelton
Kelly Street
Blackburn BB2 4PJ
(0254 62431)

Ockley Building Products Ltd
Walliswood
Nr Ockley
Surrey RH5 5QH
(0306 79 481)

Orchard Seating
Moreton Avenue
Wallingford
Oxfordshire OX10 9RH
(0491 36588)

Permafix Products
72–74 Bath Road
Cheltenham
Gloucestershire GL53 7JT
(0242 573202)

Piggott Brothers & Co
43 London Road
Stanford Rivers
Ongar
Essex CM5 9PJ
(0277 363262)

Recticel Ltd
18–22 Summerville Road
Bradford
West Yorks BD7 1PY
(0274 27370/2943)

Redland Bricks Ltd
PO Box 7
Langhurst Wood Road
Graylands
Horsham
West Sussex RH12 4QG
(0403 211222)

Redland Precast Ltd
Sileby Road
Barrow-upon-Soar
Loughborough
Leics LE12 8LX
(0509 812601)

Rosemary Brick and Tile
Haunchwood-Lewis Works
Cannock
Staffordshire WS11 3LS
(0922 412346)

Sarena Plastics
Autumn Street
London E3 2TT
(081 980 6371)

Sevenoaks Brickworks Ltd
Greatness
Sevenoaks
Kent TN14 5BP
(0732 59678)

SMP (Playgrounds and Sports
Surfaces)
Pound Road
Chertsey
Surrey KT16 8EJ
(0932 568081)

Stanton Plc
PO Box 72
Nr Nottingham NG10 5AA
(0602 322121)

Steelway-Fensecure
Queensgate Works
Bilston Road
Wolverhampton
West Midlands WV2 2NJ
(0902 51733)

Sugg Lighting
Sussex Manor Business Park
Gatwick Road
Crawley
West Sussex RH10 2GD
(0293 540111)

Tarmac Bricks Ltd
Watling Street
Cannock
Staffordshire WS11 3BJ
(05435 6085)

Tarmac Roadstone Holdings Ltd
50 Waterloo Road
Wolverhampton WV1 4RU
(0902 22411)

Thorn EMI Lighting
Thorn EMI House
Saltley Trading Estate
Aston Church Road
Saltley
Birmingham B8 1BE
(021 327 1535)

Tinsley Wire (Sheffield)
PO Box 119
Shepcote Lane
Sheffield
South Yorkshire S9 1TY
(0742 443 388)

Townscape Products
Fulwood Works
Fulwood Road South
Sutton-in-Ashfield
Nottinghamshire NG17 2JZ
(0623 513 355)

INSTITUTIONS AND ASSOCIATIONS

APPENDIX E

Aggregate Concrete Block Association (ACBA)
60 Charles Street
Leicester LE1 1FB
Tel: (0533) 536161

Agricultural Engineers Association
6 Buckingham Gate
London SW1

Aluminium Coaters Association
c/o British Standards Institution
Quality Assurance Section
PO Box 375
Milton Keynes
Bucks MK14 6LO
Tel: (0908) 315555

Aluminium Extruders Association
Broadway House
Calthorpe Road
Birmingham B15 1TN
Tel: (021) 4550311
Telex: Bircom-G-338024ALFED

Amateur Athletics Association
Francis House
Francis Street
London SW1P 1DL
Tel: (071) 828 9326

Arboricultural Association
The Secretary
38 Blythwood Gardens
Stanstead, Essex

Asphalt and Coated Macadam Association
see British Aggregate Construction Materials Industries

The Asphalt Institute
Asphalt Institute Building
College Park
Maryland, USA

Association of Swimming Pool Contractors
76 Marylebone High Street
London W1

Brick Development Association (BDA)
Woodside House
Winkfield
Windsor
Berks SL4 20X
Tel: (0344) 885651

British Adhesives and Sealants Association (BASA)
Secretary
33 Fellowes Way
Stevenage
Herts SG2 8BW
Tel: (0438) 358514

British Aggregate Construction Materials Industries (BACMI)
156 Buckingham Palace Road
London SW1W 9TR
Tel: (071) 730 8194
Fax: (071) 730 4355

British Agricultural and Horticultural Plastics Association
5 Belgrave Square
London SW1X 8PH
Tel: (071) 235 9483

British Cement Association (BCA)
Wexham Springs
Slough
Berks SL3 6PL
Tel: (02816) 2727
Telex: 848352
Fax: (02816) 2251/3727

British Commercial Glasshouse Manufacturers' Association
C/o Cambridge Glasshouse Co. Ltd
Comberton
Cambridge CB3 7BY
Tel: (0223) 262 395

British Decorators Association
6 Haywra Street
Harrogate
N. Yorks HG1 5BL
Tel: (0423) 67292/3

British Precast Concrete Federation Ltd (BPCF)
60 Charles Street
Leicester LE1 1FB
Tel: (0533) 536161
Fax: (0533) 51468

British Ready Mixed Concrete Association
1 Bramber Court
2 Bramber Road
London W14 9PB
Tel: (071) 381 6582

British Standards Institution (BSI)
Head Office:
2 Park Street
London W1A 2BS
Tel: (071) 629 9000
Telex: 266933
Fax: (Group 2/3) (071) 629 0506

British Steel Corporation Research Services (BSC)
BSC Swinden Laboratories
Moorgate
Rotherham
S. Yorks S60 3AR
Tel: (0709) 820 166
Telex: 547279

British Waterways Board
Melbury House
Melbury Terrace
London NW1

British Wood Preserving Association (BWPA)
Premier House
150 Southampton Row
London WC1B 5AL
Tel: (071) 837 8217

Building Research Station
Bucknalls Lane
Garston, Watford, Herts

Calcium Silicate Brick Association (CSBA)
24 Fearnley Road
Welwyn Garden City
Herts AL8 6HW
Tel: (07073) 24538

Cement Admixtures Association (CAA)
2A High Street
Hythe
Southampton
Hants SO4 6YW
Tel: (0703) 842765

Cement and Concrete Association
see British Cement Association

Chartered Land Agents' Society
21 Lincoln's Inn Fields
London WC2

Civic Trust
Walter House
Bedford Street
Strand, London WC2

Clay Roofing Tile Council (CRTC)
Federation House
Station Road
Stoke-on-Trent
Staffs ST4 2SA
Tel: (0782) 747256
Telex: 367446
Fax: (0782) 744102

Commons, Open Spaces & Footpaths Preservation Society
166 Shaftesbury Avenue
London WC2

Concrete Block Paving Association (Interpave)
60 Charles Street
Leicester LE1 1FB
Tel: (0533) 536161
Fax: (0533) 514568

Concrete Brick Manufacturer's Association (CBMA)
60 Charles Street
Leicester LE1 1FB
Tel: (0533) 536161
Fax: (0533) 514568

Copper Development Association (CDA)
Orchard House
Mutton Lane
Potters Bar
Herts EN6 3AP
Tel: (0707) 50711
Telex: 265451 MONREF (quote 72:MAG 30836)

Council for the Preservation of Rural England
4 Hobart Place
London SW1

Council for the Preservation of Rural Wales
Y Plas
Machynlleth
Montgomeryshire

Country Landowners' Association
7 Swallow Street
London W1

Country Naturalists Trusts
(Headquarters in each county)

Countryside Commission for Scotland
Battleby
Redgorton
Perth PH1 3EW
Tel: (0738) 27921

Crafts Council
12 Waterloo Place
London SW1Y 4AU
Tel: (071) 930 4811

Crown Estate Commissioners
Crown Estate Office
Whitehall
London SW1

Decorative Paving and Walling Association
60 Charles Street
Leicester LE1 1FB
Tel: (0533) 536161
Fax: (0533) 514568

Fauna Preservation Society
c/o Zoological Society of London
Regent's Park
London NW1

Fencing Contractors Association (FCA)
St John's House
23 St John's Road
Watford
Herts WD1 1PY
Tel: (0923) 248895

Field Studies Council
9 Devereux Court
Strand, London WC1

Forestry Commission
231 Corstorphine Road
Edinburgh EH12 7AT
Tel: (031) 334 2576

Guild of Architectural Ironmongers (GAI)
8 Stepney Green
London E1 3JU
Tel: (071) 790 3431
Telex: 94012229 GAII G
Fax: (071) 790 8517

Her Majesty's Stationery Office (HMSO)
St Crispin's
Duke Street
Norwich
Norfolk NR3 1PD
Tel: (0603) 22211
Telex: 97301
Fax: (0603) 695582

Horticultural Education Association
65 Tilehurst Road
Reading, Berks

Horticultural Traders Association
6th Floor, Cereal House
Mark Lane
London EC3

Institute of Civil Engineers
25 Eccleston Square
London SW1V 1NX
Tel: (071) 630 0726

Institute of Highways and Transportation
3 Lygon Place
Ebury Street
London SW1W 0JS
Tel: (071) 730 5245

Institute of Park and Recreation Administration
The Grotto
Lower Basildon
Nr Reading, Berks

Interpave:
The Concrete Block Paving Association
60 Charles Street
Leicester LE1 1FB
Tel: (0533) 536161

The Landscape Institute
6–7 Barnard Mews
London SW11 1QU
Tel: (071) 738 9166

Land Settlement Association
43 Cromwell Road
London SW7

Lead Development Association (LDA)
34 Berkeley Square
London W1X 6AJ
Tel: (071) 499 8422
Telex: 261286

The Mastic Asphalt Council and Employers Federation
Construction House
Paddockhall Road
Haywards Heath
West Sussex RH16 1HE
Tel: (0444) 457786

Mortar Producers Association Ltd (MPA)
Holly House
74 Holly Walk
Leamington Spa
Warwicks CV32 4JD
Tel: (0926) 38611

National Federation of Clay Industries Ltd (NFCI)
Federation House
Station Road
Stoke-on-Trent
Staffs ST4 2TJ
Tel: (0782) 416256
Telex: 367446
Fax: (0782) 744102

National Association of Agricultural Contractors (Garden Section)
140 Bensham Lane
Thornton Heath, Surrey

National Association of Groundsmen
108 Chessington Road
Ewell, Surrey

National Farmers' Union
Agricultural House
Knightsbridge
London SW1

National Farmers' Union for Scotland
17 Grosvenor Crescent
Edinburgh 12
(*see* Trade Association of the United Kingdom)

National Federation of Painting and Decorating Contractors
82 New Cavendish Street
London W1M 1AD
Tel: (071) 580 5588

National Parks Commission
8 St Andrew's Place
London SW1

National Paving and Kerb Association (NPKA)
60 Charles Street
Leicester LE1 1FB
Tel: (0533) 536161
Fax: (0533) 514568

National Playing Fields Association
57b Catherine Place
London NW1

National Trust
36 Queen Anne's Gate
London SW1H 9AS
Tel: (071) 222 9251

National Trust Committee for Northern Ireland
82 Dublin Road
Belfast 2

National Trust for Scotland
5 Charlotte Square
Edinburgh 2

National Vegetable Research Station Association
Wellesbourne
Warwick

Natural Slate Quarries Association
Bryn, Llanllechid
Bangor
Gwynedd LL57 3LG
Tel: (0248) 600476

Nature Conservancy
19 Belgrave Square
London SW1
(also Regional Offices and
Research Stations)

NBS Services Ltd
Mansion House Chambers
The Close
Newcastle upon Tyne NE1 3RE
Tel: (091) 232 9594
Fax: (091) 232 5714

Paintmakers Association of Great Britain (PA)
Alembic House
93 Albert Embankment
London SE1 7TY
Tel: (071) 582 1185

Paint Research Association
8 Waldegrave Road
Teddington
Middlesex TW11 8LD
Tel: (081) 977 4427
Telex: 928720
Fax: (081) 943 4705

Ramblers Association
124 Finchley Road
London NW3

Refined Bitumen Association
165 Queen Victoria Street
London EC4V 4DD

Royal Forestry Society of England & Wales
49 Russell Square
London WC1

Royal Horticultural Society
Vincent Square
London SW1

Royal Scottish Forestry Society
7 Albyn Place
Edinburgh 2

Sand and Gravel Association Ltd (SAGA)
1 Bramber Court
2 Bramber Road
London W14 9PB
Tel: (071) 381 1443

Society of Chain Link Fencing Manufacturers
16 Montcrieffe Road
Sheffield S7 1HR
Tel: (0742) 500350

Sports Council, Technical Unit for Sport
16 Upper Woburn Place
London WC1H 0QP
Tel: (071) 388 1277

Stone Federation
82 New Cavendish Street
London W1M 8AD
Tel: (071) 580 5588
Telex: 265763

Timber Growers' Association
35 Belgrave Square
London SW1

Timber Research and Development Association (TRADA)
Stocking Lane
Hughenden Valley
High Wycombe
Bucks HP14 4ND
Tel: (024024) 2771/3091/3956
Telex: 83292 TRADA G
Prestel: 3511615
Fax: (024024) 5487

Town and Country Planning Association
28 King Street
Covent Garden
London WC2

Town Planning Institute
26 Portland Square
London W1

Trade Association of the United Kingdom
Cereal House
Mark Lane
London EC3

Zinc Development Association
24 Berkeley Square
London W1

section

Symbol	Name
	Gravel
	Hardcore
	Hoggin
	Rock
	Rubble
	Sand
	Topsoil
	Water

UNIT MATERIALS

Symbol	Name
	Brick paving
	Brickwork
	Cobbles
	Concrete - p.c. blockwork

Symbol	Name
	Concrete - p.c. paving units
	Metal
	Setts
	Stone - natural, cut
	Stone - reconstituted
	Rubble stone - random
	Rubble stone - coursed
	Timber - dressed (wrot)
	Timber - rough (unwrot)

IN·SITU MATERIALS

Symbol	Name
	Asphalt
	Concrete - in-situ
	Mortar

plan

Symbol	Name
	Grass
	Gravel
	Hoggin
	Sand
	Soil
	Rock
	Rubble
	Water

UNIT MATERIALS

Symbol	Name
	Brick - stretcher bond
	Brick - basket weave
	Brick - stack bond
	Brick - herringbone
	Cobbles - random laid
	Cobbles - coursed
	Cobbles - flat, parallel laid

Symbol	Name
	Concrete - p.c. paving slabs
	Concrete - p.c. blocks
	Concrete - p.c. hexagonal slabs
	Setts - stack bond
	Setts - stretcher bond
	Stone - natural
	Stone - reconstituted
	Stone - random paving
	Tiled paving
	Timber

IN·SITU MATERIALS

Symbol	Name
	Asphalt
	Concrete - i.s. broom finish
	Concrete - i.s. exposed aggregate
	Concrete - i.s. trowelled finish
	Concrete - i.s. marked finish

207